BEYOND THE ADIRONDACKS

THE STORY OF ST. REGIS PAPER COMPANY

Eleanor Amigo and Mark Neuffer
Elwood R. Maunder, General Editor

GREENWOOD PRESS
Westport, Connecticut • London, England

The Forest History Society is a nonprofit, educational institution dedicated to the advancement of historical understanding of man's interaction with the North American forest environment. It was established in 1946. Interpretations and conclusions in FHS publications are those of the authors; the institution takes responsibility for the selection of topics, the competence of the authors, and their freedom of inquiry.

Work on this book and its publication were supported by a grant to the Forest History Society.

Library of Congress Cataloging in Publication Data

Amigo, Eleanor.
    Beyond the Adirondacks.

    (Contributions in economics and economic history ; no. 35 ISSN 0084–9235)
    Bibliography: p.
    Includes index.
    1. St. Regis Paper Company—History. I. Neuffer, Mark, joint author. II. Maunder, Elwood R. III. Title.
HD9829.S3A44   338.7'6762'0973   80-1798
ISBN 0–313–22735–7 (lib. bdg.)

Contributions in Economics and Economic History, Number 35

Library of Congress Catalog Card Number: 80-1798
ISBN: 0–313–22735–7
ISSN: 0084–9235

First published in 1980

Greenwood Press
A division of Congressional Information Service, Inc.
88 Post Road West, Westport, Connecticut 06881

Printed in the United States of America

10 9 8 7 6 5 4 3 2 1

Contents

Illustrations — *vii*
Introduction — *ix*

1 Watertown — 3
2 The Arm of a Giant — 13
3 Survival in Troubled Times — 37
4 Growing Up to Power — 61
5 Surviving Depression and War — 79
6 Coming of Age — 93
7 Prosperity and Turbulence — 121
8 The Move to Multinationalism — 143
9 Capitalizing on Opportunity — 161

Appendix I: *St. Regis Executives* — 171
Appendix II: *St. Regis Officers as of July 1, 1980* — 173
Notes — 175
Notes on Sources — 203
Index — 205

Illustrations

(Photo section follows page 92.)

1   Adelmer M. Bates and John E. Cornell of Bates Valve Bag Company
2   George W. Knowlton, Jr. President, 1900–1908
3   Gordias H. P. Gould. President, 1908–1916
4   Floyd L. Carlisle. President, 1916–1934
5   H. Edmund Machold. Vice-president, 1924–1934
6   A logging crew at Camp #3, St. Paul & Tacoma Lumber Company
7   A 1932 advertisement for Multi-Wall Sewn Paper Bags
8   The appointment of Roy K. Ferguson as St. Regis's fifth president
9   Former St. Regis mill at Rhinelander, Wisconsin
10 The pulp and paper mill at Deferiet, New York
11 A driver watches for snags during a log drive on the Machias River, Maine
12 The company's pulp and paper mill at Bucksport, Maine
13 Roy K. Ferguson. President, 1934–1957
14 The bleached sulfate pulp mill at Hinton, Alberta, under construction
15 The printing paper mill at Sartell, Minnesota
16 Rewinding paper at the dry end of the machine
17 Folke Becker of Rhinelander Paper Company
18 Everett G. Griggs II of St. Paul & Tacoma Lumber Company
19 Paul Neils of J. Neils Lumber Company
20 Roy K. Ferguson and William R. Adams in the early 1960s
21 View of the Roy K. Ferguson Technical Center in West Nyack, New York
22 St. Regis's kraft-making facility at Tacoma, Washington
23 The Roy K. Ferguson Mill in Monticello, Mississippi
24 The "Little Chief" paper machine
25 The *William R. Adams*
26 Planting seedlings on a pine plantation operated by the Southern Timber-
      lands Division

27   William R. Adams. President, 1957–1971

28   William R. Caldwell. President, 1971–1973

29   George J. Kneeland. Chairman of the Board, 1972 - date. Chief Executive
     Officer, 1972-1979

30   William R. Haselton. President, 1973 - date. Chief Executive Officer,
     1979 - date

Introduction

The forest as a unique renewable resource and the conversion of harvested trees into products needed by all are of particular interest today. Other alternate and complementary uses of the forest bring together for frequent contacts representatives of corporations and those with serious environmental concerns. Fortunately, wise stewardship, balancing the interests of all, appears to be an achievable goal. This book, dealing with the history of one business enterprise, is meant to contribute to the understanding of the origin and evolution of the key issues involved.

The St. Regis Paper Company began as a single newsprint mill in a small, upstate New York town in 1899 and became one of the largest industrial corporations in the United States, as well as a multinational enterprise of major stature. In 1979 *Fortune* ranked St. Regis as the 110th largest American industrial corporation in terms of total assets and 138th in terms of total sales. Within its own industry, St. Regis's more than $2.2 billion in assets rank it sixth, and only seven other companies have greater sales.

The world has been St. Regis's marketplace. The company operates 148 plants employing 31,100 in ten countries; 114 of these plants are in the United States. The company is owned by 34,000 shareholders worldwide. Growth has been supported by a policy of timberland acquisition and application of modern forest management. Today the company owns or controls cutting rights on nearly six million acres in North America. It also holds valuable oil and gas reserves and has investments in affiliated companies that operate eighty-seven additional plants in twenty-nine countries. In addition to traditional paper and paperboard products, St. Regis manufactures and markets plastic packaging, prestressed concrete, lumber products, and packaging machinery. It is also one of the largest designers and printers of packaging in the world. This book emphasizes the growth of the company and its manufacture of paper products.

The subject of paper itself, which is looked at here only obliquely, merits its own book. Annual per-capita consumption is now 638 pounds for each American, up from 450 pounds only twenty years ago. This versatile, essential, and biodegradable product, so integral to our daily lives, has thousands of uses. The daily newspaper, tablets for young scholars, shotgun shells for duck hunters, grocery bags used to provision every household, paperboard boxes to package the wares of a national economy, cups and plates for picnickers, stationery to supply bureaucracies—the list is truly impressive in length.

St. Regis and its industry are only part of a swiftly growing forest-related community. Closely allied to it are many service industries, which supply an array of machinery, chemicals, energy, and technical knowledge that can be comprehended only by surveying the trade journals and catalogs. Still faster growing are groups looking to the forest for recreation, and affluence leads to increased leisure-related uses of the forest. Thus paralleling the rise of the large corporation has been the emergence of many environmentally concerned groups.

This book is addressed to these various audiences in the hope that it may further the understanding of the role that St. Regis has played in using one of the most valuable natural resources. The company agreed to sponsor this study partly to enable its own employees to have a better awareness of the origins of many issues that we all face daily. This book is also meant to benefit historians in their research and writing.

We were inspired by the ideas of many scholars, especially those expressed by Thomas C. Cochran. They have sought to explain what Cochran calls "the effects of business roles and their institutional forms on the rest of society," and they have acted on his underlying supposition that if free enterprise is to continue to be the backbone of the American economy, its history must be known.[1]

Many have contributed to this work. The St. Regis Paper Company sponsored the effort, made its records available for study, encouraged key personnel to share recollections and impressions, and allowed us freedom of inquiry and interpretation.

Elwood R. Maunder, in consultation with company representatives, developed the project, conducted many oral interviews, and provided overall supervision. John R. Ross began the study by assembling and organizing materials. Ronald C. Larson, Timothy Coogan, and Virginia J. Dzurinko added important elements of research and organization. Ross, James E. Kussmann, and Mark H. Neuffer also conducted interviews and exchanged ideas with many active and retired St. Regis officials. Neuffer intensively researched the early years and drafted the first chapters; Eleanor L. Amigo wrote the latter portions of the book. Eleanor L. Maunder, Kristine Holtvedt, Gloria Swing, Carolyn Hernandez, and Ann Bennett transcribed numerous interviews and carefully typed the many manuscript drafts.

After the manuscript was in full draft, much help and advice were received from Paul M. Dunn, Ronald J. Fahl, W. H. Hutchinson, Mary Elizabeth Johnson, Lorraine Kashara, Harold T. Pinkett, David C. Smith, and Harold K. Steen. Robert E. Ficken deserves special thanks for a careful reading of the entire manuscript and for providing many substantive editorial comments. James E. Kussmann, vice-president of public affairs, was the company's gracious and patient liaison.

Thanks are due to J. McHenry Jones, who allowed access to especially rich materials in his personal possession. Jones, like so many others, filled important gaps in the St. Regis story.

1
Watertown

That a hamlet on the banks of a river in northern New York was named Watertown is not in any way remarkable. The focus of settlement early in the nineteenth century was—just as it is today—the turbulent Black River. The river did not evoke great poetry or prose or play a heroic role in the history of the American frontier, nor was it a river to enchant the eye. One early commentator described it as "peculiarly dark and forbidding," attributing this unwholesome aspect to the leachings of bogs and swamps and to the presence of oxides.[1] And beneath this somewhat sinister appearance there existed an awesome potential for destruction. Swollen by rain or melting snow, the river could smash nearby structures to matchwood or sweep buildings from their foundations and carry them away like corks.[2]

The Black River's headwaters are in the midst of the mountainous Adirondack forest. In its descent to the lowlands, it is strengthened by rivulets, streams, ponds, and lakes. Gaining momentum and power, the river twists northward into Lewis and Jefferson counties, describes a gigantic bend in Jefferson, and then moves on in a westerly course. Widening as it loses altitude, the river flows through Watertown and empties into Lake Ontario a few miles below the city.

Within Watertown alone, the Black River had a potential force in the 1870s of over 80,000 horsepower. Allowing for the inevitable energy loss because of friction and leakage in power developments of the time, the river's drop of nearly 112 feet still offered an impressive 30,000 horsepower to developers.[3] This potential waterpower was central to the development of Watertown and the other communities along the river. In the new Industrial Age, waterpower meant the ability to drive machines, create products, and make profits. Almost from the very beginning, Watertown residents were intrigued by the industrial promise of the river.

Watertown was settled in the first decade of the nineteenth century. Early accounts describe a typical rough-hewn frontier community, but it was not long before the industrial applications of the Black River were exploited. The river was especially attractive to textile manufacturers, who discovered that its water was "almost as soft as the purest rain-water" and that it was well suited to the manufacture of cotton and woolen goods.[4]

This discovery set the stage for the first wave of industrialization. A cotton and woolen firm was organized in Watertown as early as 1813, but this modest undertaking was not immediately successful, possibly because local demand was restricted and because of the lack of transportation to a broader market. But by 1827, Watertown's textile industry was ready to burgeon. In that year Levi Beebee constructed a large mill on the Black River island, which later bore his name. The mill was four stories high, over eighty yards long, and designed for 150 looms. Six years later, fire destroyed the mill; one writer attributed the blaze to arsonists who were not content to express their "prejudice against machinery" in words alone. This conflagration, the first of many that Watertown would survive, ruined Beebee.[5]

The momentum of Watertown's industrialization was not halted by the activities of a few incendiaries. Soon after the destruction of Beebee's mill, another textile firm was incorporated in Watertown. By 1836 textile factories were the town's major economic activity, with half a dozen mills employing about 160 workers. But by then Watertown's first industry had begun giving way to new enterprises.

Tanning, for instance, was initiated in 1823 by Jason Fairbanks, using bark from indigenous hemlock. Farm and grazing lands were opened up, and the growth of the livestock business added to the raw material supply of the tanneries. The introduction of gristmills, breweries, and distilleries pointed to the further expansion of agriculture.[6]

Development of a local paper industry was rather slow, although the business made an early start when Gurdon Caswell, a Connecticut tailor turned papermaker, moved to Watertown in 1808 and established what was known as the Pioneer Mill. Papermaking at the time was wholly unlike what it is today. The basic raw material was rags, which were beaten and boiled into pulp. A hand-held screen or sieve was dipped into the vat containing the pulp, and as water drained through the screen, the fibers began to coalesce. The resultant sheet was dewatered by a crude press and hung on a pole to dry. In this fashion Caswell's Pioneer Mill produced a modest 150 pounds of paper per day.

The small output of Caswell's mill resulted as well from lack of sufficient local residents to supply raw material and to consume the finished product. Workers also delayed production, according to one account, by "going on prolonged drunken sprees, when all work must come to a stop."[7] Caswell constructed a second paper mill in 1819 but shortly thereafter sold both plants to a Vermont printing firm. All of these properties—mills, bookstore, bindery, and printing shop—came under the control of George W. Knowlton, Sr., and Clarke Rice in 1824. The new owners created their own market for the mills by converting the paper into such books as *Webster's Spelling Book*, a gourmand's delight entitled *The Cook Not Mad*, and Alexander Pope's *Essay on Man*.[8]

During these years, technological advances began to revolutionize the paper industry. At the end of the nineteenth century in France, Nicholas-Louis Robert had designed a machine that produced a continuous sheet of paper on a long, horizontal plane. Named the fourdrinier, after Henry and Sealey Fourdrinier, its British developers, this invention was later followed by the cylinder paper machine, which produced an unbroken sheet of paper by rotational movement.

More than a quarter century after the invention of fourdriniers, Americans began importing them from Europe. Knowlton and Rice installed what is thought to be a fourdrinier at their mill in 1832.[9] Repaired after a fire in 1833, this machine continued in use until nearly mid-century, producing from a variety of rag stock an assortment of wrapping, newsprint, and book papers to meet the needs of local consumers.[10]

After nearly five decades of growth, Watertown was a bustling community with a good future. In that regard it followed a pattern of growth common throughout the United States. Urban America grew rapidly in the first half of the nineteenth century and at an even more prodigious rate in the second half as the result of what historian Thomas C. Cochran has called "the reciprocal process of industry creating cities and cities building industries." But while Watertown's industry and commerce flowered, development of its urban amenities had lagged behind. For many years, there were no paved streets, and an early chronicle describes the center of the town as "anything but a beauty spot, in fact . . . it was a common dumping ground."[11]

In 1849 a gigantic fire destroyed frame buildings and much of the central business section. Various manufactories, including the Knowlton firm, were destroyed. Some sources suggest that the conflagration was actually a blessing in disguise, despite the resulting devastation. One observed that the new Public Square became a "garden of beauty," while another asserted that the fire of 1849 and a succession of lesser blazes imposed a necessary facelift. Banker Wooster Sherman was one victim of the fire who was not about to mourn the destruction. When flames leaped across Court Street and set fire to the building that housed his bank, "that redoubtable citizen succeeded in escaping with the bank's assets in a wheel barrow but lost his hat and singed his whiskers in the process."[12]

Watertown's paper industry continued to grow following the fire. The Knowlton firm rebuilt its mill and then, in 1854, active management of the company passed into the hands of a new owner. Seven years later, however, the two Knowlton sons, John C. and George W., Jr., regained control of the firm and named it Knowlton Brothers. John had acquired financial experience while working in Wooster Sherman's bank, and his younger brother had worked in the mill since the age of fifteen.[13]

The almost unbroken hegemony of Knowlton papermakers in Watertown ended when two other families founded their own firms. The first infusion of new blood came from the Remington family. Illustrious Remington, born in 1791, had operated a cotton mill in Manlius, New York, and a paper mill at Fayetteville. The oldest of his three sons, Alfred, induced the migration of the Remingtons to Watertown. This family's first mill there began operating in 1855, and within two years A. D. Remington had his machine running half again as fast as those of his competitors. Over the next three decades, the Remingtons added mills in Watertown and downriver in Glen Park.[14]

The Taggart family entered the paper industry of Watertown about a decade after the Remingtons. About 1864 Byron Benjamin Taggart, Sr., a member of a farming family, began producing paper bags in partnership with A. H. Hall. The Taggart-Hall enterprise, capitalizing on a shortage of food sacks made of cotton during the Civil War, made small hand-pasted bags from manila paper stock purchased on the open market. Taggart then moved to a building formerly occupied by a distillery, adding a fourdrinier paper machine to manufacture newsprint as well as manila. Eventually B. B. Taggart was joined by his brother, lawyer William W. Taggart, and the Taggart Brothers firm was organized.[15]

As the paper industry grew, so did the gathering of rags to make pulp. Imaginative advertisements encouraged housewives to sell their rags directly to the mills or to middlemen. One appeal begged the "sweet ladies" not to take offense at the request for rags and to overlook "the jest of sneering wags." Such doggerel was supplemented by inventive admonitions: "If the necessary [rag] stock is denied paper mills, young maids must languish in vain for tender epistles from their respective swains." Advertisements stressed the "ugly duckling" theme, pointing out that unsavory raw material would be transformed into a beautiful finished product.[16]

One Watertown firm was more systematic in collecting rags. A tinsmith named Holden came to Watertown in 1852 and was soon joined in business by John M. Tilden and David M. Anderson, the latter a graduate of Brooklyn Polytechnic Institute.[17] Sensing the mercantile promise of the rag business, the partners hit upon the notion of exchanging tinware as well as cash for rags. Their red carts equipped with large rag containers became a familiar sight on village roads and city streets in the North Country. At the conclusion of a successful tour of the countryside, the rag stock was sold to local papermakers.

By the Civil War, the paper industry was ready for additional technological advances, as the demand for paper was increasing faster than the availability of rags. A larger and more literate population and the increasing scope of the federal government, in particular, meant ever greater paperwork and thus a need for more paper. Historian David C. Smith asserts that the Civil War exerted a "great drain on paper," and was the "catalytic agent" in finding a solution to the problem of supply.[18] Indeed the rag shortage had been growing for some time. The Knowlton firm, for example, consumed forty-five tons of rags in 1835; eleven years later its consumption had risen to seventy-five tons. The price of rags soared as demand increased. Between 1862 and 1868 the Knowltons had to double what they paid for rags. And, of course, the mill men passed on the increased cost to their customers. American papermakers met this crisis by tapping foreign rag sources; India,

China, and Japan became major suppliers by the end of the Civil War.[19]

Access to international sources of raw materials was made possible by the rapid growth of transportation systems: roads, connecting rail lines and barge canals, and larger and more seaworthy ships. These developments opened new markets and led to an explosion of advertising, with profound implications for papermakers.[20]

Another solution to the supply squeeze was sought through experimentation with new fiber sources for pulp, including such items as straw, tobacco, sugarcane, cornhusks, and wood. For over a century, such materials had been tested as substitutes for rags, and an example already existed in nature for the use of wood. The common wasp could transform wood fiber into a paper nest, and papermakers sought to refine and implement this process on a large scale. The basic challenge was to perform, at faster speed, what the wasp accomplished with apparent ease: the separation of a solid mass of cellulose into its component fibers and then reweaving them into paper.

Three methods of commercial wood pulping became increasingly popular in the two decades following the Civil War. The first was the soda process, which employed sodium hydroxide (caustic soda) to dissolve lignin, the natural agent binding wood fibers into bundles. By the mid-1860s some paper mills were using this system, often mixing poplar wood pulp with rag pulp. The second method of wood pulping, the sulfite process, employed sulfurous acid as the delignifying agent. This pulping method was used experimentally during the 1860s and achieved more general acceptance during the ensuing two decades as refinements in technique made it more practicable.

Mechanical grinding of wood fiber was the third method of separating wood fibers from their natural structure. Heinrich Voelter had developed a grinder in Germany that shredded wood into tiny, stiff strands. The first Voelter grinder in the United States was used in March 1867 at Curtisville, Massachusetts. Within a decade it was clear that this system would have a profound effect on the American paper industry. Smith describes the Voelter process as the great breakthrough in the production of cheap newsprint, since the decreased cost of paper allowed publishers to print an increased number of pages.[21]

The wood pulp revolution had a significant impact upon the paper industry. Paper was no longer scarce, as it had been when rag pulp was the principal component. Paper prices dropped, and competition among papermakers was greatly increased. Papermakers recognized that they needed access to large supplies of timber to guarantee a supply of the primary raw material. High prospects appeared for mills close to the forests, but an uncertain future confronted those that had been constructed near great urban centers when rags were the main ingredient of paper.

The new wood pulp technology delivered a galvanic shock to the paper industry of the Black River Valley, particularly as spruce became the dominant source of wood fiber. The great forests of northern New York had earlier attracted lumbermen, and their softwood cut gradually extended from Lake Ontario to the Adirondack Mountains. As the choice stands of trees disappeared, lumbermen migrated westward, leaving in their wake vacant mill and waterpower sites and spruce too small for lumber but adequate for pulping.

The North Country lumber industry had reached the point of extinction, but the stage was set for a new phase of industrial development. A New York paper industry historian asserted in 1920 with some exaggeration that "where there is a paper mill now there was once a saw mill."[22] In northern New York the pulp and paper industries fell heir to one of the state's richest natural resources, unique in its capacity for renewal. It remained to be seen if the papermakers would use the forest more wisely than had the lumbermen.

Reluctance to accept radical change on the part of both producers and consumers of newsprint prevented wood pulp from supplanting rag pulp prior to the 1880s. Indeed in the early years of the wood pulp revolution, groundwood pulp had to be combined with rag pulp in the manufacture of newsprint in order to achieve the desired quality. Some newspaper publishers experimented for years before shifting to all-wood paper. In 1878, over twenty years after the introduction of Voelter grinders in the United States, Taggart Brothers still used six parts rag pulp to four parts wood pulp in their newsprint. A. D. Remington discovered that more than 75 percent groundwood made a poor sheet of paper, and even Warner "Wood Pulp" Miller, one of the most aggressive early advocates of wood paper, used some rag material in his groundwood paper.[23]

An additional development in wood pulp technology was required to eliminate rag pulp completely in newsprint and other paper produced in large volume. Refinement of the sulfite process in Europe in the 1870s and 1880s provided the breakthrough, and A. D. Remington was the first to use the improved sulfite pulp in Watertown. After a trip to Sweden and Germany in the 1880s, he purchased the foreign pulp, shipped it to the United States, and, combining one part sulfite to three parts groundwood pulp, succeeded in producing a good-quality all-wood newsprint. Remington continued to import European sulfite until about 1890, when he constructed a sulfite mill near Watertown and became totally self-sufficient in the raw materials required for newsprint production.

The wood pulp revolution in the Watertown area was now complete, and it remained only for others to capitalize on it. One who did was John M. Tilden, who organized the Tilden Paper Company at Glen Park and began construction of a mill in 1887. Among the firm's backers were David M. Anderson and George W. Knowlton, Jr. Knowlton persuaded his fellow directors to install auxiliary rag machinery in the mill in case all-wood paper was not a market success. The facility commenced operation in 1889 on that basis. Because the groundwood-sulfite combination proved to be a lasting innovation, however, the rag engines were later scrapped. By that time, Tilden had left the firm, and it was renamed the Ontario Paper Company.[24]

Not long afterward, Anderson departed to join a new enterprise formed by the Taggart family. The Taggarts Paper Company was formed by Anderson, B. B. and W. W. Taggart, and George C. Sherman. Sherman had already acquired some manufacturing experience while working for the Watertown Steam Engine Company, in which his father, Charles Augustus Sherman, had been involved. In 1886 George Sherman married William Taggart's daughter Alice and became involved in the Taggart bag manufacturing operations.[25]

The Taggarts Paper Company constructed its first plant at Felts Mills on the Black River, a site formerly occupied by a tannery and a sawmill. Valuable power rights were available because a nearby factory, possessor of the riparian rights, had been destroyed by fire. The winter of 1889-1890 was mild, and construction of the paper mill progressed at such a pace that start-up was possible late in the summer of 1890. As with the Ontario mill, rag machinery was purchased but never used. From the start, Felts Mills produced all-wood newsprint and poster papers.

The Taggarts Paper Company was reasonably successful. Seven years after its inception, the company acquired the mill of the Great Bend Paper Company a few miles upriver. Originally the mill had run straw stock for parcel wrapping paper but later switched production to wallpaper. When wood pulp was still encountering consumer resistance, the mill had quietly increased the percentage of wood pulp in its paper. By the time Taggarts acquired the Great Bend mill, it was fully equipped to run all-wood wallpaper.[26]

In the meantime Watertown had become a city in which business-men played important leadership roles. In 1869, Colonel George W. Flower was elected the first mayor of Watertown. Roswell P. Flower, the colonel's brother, brought prominence to the city by winning election as governor of New York in 1892. As evidence of the rising influence of the Taggart family, B. B. Taggart was later elected for two terms as mayor, and W. W. Taggart served as a member of the board of education. The Carlisle family also achieved local and then national notoriety. William S. Carlisle, a Civil War veteran, held a modest position as a mechanic in Watertown's Davis Sewing Machine Company, but his oldest son was marked for a career in the public eye. After studying and then practicing law, John N. Carlisle sought and won power in local and state politics. As a young man he headed the Democratic State Executive Committee. The second son of the Carlisle family died at an early age, and the third son succumbed to wounds received during the Spanish-American War. The youngest son, Floyd Leslie, ultimately brought the Carlisle prestige and prosperity to its zenith.

Watertown held a Labor Day celebration in 1899, the year St. Regis was incorporated, and a handsome illustrated booklet was prepared for the occasion. The authors proudly emphasized that their booming city of twenty-five thousand persons had not neglected education, culture, or charity during its commercial and industrial growth. The public school library boasted seven thousand volumes, and area residents were kept informed of current events through two daily newspapers and numerous weekly, biweekly, and monthly periodicals. Enlightened citizens had constructed an opera house, and entertainments and lectures were held at the city hall. Also described were the facilities and services of numerous churches, charitable institutions, and hospitals.

The ultimate purpose of the booklet, however, was neither to discuss cultural advances nor to extol past accomplishments. The focus was on the years to come:

> The past of Watertown having furnished a record of continuous growth, it is fair to presume that the future will present results of proportionate advance on well accelerated expansion. In the utilization of the resources which Nature has furnished or Science

unveiled, there is every reason to believe Watertown will be fully abreast with the most enterprising cities. It has no lack of men with business sagacity equal to the improvement of every opportunity, and it is safe to predict that the historian of the industries of the future will be able to point back to those of today as the auspicious beginning of a greater and brighter destiny.[27]

As the nineteenth century came to an end, Watertown's commerce and industry were thriving, and there was every reason to think about the future with optimism. Retail businesses were crowded with customers from the city and from outlying villages and towns as well. Abundant natural resources made Watertown and its environs a major dairy center. The richly varied industry of the city included an air-brake factory, major carriage manufactories, textile and flour mills, a first-class brewery, a major manufacturer of heavy machinery, and, finally, what the city fathers claimed to be "the largest print paper mills in the world."[28]

What emerged most clearly from the Labor Day program was a recognition of the vital, ever-active force that linked the city's past, present, and future:

> It is well known that Watertown owes its prosperity wholly to the power furnished by the never-failing waters of Black River. . . . From the remotest headwaters of the river in the distant Adirondacks to the bay may be seen an almost continuous line of industrial establishments, furnishing employment to thousands and thousands of mechanics, and also employing millions of dollars in capital and every day bringing comfort to thousands of God's creatures.[29]

The paper industry of the Watertown area was the product of natural resources such as the power of the Black River and the surrounding stands of spruce, of scientific advances such as the fourdrinier and cylinder paper machines, and of the technological capacity to utilize wood pulp. Yet the critical factors that determined the success or failure of any new paper business were business sagacity, foresight, creativity, and stubborn refusal to quit in the face of adversity. It was this interaction of man, nature, and technology that led to the establishment of the St. Regis Paper Company.

2
The Arm of a Giant

"Civilization and factories and railroads and population," George C. Sherman observed in 1908, "must grow to . . . water power."[1] With other contemporary Watertown industrialists, he had seen the city's pulse quicken as manufacturers harnessed the Black River to spin their turbines. Sherman had directly participated in the Taggart family's growth to waterpower in the years following 1886. As the Taggarts expanded their initial bag operation and its successor within the Watertown city limits, they had also begun to extend their reach upriver. In 1889 the first Taggarts Paper Company mill had been constructed at Felts Mills, and in 1896 they had acquired the Great Bend mill, still farther upriver.

Whether by chance or by design, Sherman and David Anderson continued to search for good millsites upriver. The large S-shaped coil in the course of the Black River above Great Bend seemed to have tremendous potential, and the two men decided to construct a newsprint mill there. This decision led directly to the incorporation of St. Regis Paper Company in 1899.

There are only vague impressions of how the founders' initial vision was translated into reality. Neither Sherman nor Anderson nor their partners left personal or business records. The only letters known to exist are in the St. Regis records center in Watertown and in the National Archives, and all postdate the incorporation. Sherman and Anderson were by nature disinclined to reveal the most intimate details of St. Regis's founding and early years. Anderson became preoccupied with the production-oriented responsibilities of general manager and served as company spokesman only when necessary. Sherman maintained a considerably higher public profile, but his desire for secrecy motivated him in later years to withhold production and cost data even from certain St. Regis directors.[2]

Despite obstacles to a fuller understanding of the St. Regis story, fragmentary evidence does permit a personal glimpse of Sherman and Anderson. David M. Anderson was born in Harrison, New York, and the pulp and paper mills of the north were far removed from the area in which he spent his youth. Still he developed a strong conviction that papermaking was a growing industry. After receiving his education at Brooklyn Polytechnic Institute, he worked for a short time in New York City. Soon thereafter, Anderson made the decision that shaped the course of his life; gathering together modest savings, he moved to Watertown with his wife and infant daughter, where he found employment with John M. Tilden.

The art of papermaking fascinated Anderson. After a day's work with Tilden, he often made the short downriver trip to Glen Park to watch C. H. Remington and his men building their new mill. Apparently Remington was the right man to excite Anderson's interest in paper manufacture. Although descended from mill owners and managers, Remington "got his hands dirty," whether in pulpwood camps or at the construction site of a new mill. Anderson's practical knowledge of papermaking matured under Remington's informal tutelage. Infected with Remington's enthusiasm, Anderson in 1887 joined Tilden in a mill venture at Glen Park.[3] Still later Anderson was appointed general manager of Taggarts Paper Company, beginning his involvement with George Sherman.

Although an unobtrusive presence in the paper industry, Anderson nevertheless received credit for being "one of the brightest men in the business."[4] His countenance perfectly matched the stereotype of the "manufacturing man": firm jaw, cropped mustache, and pale, analytical eyes. But this severe mien represented only one side of the man. Quietly charming, Anderson was described by one contemporary as "a great mixer." Another of his peers recalls his social energy once the week's manufacturing concerns were laid to rest:

> The Shermans and the Andersons were society people. They liked parties, liked to dress up and do the right thing. . . . Yachts

were stylish on the St. Lawrence so they had a yacht together and they took turns using it. . . . Never have I known people lovelier to anybody than the Andersons were to me. And they were on the other side of the camp as far as business was concerned but a very likeable couple with a lot of the milk of human kindness in their systems.[5]

George C. Sherman had a different kind of business background from his partner. Growing up in a banking family, he gravitated to the financial and administrative end of the paper business. More so than Anderson, he participated in broad industry concerns, serving as vice-president of the American Paper and Pulp Association's News Division from 1896 to 1899. Records of Sherman's involvement in public affairs reveal a great deal about his character and temperament. Intense, energetic, and independent, he was clearly a leader. Pictures of him as a young man hint of the dandy: a certain refinement in dress, meticulously parted hair, a carefully waxed and curled mustache. Pictures taken in later years suggest high seriousness and the chastening effect of experience but also imply creativity, flair, and deep sensitivity.

Sherman had a good business presence, was an effective salesman, and possessed sound fiscal sense. These talents complemented Anderson's production and mill management abilities. Sherman's disposition and abilities, however, on occasion did harm. A strong ego contributed to his being a rebellious subordinate when confronted by what he considered plodding management. One effect of these traits was that Sherman could not long be satisfied with any business unless it was in large part his own. And so a complex chemistry of personalities and circumstances led Sherman and Anderson to begin accumulating small parcels of land along the Black River.

The circumstances were as important as the personalities in determining the success of the two men's venture. As the nineteenth century drew to a close, a swelling American population and an increasing demand for entertainment and knowledge provided the allurement to papermaker and publisher alike. Between 1880 and 1900 the number of daily newspapers doubled, while the circulation of weeklies and biweeklies increased by 50 percent.

Success in the papermaking field was linked inextricably with social change and rapid population growth. But it was linked as well to the technological revolution of the late nineteenth and early twentieth centuries. This revolution transformed the paper industry between 1840 and 1900. Not surprisingly that transformation was paralleled by the growth of printing and publishing. The development of the fourdrinier machine in the 1830s opened the way for the penny press, just as later in the century wood pulp processing discoveries by Voelter and others made possible the publication of mass-circulation daily newspapers.

Technical triumphs in papermaking were matched by inventions in printing and new methods of news gathering and distribution. The American firm of R. Hoe & Company brought out a succession of new rotary presses, which greatly speeded the process of printing newspapers. German immigrant Ottmar Mergenthaler contributed perhaps the most important invention of all when he produced between 1884 and 1889 a machine permitting a skilled operator to set three or four times as much type in an eight-hour day.[6]

The growth in printed media reflected America's developing sense of its importance as a new world power. Newspapers and magazines played upon this theme, often irresponsibly. This was never more dramatically demonstrated than in press coverage of the Spanish-American and Boer wars at the end of the century. Newspaper circulation increased dramatically during the 1890s, especially during the last three years of the decade when Sherman and Anderson were working out their plans for a newsprint mill.

The Spanish-American War established the sensational front-page headline as a circulation builder. Of almost equal importance were the emergence of color supplements and less expensive processes for reproducing pictures. When the New York World splashed the banner headline, "DECLARATION OF WAR," across its front page on April 17, 1898, circulation jumped to a record high of 1.3 million; as recently as 1896, the World's circulation had been only 370,000. Mushrooming circulation increased both the demand for and the cost of advertising. Newspaper publishing had arrived as a big business in America.[7]

Sherman and Anderson clearly saw the boom in newsprint consumption and sought to capitalize upon it. Newsprint mills ran full tilt, and publishers, anxious to cash in on favorable conditions, paid generously for paper. The future of the newsprint industry looked promising enough for these reasons alone. In addition, as a major industry spokesman stated, American business generally was "on the threshold of a period of national expansion."[8] Other factors, however, offered warnings to even the most optimistic investor in newsprint manufacture. Some cautions were tacit, but others were impossible to overlook. The wood pulp revolution dramatically changed the nature of the paper business, both in terms of raw material supply and in terms of pricing.

During this period apprehension was voiced about the timber available for exploitation by the forest products industry. One northern New York correspondent predicted the extinction of privately owned Adirondack spruce due to extensive cutting by softwood lumber and pulp and paper manufacturers. Gifford Pinchot, soon to become the most influential figure in the American conservation movement, established in 1893 a forestry consulting firm in New York City. "His concern here," notes historian Harold T. Pinkett, "was to save the Adirondack forests from destructive use, which had begun with extensive lumbering of virgin pine, and by 1893 was resulting in widespread loss of commercially valuable spruce."[9]

The pulp and paper industry did not fail to see the significance of these warnings. At the 1898 convention of the American Paper and Pulp Association (APPA), Pinchot delivered an address based upon his work in the Adirondacks. He described the hazards facing the forest products industry and argued that the pulp industry was devastating the landscape even more than the lumbermen because it was not limited to the larger trees. Spruce was heavily cut for many uses, and only inferior stock was left for reproduction.[10]

Pinchot was not alone in expressing these concerns. In late 1898 the New York State College of Forestry at Cornell University was founded under the leadership of America's first professional forester, Bernhard Eduard Fernow. It set up experiments in silviculture on thirty thousand acres of land in Franklin County purchased from the Santa Clara Lumber Company.[11]

The long-range plans of foresters who had studied the results of European forest exploitation were difficult to sell to American businessmen seeking short-term profits. There were really only two sources of raw material supply: land held in fee simple by the manufacturer and logs bought on the open market. By 1898 newsprint manufacturers in the United States faced a steadily declining supply of domestic spruce logs and resultant rising log prices. This led to the importation of logs from Canada. But as the reliance on wood from north of the border grew, so also did anxiety as to how long this importation would be possible on terms advantageous to American buyers.[12]

The industry's pricing problems also derived from the wood pulp revolution. Despite warnings of future timber supply problems, wood was not yet the major scarcity item that rags had been when they were the primary component of paper. With the advent of easily produced wood pulp, the paper industry began to suffer from overproduction and savage competition. More often than not, the industry's price structure was in shambles. In the 1880s and 1890s, newsprint manufacturers enjoyed only brief periods of strong profits amid long spells of marginal returns.[13]

Sherman kept close watch on the newsprint industry as vice-president of the APPA's News Division. He participated in the elation that accompanied the boom created by the Spanish-American and Boer wars, but he remembered earlier droughts. He later described the year 1897 as "perhaps the hardest ever experienced by the newspaper manufacturers." He also placed boom periods into perspective by emphasizing their inevitable aftermath:

> The . . . war with Spain caused, of course, an extraordinary local demand for paper . . . newspapers and mills were all carrying small stocks. Consumers at once ordered wildly and far in excess of their printing possibilities. . . . When the dull season finally occurred and hostilities ceased, publishers found themselves with very large stocks and merely a nominal consumption. If . . . we could fairly average the effect of the war upon the amount of business we would otherwise have received for the year, it seems to me that the extra quantity consumed will be found to be less than generally supposed.[14]

Mergers seemed to offer relief from distorted production and pricing through combination. In 1898 the International Paper Company (IP) was organized by combining twenty mills in New York, Massachusetts, Maine, Vermont, and New Hampshire. Its daily production of more than one thousand tons of newsprint and printing paper was backed by extensive timberlands. At one point, IP claimed control of three-quarters of American newsprint production.[15]

Elimination of competition through consolidation did not in the long run mitigate the newsprint industry's pricing problems. Although prices strengthened during 1898 as a result of the war and IP's incorporation, these beneficial effects were transient. The newsprint industry soon reverted to a period of unimpressive earnings, and George W. Knowlton, Jr., lamented in 1902, "There is no business that makes such a small return for the capital invested in it and the intelligence used in it as the newspaper mill of today."[16]

The hopes that combination would produce an enduring run of better prices were also dashed by the press lords. Newspaper publishers were tough negotiators who enjoyed the advantage of being able to use their editorial pages to attack suppliers. The publishers expressed hostility immediately after the formation of IP. John Norris of the *New York World* advertised for "a free, anti-trust paper mill" and offered a ten-year contract and funding to any firm outside of what he called the "paper trust." The terms of the offer indicate that Norris was serious. IP reportedly regarded the entire affair as a bluff to create price leverage, since the facilities that supplied the *World* were part of the paper trust. The *World*, though, launched an attack on IP, describing it as "a conspiracy to tax knowledge, to levy tribute on education, to blackmail intelligence itself."[17]

This agitation over pricing and trusts, as well as the general concern over domestic pulpwood supply, focused attention on the tariff duties on Canadian pulp and newsprint. Although desire for reform of the duties had been registered as early as 1879, American manufacturers continued to be protected by tariff barriers. Free importation of Canadian pulpwood was permitted, whereas duties were levied upon Canadian pulp and newsprint. The sheltered American industry faced a double threat. First, U.S. publishers began an active campaign for removal of the tariff in the belief that cheap Canadian pulp and paper would drive American market prices down. At the same time, some Canadians pressed for an export duty on pulpwood shipped to the United States, arguing that pulp and paper should be made in Canada by Canadians, with the profits going to Canadians. American newsprint producers discussed the threat at their 1899 annual meeting. Sherman declared that if Canadian paper and pulp were given free entry, it would force the closure of American mills and "the transfer of this great industry to a foreign land." He minced no words in declaring his belief that the newspaper publishers were pursuing a policy that was "unreasonable and wrong."[18]

As Sherman and Anderson moved to build their new newsprint mill at the turn of the century, they were not unmindful of the factors affecting their decision. They were especially concerned with the impact on product pricing of the recently created IP combine. During the congressional investigation of the pulp and paper industry in 1908, Sherman discussed IP's influence. He testified that IP set the trend in pricing, one that other and smaller manufacturers tended to follow.[19]

Another major impact of IP was its sweeping entrance into the Black River Valley in 1899. An initial foothold was secured early in 1898 through acquisition of former New York Governor Roswell P. Flower's Piercefield Paper Company. Rumors followed that the Gould Paper Company, the Ontario Paper Company, and some of the Remington mills would follow Piercefield into the combine. International's news magnates traveled to Watertown in May 1898 to scrutinize the Ontario, Remington, and Taggarts properties. In early 1899 their designs on the Remington and Ontario properties were confirmed when the mills were absorbed by the combine.[20]

The presence of IP in the Black River Valley in 1898 and 1899 offered the prospect of a battle for waterpower rights. Sherman and Anderson had about completed acquisition of their millsite. They held options on two key properties owned by the Freeman family and farmer Frank Reynolds, and there was conjecture that IP sought to increase the option price, acquire the two tracts, and thereby prevent construction of an independent mill in the area.

Another account indicates that Flower, now one of IP's directors, sought to acquire the Reynolds site for the combine:

> Anderson . . . was a good friend of Frank Reynolds. Reynolds lived at Deferiet and owned that 645 acres of farmland where the Deferiet mill is now. When Anderson heard that Flower was after this, and they [IP] had been thinking about that site as a power development, he went to Frank Reynolds. He made a deal with him for less money than Flower offered him, so the story goes, because of their friendship. Anderson was a great man in that way. And the understanding was that Reynolds was to have the use of all the farmlands that St. Regis didn't want to use for as long as he lived.[21]

Whether such stories are true or not, the important point is that by 1899

Sherman and Anderson held clear control over the land and power rights for their mill.

Having established firm claim to two essential components, Sherman and Anderson turned to assuring a third, the timberland that would guarantee their new mill a steady flow of raw material independent of the log market. It seems unlikely that they would have committed so much capital and energy to their enterprise without having given prior consideration to the source of wood. This must have led them to a systematic search of major ownerships within range of their millsite. The firm of Dodge, Meigs and Company was widely known at the time as both a developer and operator of timberlands from Canada to Georgia. It operated several lumber mills, including the Santa Clara Lumber Company, with lumber mills at St. Regis Falls and Santa Clara in Franklin County. It also owned a railroad capable of transporting pulpwood to the Sherman-Anderson millsite.

The process by which Sherman and Anderson became partners with George E. Dodge, Titus B. Meigs, and Ferris J. Meigs remains obscure, but it is known that the arrangement was completed prior to the incorporation of St. Regis. Dodge was the heir of philanthropist William E. Dodge, described by one historian as "the last of the merchant princes."[22] He had served for twenty-five years as New York State commissioner of Manhattan State Mental Hospital, which housed nine thousand patients. He also organized support for a sanitarium in the Adirondacks. Titus Meigs was a longtime business associate of both Dodges. Ferris Meigs, Titus's son, managed the Dodges' affairs in Franklin County, which included ownership of a considerable body of timber. His father and George Dodge supervised the larger interests of Dodge, Meigs and Company from offices in New York City.[23]

Early in 1899 the five partners incorporated the St. Regis Paper Company. The name was suggested by the river and falls dominating the Santa Clara timberland that was formally deeded to the paper company later in the year. How "St. Regis" became linked with the river and falls is suggested in several sources. Jean François Regis, born in France in 1597, was a Jesuit priest highly admired for his reputed performance of miracles. He died in 1640 and was canonized in the following century.[24] François Regis never realized his desire to be a missionary in the New World. Other Jesuits, though, traveled to North America to convert the Indians. One of their number reached a village of the Caughnawaga Indians, and after converting the inhabitants, renamed it St. Regis in honor of the saint. In due course, this offshoot of the Caughnawaga tribe, the nearby river, and the falls all acquired the same designation.[25]

Sherman, Anderson, Dodge, and the Meigses drew up the articles of incorporation of the St. Regis Paper Company in New York City on 26 January 1899, and filed the certificate on 4 February. The total capitalization of $1 million was divided equally between five thousand shares of common and five thousand shares of preferred stock. The dividend on preferred, 6 percent annually, was made payable beginning three months after the mill commenced operation. Of the remaining earnings, $25,000 was to be paid into a surplus fund each year and the balance distributed as dividends on common stock. The incorporators became the first St. Regis board of directors. At the initial meeting in March 1899, George E. Dodge was elected president and Titus B. Meigs and W. W. Taggart were named, respectively, first and second vice-presidents. Anderson became general manager, Sherman the treasurer, F. J. Meigs the secretary, and Frederick J. Soper the assistant secretary.[26]

Three of the five founders played active roles in St. Regis's first year. Responsibility for raising capital and constructing the mill was delegated to Sherman and Anderson. Timberland fell within the purview of Ferris Meigs, acknowledged authority on the land Santa Clara planned to transfer to St. Regis. Dodge, Titus Meigs, and Soper remained in New York City and, aside from participation in board meetings, seem to have engaged very little in company affairs. William W. Taggart was seventy-five years old, and board minutes clearly show that he was a valued adviser, especially in matters of finance and assignment of dividends. His election each year as second vice-president carried no defined responsibilities.[27]

Plans for the capacity of the St. Regis mill were largely based upon data assembled by the younger Meigs, who asserted that eighty thousand acres of Dodge-Meigs land would provide St. Regis with an average yield of five cords per acre, or a total of four hundred thousand cords. On the basis of these calculations, it was decided to build a two-machine mill that would produce fifty tons of product a day. The mill would consume twenty thousand cords per year and so had an assured raw material supply for two decades of operation. Additions of a third machine at the end of the first year and a fourth after the second year

of operations were projected. There seems to have been no recognition given to the fact that increased mill production would cut short the flow of logs from company lands and necessitate the securing of raw material from other sources.[28]

Ferris Meigs's cordage estimate also determined plans for the financing of the new facility. Standing pulpwood was valued at $1.25 to $1.50 per cord, so the company's timber could be used to secure a $500,000 issue of twenty-year bonds. The capital raised in this fashion would cover the cost of mill construction and waterpower development. A sinking fund, scheduled to terminate after accumulating $500,000 through twenty annual payments of $25,000, would pay the principal on the bonds. The basis for Meigs's estimate later became the focus of growing dissension among the founders and involved Gifford Pinchot, the chief forester of the U.S. Division of Forestry.

In the meantime, Sherman and Anderson devised the plan for developing waterpower. Damming the river might flood adjoining land, so it was decided to divert the stream through a canal cut across one gooseneck of land formed by the river's S-curve. Excavation of a canal fifty-seven hundred feet long was to be completed by the end of November 1899.

St. Regis moved toward implementation of these plans. Late in March 1899 a contract was signed with Manufacturers Paper Company for marketing the combined output of the St. Regis and Taggarts paper companies. This sales agency, headed by Kenneth B. Fullerton, had developed from combination of the sales departments of three paper companies absorbed by IP. To receive a 5 percent commission on paper sales for five years, Manufacturers guaranteed the accounts and agreed to pay St. Regis and Taggarts in weekly installments. The contract was to become effective upon completion of the St. Regis mill, probably late in 1899 or early in 1900.

Shortly thereafter St. Regis sealed a contract with the Santa Clara Lumber Company for fifty-seven thousand acres of timberlands in Franklin County, valued at approximately $359,000, with payment made in preferred stock. An additional twenty-two and a half thousand acres valued at about $141,000 were acquired from the Forest, Land and Mill Company, of which Ferris Meigs was president. Since the Dodge-Meigs interests received payment for this latter acreage in preferred stock and demand notes, its ownership seems obvious. Later, payment for this tract was altered to preferred stock only.[29]

Sherman and Anderson were reimbursed in cash for their millsite and waterpower rights. After these transactions were completed, Dodge and the Meigses possessed all of St. Regis's preferred stock; in addition, they divided one-half of the common stock among themselves for services rendered in connection with the timberland acquisition. The other half of the common stock was given to Sherman and Anderson for their work on the millsite. This division of common stock was simply an arrangement for equitable distribution among the founders of profits remaining after preferred stock dividends and sinking fund payments had been made.[30]

With timberland, waterpower, and millsite now officially in possession of the company, St. Regis's founders began to raise the capital for the undertaking that lay ahead. Late in May the directors mortgaged the company's land, waterpower, and mills to the Colonial Trust Company of New York City. By midsummer a $500,000 mortgage had been executed, and, with Colonial as trustee, the first St. Regis mortgage bonds were ready for sale to the public.

Anderson's business connections were used to contact one prospective purchaser of bonds. As a director of the Agricultural Insurance Company of Watertown, he convinced his associates to invest in the venture. By mid-May the insurance company was contemplating subscription to $100,000 of St. Regis bonds, and, because the security of the bonds was intimately tied to the value of St. Regis timberland, Ferris Meigs was called to Watertown to confer with insurance company officials. By mid-July, Sherman was able to report an "informal agreement" with this investor.[31]

Construction had begun while these financial transactions went forward. Civil engineer Frank A. Hinds of Watertown surveyed the canal site in March, and bids were opened in mid-April. Belden and Seely of Syracuse won the excavation contract, and on April 20, 1899, President Dodge signed the agreement. The contractors posted bond against successful completion of the canal by the end of November 1899. Belden and Seely shipped graders and other equipment to the millsite in May, and the basic lines of the canal and a branch railroad line were laid out. Borings were made to determine the depth to which mill foundations had to extend.

What Sherman estimated as one-fifth of the earth to be excavated was removed by midsummer, and construction of a permanent village for mill workers was begun. A hotel, store, and post office were erected, followed by construction of residential housing. The millsite was cleared, and rapid progress was made on the railroad line. Graders, each driven by twelve teams of horses, sheared away tons of soil in grading the roadbed. Groups of men sledged ties and rails into place. Workers, horses, and equipment were shifted to canal excavation as the railroad right-of-way neared completion.

Estimates were received on stone masonry and brickwork for mill construction. Contractors from Rochester, Utica, Syracuse, and Watertown placed bids, and George J. Benson of Watertown won the contract by bidding $7,000 less than the closest competitor. A contract for the mill's steel beams was negotiated with the Carnegie Steel Company. By late July the railroad switch was completed, opening a major means of delivering building material to the site. Five hundred men and three hundred horses toiled on the various projects.

As fall approached, signs were auspicious for successful and rapid completion. Construction of the mill's foundation and chimney commenced and was fed each day with twelve carloads of building materials. Hopes for timely completion of construction were further buoyed by progress on the canal and work on the dam, both aided by low water in the Black River.[32]

By mid-autumn, St. Regis received the first indication of troubles ahead. As soil was scooped from the canal and blasting of the underlying limestone commenced, the magnitude of the task became apparent. A great deal of rock would have to be extracted from the raw scar in the earth that had so far grown swiftly in length and depth.[33] New contractors were granted an extension of time until 15 July 1900. This was, of course, a major revision of the original schedule, resulting in extra inconvenience and cost. Hope focused on the new date, but more problems lay ahead. Even by July 1900 it could not be reasonably said that the end of the canal job was in sight.[34]

Materials problems were compounded by the failure of Sherman and Anderson to communicate to their associates a major change in building plans, increasing the size of the plant to a four-machine, one-hundred-ton mill. Ferris and Titus Meigs objected, pointing out that an increase in cost from $500,000 to $750,000 would be incurred if the new plan was followed. Adding two machines would necessitate greater pulp capacity and more extensive waterpower development, and the pulpwood supply on St. Regis's eighty thousand acres of timberland would be more quickly diminished. Ferris Meigs was pointed in his complaint, speaking against incurring "large bank indebtedness."[35]

The St. Regis minutes indicate confusion over the cost of the altered plans. Sherman estimated that an increase to $750,000 would cover only additional power development and greater mill capacity. Computing the cost of the third and fourth machines, Sherman pushed for an even million dollars, twice the capital provided by the original bond issue. After various estimates were discussed, the directors resolved to build a mill with space for four machines but with initial installation of only two machines. Sherman won concessions on the other increases in capacity, and the total price tag was raised to $700,000 to $750,000.[36]

The proposed doubling of capacity and the preparations for St. Regis's first bond issue created a need to ascertain the exact quantity of raw material on the company's new timberland. But there would be persistent misunderstanding about the cordage this acreage could yield when cutting commenced: four cords per acre (a total of three hundred and twenty thousand cords on eighty thousand acres) or five cords per acre (a total of four hundred thousand cords). And on the issue of that discrepancy, correspondence between the founders abounds with confusion. Efforts to communicate were doomed by the founders' inclinations toward obscurity in their business affairs.

Financing the mill through the issuance of mortgage bonds required precise information on the quantity and value of the wood standing on company land. In considering a purchase of $100,000 in bonds, for instance, the Agricultural Insurance Company demanded a guarantee of the available cordage. This request triggered further dissension. Sherman and Anderson had accepted, on the authority of Ferris Meigs, the original estimate of four hundred thousand cords. But because Dodge and the Meigses were uncertain about the actual cordage, they formulated a safety plan for provision of adequate raw material. For the first two or three years of the mill's operation, Santa Clara Lumber would supply St. Regis with pulpwood from its own land. The cordage thus delivered would be credited to the three hundred and twenty thousand cords Santa Clara had guaranteed on what was now St. Regis land.

Neither Sherman nor Anderson would budge in their commitment to a four-machine mill. In August Sherman placed orders with the Bagley and Sewall Company of Watertown for four machines. As a consequence of this increase in capacity, St. Regis shortly thereafter entered into a new pulpwood contract with the Santa Clara Lumber Company. This agreement, totally distinct from any arrangements made earlier, stipulated that Santa Clara would deliver from its own lands to the paper company twelve thousand cords of rossed wood annually for ten years at $9.00 per cord, with an option to extend the contract for an additional ten years at $12.00 per cord.[37]

Thus Sherman and Anderson's plan for increased capacity went forward at a high cost in capital and in division among the founders. The Meigs's immediate objection to expanded capacity boiled down to a matter of dollars and cents. Almost from the beginning, they expressed concern about their cash payoff for the timberland that Dodge, Meigs and Company had deeded to St. Regis. Dodge and the Meigses had initially received in exchange for their timberland all of the paper company's preferred stock, totaling $500,000. The only cash reimbursement Dodge and the Meigses would receive in the short term was a 6 percent dividend on their preferred stock, this being payable only after mandatory interest payments on the St. Regis bonds had been made. No provision was made to pay them for their preferred shares at par, the stated value of the land they had surrendered. As Titus Meigs complained, "The title to 80,000 acres of forest lands has been parted with for an unguaranteed payment of interest at 6% on the amount of purchase with no provision for payment of principal."[38]

Sherman and Anderson responded to this apprehension by agreeing to purchase one-fifth of the St. Regis preferred at par, an outlay of $100,000. This concession placated their partners, at least until the issue of adding two machines arose, with the commensurate doubling of capital requirements. The inevitable increase in outside financing posed the threat of another bloc of investors clamoring for dividends in line ahead of the Dodge-Meigs interests. Dodge suggested a resolution that seemed to benefit everyone. Since the Meigses were apprehensive about reimbursement for their portion of the preferred stock, Dodge bought out all their preferred holdings at par. He then purchased the Meigs's common shares at $30.00, $70.00 under par. In return, Dodge turned over his 60 percent interest in Santa Clara Lumber to the Meigses, thereby giving them complete ownership of the lumber firm. It is easy to speculate that it was stipulated that Santa Clara enter into a long-term pulpwood supply contract with St. Regis.[39]

Dodge now owned four-fifths of the St. Regis preferred and one-half of its common stock. He thereby controlled half the voting stock and could ultimately cash in on four-fifths of the value of the timberland, receiving a 6 percent dividend on the preferred before he did so. The Meigses had dispensed with their stock, believing that the success of the venture was imperiled by indebtedness. Although the formal severance of their St. Regis directorships did not come until November, their only actual link with St. Regis now was the long-term supply contract, which was made at what appeared to be a fine price for Santa Clara. Sherman and Anderson also must have been pleased by the supply contract, despite the fact that it was made at an apparently heavy price.

Sherman and Anderson gambled that the soaring market price of pulpwood would soon exceed the long-term contract price, thereby justifying the excessive cost in the short-term future. Dodge placed his reliance on the fact that the St. Regis timberland represented by his preferred stock was valuable. And the Meigses, perhaps realizing that ultimately they might not profit from the supply contract with St. Regis, were at least full owners of Santa Clara. They could make a killing on the St. Regis contract as long as their prices were above market, and they also had the Santa Clara land and mills as sources of additional income.

Still another shot remained to be fired in the internecine war between the founders of St. Regis. It is rather ironic that the final act resulted from one of the first efforts to employ professional forestry in the management of an American forest products company. Two of the first Americans to earn forestry degrees in Europe were Gifford Pinchot and Henry Solon Graves, both Yale University graduates who had continued their graduate studies at the famed French forestry school in Nancy. In the 1890s, Pinchot and Graves began working as consultants to private timberland owners in the Adirondacks, among them the Santa Clara Lumber Company. During this period, Pinchot and Graves briefly examined Santa Clara timberland, as well as Webb and Whitney tracts. In March 1897 Graves submitted to Ferris Meigs a brief report on "two . . . areas where the conditions were most favorable for the growth of spruce." These observations were applicable to only two sample plots of slightly more than one acre, not to Santa Clara lands at large. Both were prime growing sites, and Graves reported finding nearly twenty cords of growing spruce.[40]

At the same time, Santa Clara made its own survey of the pulpwood harvest on two thousand acres of its land. The findings showed a yield of only one and one-half cords per acre, a sampling later verified by Overton Price of the federal forestry division in a November 1899 report to Ferris Meigs. It therefore becomes evident that there was deception on the part of Dodge, Meigs and Company in their dealings with Sherman and Anderson and in their valuation of company forest-lands in the St. Regis bond prospectus. Shadow is also cast on the role played by Gifford Pinchot, since he endorsed the glowing statements in the prospectus. Pinchot wrote Ferris Meigs on 12 April 1899, giving his approval to the statement that "the Division of Forestry, United States Department of Agriculture, has informed us officially that these lands are admirably adapted to the growth of spruce timber, and that under proper and intelligent cutting they would readily produce a large annual supply of pulpwood." Pinchot left it to Meigs to decide whether Pinchot's name would be used in the statement. Pinchot did ask that a statement be added that "the lumbering on this tract would be done under the management and control of this Division." Pinchot was attempting to get private owners to submit voluntarily to federal control of their timber cutting, and in this instance he was successful. Within a month, Pinchot wrote again to Meigs, thanking him for "the very interesting and satisfactory statement concerning the St. Regis Paper Company," and asking for half a dozen extra copies. "The fact that great lumber companies are availing themselves of our offer of assistance is going to help us very much indeed."[41]

It is difficult to understand Pinchot's enthusiasm for the statements made in the St. Regis prospectus. He was not unfamiliar with the character of the land in question, nor could he have been unacquainted with the fact that the findings of his friend Graves were based upon a very limited sample. Pinchot selected Overton Price to oversee the St. Regis project. By early summer 1899, Price and a crew of young foresters were devising a working plan for the pulpwood cut that St. Regis would need once it went into operation. At the same time they also engaged in an experimental study of the growth rate of hardwood on the property. By November Price had discovered how sparse the timber actually was. His report confirmed the earlier private Santa Clara survey, and it was now impossible to hide the situation from St. Regis.[42]

The Price report caused Dodge to write a long letter to lawyer

John P. Badger on 22 November, the purpose of which was to absolve himself of any wrongdoing and to put the full weight of guilt upon Ferris Meigs:

> As you very well know, the St. Regis Paper Company purchased what they supposed was 80,000 acres of land from the Santa Clara Lumber Company. This purchase was made entirely on the representations of Mr. Ferris Meigs; that these lands were valuable and contained at least 300,000 cords of spruce wood.
>
>   It is now found that a positive fraud has been committed by Ferris Meigs. . . . A Government expert has been over the lands and after a careful study of them for more than four months, makes the report that there is [sic] at least 17,000 acres of waste and swamp lands, and that more than 12,000 acres have had all the small spruce wood cut off of them. . . . This leaves about 50,000 acres of land with spruce on it, and this has only a cord and a half to the acre, making about 100,000 cords of wood on the property instead of the 300,000 to 400,000 as always claimed by Ferris Meigs. . . . Ferris Meigs constantly spoke of the full 80,000 acres. He said nothing as to the waste and barren land and nothing as to the land he knew perfectly well had been cut over.[43]

But who among the Dodge-Meigs group was innocent of misrepresentation? It seems unlikely that any of the owners of the Santa Clara Lumber Company were uninformed of the true worth of their forest holdings. They had their own experts check harvest potential at least a year before entering into their partnership with St. Regis. Despite the indignant tone of Dodge's letter to Badger, his plea for respectability in an April 1899 letter to Sherman is as provocative as it is ambiguous:

> I am very glad to note by your last letter just received that you have decided not to print the Prospectus as to the bonds in any of the papers just as present, for this falls in line with what I had the pleasure of writing you yesterday.
>
>   My whole hope in all this matter is to carry it through with as little publicity and with as little noise and brass bands as we can, for it would be so much more dignified and will make our posi-

tion so much more respected by the Banks and by the Paper Trade.

We are sending the Prospectus back to you today with a few corrections and additions that we hope will be satisfactory to you.[44]

The management and organization of St. Regis crumbled rapidly in the fall of 1899 and early 1900. The Meigses resigned as officers and directors in November. Dodge agreed to return much of his preferred stock to the company treasury. He retained 1,786 of his 4,000 shares, this reduced holding representing the actual amount of pulpwood multiplied by the market price of $1.50 per cord. Most of his common stock—2,250 of his 2,500 shares—was also returned.[45]

The controversies of 1899 sullied personal reputations, emptied directors' chairs, and revealed a massive raw material supply problem. It also, as Dodge indicated in his letter to Badger, precipitated a financial crisis:

> See the injury it [the controversy] has done. It has stopped at once all sale of our [St. Regis] Bonds and brought our Paper Company to a standstill. Do you suppose for one moment that Sherman and Anderson and myself are going to see positive ruin staring us in the face and make no effort to obtain redress?[46]

By April 1900 there were only reminders of the Dodge-Meigs collaboration. Dodge resigned as president and remained a peripheral figure on the St. Regis board, finally severing this involvement in 1902.[47]

The management turnover and the bond crisis opened the way for the infusion of new managerial blood. George W. Knowlton, Jr., replaced Dodge as president. Knowlton was a revered figure in the industry, a man who had worked in machine rooms, mill offices and, finally, had headed Knowlton Brothers. Shortly after his election to the St. Regis presidency, his reputation in the paper business was recognized by his election as vice-president of the APPA's News Division. In 1903 he became that organization's president. Knowlton's reputation brought relief to St. Regis's financial difficulties. He assumed responsibility for placing the remaining unsold bonds, raising the interest rate to 6 percent, and guaranteeing payment of the interest and principal by the

Taggarts Paper Company as inducements to investors. Knowlton was aided in bond placement by his friend, Albrecht Pagenstecher, an IP director. At that time such assistance was not seen as a conflict of interest.[48]

Others who joined the St. Regis directorate were K. B. Fullerton and Alvah Miller of H. G. Craig and Company, a sales agency. Sherman had used the Craig agency since 1894 to sell the Taggarts Paper Company's specialty production, and Miller represented them on the St. Regis board. He also became a major individual shareholder; in fact Sherman described his relationship with Miller as "almost a partnership."[49]

St. Regis took an additional step to secure its financial position by selling twenty-two thousand acres of its land to William Rockefeller. Finally it agreed to sell a volume of hardwood on its remaining fifty-eight thousand acres to the Weidmann Stave and Heading Mills. Proceeds from the timber sales were diverted to the sinking fund to repay the principal on the company's mortgage bonds.[50]

As spring came to the Black River Valley in 1900, work on the St. Regis mill began again, but then without warning, canal excavation was halted by Metropolitan Paving. On the night of 31 March, Metropolitan pulled six railroad cars onto the branch line at the millsite and loaded them with dump wagons, wheel scrapers, and shovels. Early the next morning, a locomotive moved this equipment to the village of Carthage, where it was hidden in a building. St. Regis now lacked both a canal contractor and some of the basic equipment needed to complete the work. Metropolitan Paving's act stemmed from the fact that it was in serious financial condition, compounded by mortgages held by a Schenectady bank on its construction equipment. St. Regis obtained an injunction preventing removal of any additional earth-moving equipment. Even so, Anderson estimated that each day of idleness on the canal project cost the company $1,000.[51]

Within a month Sherman and Anderson secured the services of the Engineering Contract Company, and work was under way once again. As canal work reached a high pitch, a new threat emerged, this time in abrogation of the pulpwood supply contract of August 1899 between St. Regis and Santa Clara Lumber. The absolute terms of the contract—duration, price, and wood quantity—were not called into question, but the matter of advance payments was. The advances, designed to cover the immediate expense of cutting the wood, had been paid by St. Regis at the rate of $2.00 per cord, providing Santa Clara with approximately $25,000. Ferris Meigs, however, claimed that advances should have been made at $3.00 per cord, leaving an unpaid balance of $15,000. Sherman claimed there was an arbitration clause in the agreement, but Meigs insisted there was not. Upon failure of the paper company to pay the contested amount, Meigs revoked the contract and attempted to sell the land subject to this agreement to the Brooklyn Cooperage Company.[52] St. Regis secured an injunction against the sale to Brooklyn Cooperage, but by the summer of 1901 the complaint was dismissed.[53]

Sherman remained determined to defeat Meigs. His onslaughts against Santa Clara Lumber stemmed mostly from his concern for raw material supply, but there was also an important economic incentive. A major inducement for Santa Clara Lumber when the contract was signed in 1899 had stipulated that St. Regis would pay fifty cents per cord above market. Sherman had gambled that the handsome short-term bait would be more than counterbalanced by an increase in the market price for pulpwood, and he was right. Had the St. Regis-Santa Clara contract been in force in 1908, St. Regis would have still been paying $9.00 per cord, fully $3.50 less than the market price. Sherman ultimately won his case after seven years of litigation; but this triumph did not solve the raw material supply issue, and one critic, examining the terms of the settlement, considered the victory to be a hollow one.[54]

In 1900 St. Regis pushed ahead with construction work. The construction force was increased to seven hundred and then to a thousand workers in the hopes that the canal would be completed by the end of the year. Work on the mill now progressed rapidly, but again the canal presented problems. Quicksand-like material was encountered in the tailrace, which made the use of heavy machinery very difficult. As the year drew to a close, a major effort was made to complete the project before the onset of freezing weather. By the beginning of November, the boiler house, finishing room, and two of the machine rooms were under roof, and foundations were being built for the groundwood mill. In the last month of the year, all but the groundwood and sulfite mills were under roof, and the paper machines were on their way to the mill. Cold weather caused discontinuation of the night shift, and the labor force was reduced to five hundred. St. Regis would not start up during 1900.

The bitter cold of winter set in, but in some respects this was a blessing because the freezing temperatures hardened the soil around the tailrace, rendering it a much easier surface on which to work. By the end of February 1901, two paper machines were partially installed, and the sulfite plant digester house was completed. In early March, the major portion of the canal and tailrace excavation was completed, leaving only cleanup and work on the sloping walls before it would be ready. Also to be finished was installation of the two smaller machines and completion of the groundwood mill.[55] Finally, on 30 July, the mill started up and the four machines, measuring 145, 126, 110, and 90 inches, began to spin out broad rolls of newsprint. As George C. Sherman and David M. Anderson watched the finished product emerge from the machines, they must have felt a surge of great pride and relief, confirmation having come at last that the agonizing struggles had been worthwhile.

The company bore the name of a French saint, and by 1901 St. Regis's first mill and the nearby village had also received a French name. Originally the town built around the mill had been named Eggleston in honor of the company's first president, George Eggleston Dodge. The local citizenry, however, disliked the name. The ruin of what had been a magnificent mansion known as the Hermitage was nearby. It had been built in 1824 by Jenika De Feriet, reputed to have been a lady-in-waiting to Marie Antoinette. Madame De Feriet was forced to leave France during the Revolution, but it was not until 1816 that she settled in the North Country. Despite the sumptuous furnishings of her mansion, the wild beauty of the natural setting, and the lively socializing, Madame De Feriet suffered from loneliness and finally returned to France. The De Feriet mansion was destroyed by fire in 1871, but the people of the area remained firmly attached to the ruined landmark. In 1901 they persuaded St. Regis to change the name of their town from "Eggleston" to "Deferiet."[56]

The Deferiet mill and village were destined, unlike the woman after whom they were named, to remain and prosper in the North Country. The *Watertown Daily Times* celebrated the start-up of the mill in 1901 in a special issue. The editor and his staff waxed eloquent in their accounting of the building of a "Mammoth Papermaking Plant." The new mill upriver from Watertown was the largest built in the region, and its importance to the North Country was heralded with all the fanfare and public applause typical of the day. The great foresight of

the company's founders, their grand plans, the great obstacles overcome: all were given an exhaustive recounting. Not forgotten was the
land and its physical resources, which served to provide opportunities
for such heroic accomplishment:

> Facing north and looking from a commanding hill on the south
> side of Black River about two miles above the village of Great
> Bend, in the town of Champion, a panorama stretches out from
> east to west, the river circling sharply to the south, swinging
> close to the base of the hill on which the observer stands, and
> falling in a succession of rapids as it swerves back towards the
> north until it finds the lower level and takes its general direction
> again. It is like the bend of an elbow, and it is the arm of a giant.[57]

3
Survival in Troubled Times

The twentieth century marked much more than a shift in calendars. It was the time when more Americans lived in urban than rural settings, a result of industrialization. Family-owned firms were becoming less common; now boards of directors answered to stockholders who were primarily interested in dividends. A decade earlier, the Census Bureau had proclaimed the end of the American frontier; the land-rich nation seemed to be running out of its most abundant resource. These shifts were not dramatic and undoubtedly only unconsciously perceived by those who lived their lives from day to day. But the cumulative impacts were dramatic.

As part of this drama, President Theodore Roosevelt broke with tradition by turning the executive branch into an aggressive arm of government. Notions of laissez-faire were challenged as Roosevelt took on the "malefactors of wealth." Not to be outdone, Congress too abandoned status-quo politics and by resolution in 1907 asked the Bureau of Corporations to investigate American enterprise, including the lumber industry, and it began its own look at the paper industry. A six-volume report, *Pulp and Paper Investigation Hearings*, appeared in 1908.

Trade associations, formed a decade or two earlier to agree upon prices and to deal with unfair competition, at first stubbornly opposed Roosevelt's trust-busting campaign and Congress's concurrent efforts. "We stand for liberty and opportunity," an official of the American Paper and Pulp Association insisted in 1908. "We want freedom, not

restrictions; we want the Government to let private enterprise alone."
The speaker was reacting to the new times and singled out the Sherman antitrust law, an important weapon in Roosevelt's arsenal, which
was an "engine of oppression" that had been "enacted in ignorance."[1]
But there was no turning back, a painful fact that was punctuated by
a downturn in the economy, and from that point on mergers and other
combinations of corporate wealth were undertaken more carefully.

In general, times were good and getting better. Every major manufacturing enterprise except papermaking increased the volume of its
profits. The price of newsprint fell "to a much lower point than the
average of all commodities," according to the American Protective
Tariff League, and "made practically no recovery at all" while the
general price level advanced at least 10 percent above that of 1890.[2]

This observation revealed an apparent inconsistency in favor of
protecting manufacturers in general but denying price protection to
print papermaking. Although publishers protested loudly about restraint of trade and unfair prices, the contrast between those who
produced and those who bought paper is striking. Publishers enjoyed
great prosperity as population continued to grow rapidly and education advocates demanded more books, periodicals, and paper supplies.
American papermakers would have witnessed this growth with equal
enthusiasm had it not been for contrary economic factors.

Papermakers were trapped by rising operating costs. Pulpwood supplies in the north-central and New England states were running low.
As supply diminished, the cost per cord rose, especially as the distance
of the haul to the mill increased. So also did the price of timberland
south of the Canadian border. The rising cost of labor exacerbated
these difficulties. Union organization entered a new phase, shaking the
foundations of American capitalism. Labor became a cost factor of
critical importance. Most important was the demand of unions for a
three-tour, or eight-hour-shift, system. Each employee would work
eight hours a day but be paid the same wage previously received for
working twelve hours on the two-tour system. In order to maintain
production, manufacturers had to employ a complete extra shift. Increased labor benefits increased papermakers' costs by at least one-third.

In addition to the need for an expanded labor force, actual wages
increased substantially. The average daily per-capita wage in 1897 was
$1.25; by 1906 that figure had risen to $2.00. The increase, however,

was compensated by increased output of the mills, greater efficiency in production because of enhanced labor discipline, and the use of labor-saving devices. The net result was that although more labor was required overall, less labor was expended per unit of production. Still the problem of competition in the open market became more difficult. Prices of all manufactured items rose on the average about 54 percent, but paper secured only a 15 percent increase. Its position in relative terms was bleak compared to all other types of manufacturing.[3]

Congress had found no conspiracy by paper manufacturers to restrain trade, despite allegations to the contrary by the American Newspaper Publishers Association. Congressional investigators did note, however, that there was evidence that "might excite suspicion." Price increases for paper, modest though they might be, were judged to result mainly from the rising cost of pulpwood and the introduction of the eight-hour day, another Rooseveltian reform.[4]

St. Regis quickly established itself as a competitive paper company, capitalizing on a strong market for its products. One year after production commenced at Deferiet, the mill was producing ninety tons of paper every twenty-four hours and also manufacturing a considerable quantity of groundwood and chemical pulp.[5] Operations ran smoothly for the most part, and there was a minimum of malfunction. A temporary break in this run of good fortune occurred in December 1901 when the acid plant was inactivated by an accident, but this minor problem did not prevent St. Regis from celebrating its first full year of production.[6]

By 1907, however, the company was experiencing mixed results. From a purely cash standpoint, its position had improved, bolstered by successful resolution of the legal dispute with the Santa Clara Lumber Company and by a profitable lumbering operation. But 1907 was a year of economic disaster for the nation, and St. Regis was not immune. The stock market took a steep plunge in March, and business failures multiplied throughout the spring and summer. When the Knickerbocker Trust Company of New York suspended operations, President Theodore Roosevelt imposed emergency measures to quell the panic.[7] In the aftermath, St. Regis felt the brunt of the depression and underwent costly production stoppages.

The slump was not of great duration, though, and by 1910 the directors authorized the purchase of a new digester and construction of a new finishing room. At the stockholders' meeting in May 1911, Sherman's optimistic assessment of the company's status was supported by action to increase capitalization to $2 million.[8]

In the years leading up to America's entry into World War I, St. Regis's economic fortunes were buffeted by strikes, government regulation, confrontation with publishers, and repeal of tariff duties in 1913. By 1917, these and other events caused the management of St. Regis to turn the company in new directions.

The most haunting problem faced by St. Regis and other northern New York paper manufacturers was that of an adequate supply of raw material. St. Regis's own experience with the problem of procurement had begun with the scrapping of their contract with the Santa Clara Lumber Company in 1900. After a lengthy legal battle, the court of appeals decided in 1906 that the contract must be honored or damages paid to St. Regis.[9] Attorneys for the two companies agreed that $250,000 would be paid, on the basis of $50,000 each January for five years.[10]

The court victory was supplemented by the acquisition of what was believed to be an ample supply of pulpwood. In 1906 St. Regis purchased from Mary L. Fisher timber on eighty thousand acres of land bordering the Black River in the Adirondacks. This raw material, together with wood from land earlier purchased from the Meigses, comprised a supply estimated to last twenty years. The logs from the Fisher tract could be economically delivered to the mill by floating them downstream. Armed with such an apparent advantage, St. Regis purchased the plant of the Carthage Lumber Company in 1907. St. Regis planned to rebuild the old Carthage mill, increasing its capacity to four hundred horsepower and installing fifteen barkers. The mill would be supplied from the Fisher timber and ship the wood by rail to Deferiet. The availability of rail transportation was a boon for St. Regis because low water had impeded the floating of logs.[11]

The problem of ensuring a continuous wood supply, though, was not easily solved. The correct long-term solution depended upon individual perspectives, and here conservationists and timbermen came into conflict. The former argued that providing a continuous supply of timber required scientific management of woodland, which meant harvesting trees on a selective cutting basis and replanting cutover land. Most timbermen, however, saw this approach as economically impractical.

The struggle between foresters and lumbermen over land use stemmed from the region's lumbering history. In earlier years, lumbermen had cut only spruce, pine, and hemlock because the hardwoods were too heavy to float to their mills and because the market preferred the more easily worked softwoods. The building of railroads brought a transition from water transportation to rail, enabling timbermen to cut the previously unexploited hardwoods. Still, only the larger trees were cut for lumber during these early years. With the entrance of the pulp and paper industry into the area, however, trees of any size became desirable. At first only poplar was used, but it was shortly discovered that excellent fiber could be derived from spruce and later from hemlock, pine, and balsam.[12] These cutting practices began to denude the forests. "If timber cutting and timber waste goes on at the present rate," wrote Secretary of Agriculture James Wilson, the president of the American Forestry Association, "and there is no forest planting in the meantime, we will in twenty-five or thirty years be a treeless nation."[13] Such rhetoric was picked up and echoed by the press.

Cornell University had purchased thirty thousand acres in Franklin County from the Santa Clara Lumber Company for use as a demonstration forest. To operate this tract, Cornell entered into a contract with the Brooklyn Cooperage Company in 1900. The latter agreed to erect and maintain two factories, one to produce staves and headings and the other to manufacture products of wood distillation. The timber was to be cut by the college and delivered to the manufacturer, with the cooperage company providing railroad facilities. Trees in leaf along streams, highways, and fire lines were reserved by the university in respect for aesthetic and protective considerations.[14]

The state eliminated funds for the state college of forestry in 1903 following a controversy over management of the experimental forest. Cornell's president attributed this decision to failure of the state to understand project director Fernow's activities. These activities largely focused on a decision to replace old and rotten hardwoods with faster-growing merchantable softwoods like pine and spruce. Replacement of hardwoods meant denuding of the land until a newly planted crop of softwood could be established. Critics of the experiment, failing to understand that replanting meant temporary unsightliness, spoke against the project. As a result, a practical experiment was terminated before its long-term utility could be proven.[15] Fernow believed there were thirty different silvicultural methods available for use by foresters and objected to the argument that selective cutting was the only scientific method.[16]

After the forestry school was discontinued, Brooklyn Cooperage continued to cut timber in the demonstration forest.[17] Speaking at a legislative hearing in 1912, Gifford Pinchot termed Brooklyn Cooperage's operations "the worst case of vandalism with which I am acquainted east of the Rocky Mountains." He stated that its replanting efforts were tokenistic and that the company's methods had done an "incalculable injury" to the state of New York.[18]

A notable exception to the practices of private woodland owners was the effort of C. H. Remington, who by 1905 had undertaken an extensive planting program, setting out six hundred and fifty thousand Norway spruce seedlings in that year alone. As his daughter later recollected, the trees died, "but he made the effort, he tried. . . . He saw it [the value of reforestation] and the trouble is he didn't know enough. It sounds awfully easy to plant a tree . . . but it's not always easy to make them grow."[19] Despite this failure, Remington continued to agitate for a new attitude toward the forest. "In the past no provision was made for the future," he argued,

> the only consideration being that forest land be cheap enough so that the wood could be put into pulp and paper, at a price that would allow the land to be stripped and then be sold for taxes, . . . yet sell the paper cheap enough to please the publishers without any regard to posterity.
>
> Now many millions of gold dollars have been given to publishers by robbing our forests. . . . Let us adopt an intelligent system of forestry.[20]

Such ideas were sound and creative, but the cost involved was a major obstacle to implementation. In the case of St. Regis, plans for long-term forest management were derailed at the very beginning. The accepted strategy was to save the company's timber for future use, supplying Deferiet's immediate needs from outside sources. "I believe that it [reforestation] is perfectly feasible but not for the individual corporations," testified George C. Sherman in explaining St. Regis's position at the 1908 pulp and paper hearings. He continued:

Indeed, Mr. Pinchot made a complete working plan for 80,000

acres of our land in the Adirondacks, and the Government paid
several thousand dollars for making the working plans, and I was
extremely mortified to find that we did not feel we could afford
to follow out that working plan, and I came to Washington and
explained it to Mr. Pinchot, and he said I was perfectly right; that
it would yield perhaps 1½ percent interest to us if we undertook
to do it. I think it should be done, beyond any peradventure, but
the States or the General Government will have to undertake it.[21]

St. Regis purchased the cutting rights on several tracts of land, becoming by 1909 the third largest paper company in terms of timber
holdings, with ninety-eight thousand acres.[22] By that year, the bulk
of pulpwood came from Canada. St. Regis continued, as it has throughout its history, to follow a policy of conservative cutting on company-
owned land. Company timber was held in reserve "against a possible
change in conditions that would make business unprofitable were
they to depend on Canada for supplies." This practice of purchasing
a large percentage of pulpwood from Canada became an industry-wide
characteristic.[23]

Another problem loomed even larger than that of gaining a continuous flow of raw materials: that of attaining a new relationship
with the laboring men and women in the woods and mills. As the
paper industry boomed and the industry's labor force swelled, so did
the opportunity for unionism. The industry labor movement had its
origins in 1884 with the formation of Eagle Lodge in Holyoke, Massachusetts. At its inception, the lodge was social in nature and selective
in membership, admitting only machine tenders to its ranks. As the
years passed, similar organizations appeared in other paper-producing
communities. In 1893 the United Brotherhood of Paper Makers, with
a charter from the American Federation of Labor, was formed. While
more activist in nature than its Holyoke antecedent, the UBPM still
maintained a narrow craft orientation and confined membership to
machine tenders and beater engineers.

After the turn of the century, UBPM had reorganized as the International Brotherhood of Paper Makers (IBPM) and focused its efforts
on increasing membership and establishing new locals. At the same
time, agitation to shorten the hours worked per week increased. This
included limiting the total number of days the mill ran and reducing
shift time from twelve-hour to eight-hour tours. Accomplishment of

this latter objective required hiring a complete new shift of workers.[24]

Great obstacles had to be surmounted before any of these objectives could be secured. Traditional entrepreneurs held the reins tightly and asked whose job it was to run the business: labor or management? Institution of three tours was especially objectionable, since a laborer would receive the same gross income for working shorter hours. Not only would management have to hire a third tour, but it would also have to pay a higher hourly rate to all workers, a grave problem for mill owners. Costs had to be controlled somewhere, and it was not unusual to find employers holding the line on wages. The workers themselves may not have been unanimous in favoring an eight-hour day. Many feared that employers would not be able to hold gross weekly wages at the former level because of the cost of a third tour.[25]

St. Regis had its conflict with organized labor in 1903 when a difference arose between W. E. McIntyre, a machine tender, and the mill superintendent, a man named Decker. One account suggests that the dispute arose over the quality of McIntyre's work, while another indicates that his expulsion was caused by his efforts to organize the mill. Twenty-four machine tenders struck the Deferiet mill on 16 March, and with three machines down, Anderson, Sherman, and Decker began negotiations with James Mackey, president of the IBPM. These talks were not fruitful, and Mackey threatened to extend the strike to the Taggarts Paper Company unless St. Regis agreed to McIntyre's reinstatement. The effect of this would have been serious because the Taggarts facility was meeting St. Regis's contractual obligations during the strike at Deferiet. Sherman and Anderson brought suit against Mackey, won an order restraining him from calling a strike at Taggarts, and, after ten days of downtime, the machines at Deferiet started up again, run by the former employees. The short strike was a prelude to the union problem of the next dozen years.[26]

Eastern paper and pulp mill employees earned average wages of $1.375 per day in 1903 compared to $1.75 in the West. As wages rose over the next two years, St. Regis became in June 1904 the second major paper company to adopt the three-tour system, under an agreement with the IBPM.[27] St. Regis returned to the two-shift plan in 1905, even though demand by workers for the eight-hour tour had become more strident. The year was economically unsatisfactory for paper manufacturers as a result of overproduction and a decline in price.

The year 1907 saw several changes in implementation of the new work schedule, with both Taggarts and St. Regis returning to the three-tour system. International Paper, the largest employer in New York State, began to substitute the eight-hour day. However, in September St. Regis joined a number of other large mills in once again abandoning the three-tour schedule. By the end of the year, few eastern mills remained on the three-tour plan. *Paper Trade Journal* figures for the entire country noted the following breakdown: 18 mills on one tour, 215 on two, and 29 on three. St. Regis management settled the issue in the spring of 1908 when they reinstituted the three-tour system.[28]

In October 1908, four hundred St. Regis employees voted on the question of support for the eleven-week-old IBPM strike against the International Paper Company. They unanimously decided not to heed the call for an industry-wide strike by J. T. Carey, the union's president.[29] Carey had tried to obtain support from all of the independent mills, but workers from only three complied. Since Watertown was considered the stronghold of the IBPM, the impotence of the union was clearly shown when most of the members at St. Regis and other mills remained on the job.[30]

The controversy over implementation of the three-tour day became one of the major issues of dispute in the 1908 hearings of the House Select Committee to Investigate the Pulp and Paper Industry. The actual increased cost resulting from transition to eight hours came into question as a cause for the increased price of newsprint. The suspicion cast upon the newsprint industry, though, was based more upon its sales methods than upon its labor costs.

Following the lead of International Paper in the East, twenty-six mills in Wisconsin, Michigan, and Minnesota had formed a selling agency, the General Paper Company, in 1900. Its purpose was to eliminate competition and stabilize prices. Although sales organizations brought stability to the newsprint market, they aroused the ire of the newspaper publishers. When the General Paper Company was found to be in violation of the antitrust law in 1906, this was considered an outstanding victory for publishers.[31]

The General Paper Company affair provides a capsule view of the paper industry during this period. First, it symbolizes the tendency of papermakers to form combinations designed to combat the effects of competition (as had already been done in the East by IP and Great Northern). Second, it demonstrates the rising strength of publishers in their duel with the manufacturers over prices and the tariff. Finally, and importantly, it indicates that the sales agency made papermakers vulnerable to charges of monopoly. Despite the hazards intrinsic to sales combinations, however, the benefits were great and the practice continued.

During St. Regis's formative years, its sales efforts underwent a series of changes under the guidance of George Sherman. Originally Sherman had enlisted the services of outside selling agents, but he soon devised a sales operation within St. Regis itself. The first step in this direction was the organization of a sales committee among three of the company's directors: Sherman, K. B. Fullerton, and Alvah Miller. The committee was empowered to make short-term contracts supplementing the large sales made by the Manufacturers Paper Company and H. G. Craig and Company. St. Regis continued to assert greater independence in sales, however, and in 1904 its directors passed a resolution allowing it to bill customers directly. This action essentially eliminated Manufacturers Paper from all future sales. St. Regis now assumed the credit risk on sales and received payment only on delivery of contracted tonnage, which obviated the need for Manufacturers Paper. The latter organization's representatives, Fullerton and A. C. Scrimgeour, resigned their positions on the St. Regis board of directors, and a man named Gordias Henry P. Gould filled one of the vacancies.[32]

Sales continued to be an uncertain and costly proposition. For release from its sales contract with Manufacturers, St. Regis paid $36,000 and established its own New York City sales office with James T. Mix as manager. This was an expensive decision, but the company evidently felt that its own sales office could do better than its former agent. This supposition proved incorrect, and after a year and a half of operations, the sales office was closed. Sherman settled upon marketing the company's products through the independent sales agencies of H. G. Craig in the East and J. W. Butler in the West.[33]

St. Regis and other companies negotiated the best deals possible, and prices varied from customer to customer and year to year. After the panic of 1907, prices were high despite an excess paper supply, and publishers became anxious to bring them down. This agitation played a part in inducing Congress to undertake an investigation of the paper industry and its selling agencies in 1908.[34]

At the center of the controversial hearings was John Norris, who

left his position with the *New York Times* to become full-time spokesman of the publishers in Washington, D.C. Norris insisted that the
manufacturers and their sales agents had created a price-fixing monopoly, which could be destroyed by placing imported newsprint on
the free list. The tariff provided dual benefits for the paper manufacturers, permitting free importation of Canadian pulpwood and at
the same time imposing duties on Canadian pulp and newsprint. Free
importation of Canadian pulp and paper, Norris argued, would restore
competition to the paper market and drive prices down to proper
levels. A further beneficial effect of this policy, he contended, was that
domestic timber resources would be conserved. In an earlier attack on
the papermakers, Norris had insisted that the industrialists were part
of a conspiracy to "tax knowledge and diminish the educational possibilities of the newspaper press," and in his statements before the congressional committee he resorted to the same rhetoric. The newspaper
industry, said its spokesman,

> has been menaced by an extraordinary aggregation of law-
> breakers. . . . We will produce evidence of broken promises to
> Congress . . . oppression upon the public, and wrongs to labor.
> . . . The American Paper and Pulp Association . . . [is] a group
> of lawbreakers, with cunning methods of evasion of the criminal
> statutes.[35]

The principal target of these attacks was International Paper, but
H. G. Craig and other selling agencies were also indicted by Norris.
He contended that single mills such as those in northern New York
were not independent producers engaged in healthy competition.
Rather, he claimed, the various mills were consolidated into alliances
through agencies like H. G. Craig. He named the following companies
as part of the sales apparatus managed by Craig: Gould, Outterson,
Norwood, Raymondville, Remington-Martin, St. Croix, and St. Regis.
Such informal consolidations, Norris concluded, exercised the same
kind of price control imposed by International Paper. Norris insisted
that the agencies controlled production, thereby creating artificial
scarcities of paper and high prices. This particular contention he baldly
stated before the committee: "The selling agent . . . gets a commission
upon the sales of all the output and controls the direction in which it
shall go."[36]

The testimony of Syracuse publisher W. E. Gardner pointed an

even more accusing finger at St. Regis. Gardner had negotiated an
extremely inexpensive contract with St. Regis in 1906 and 1907 and
ascribed the low price to competition between St. Regis and a new
rival mill in the North Country. Seeking to supply his needs for 1908,
however, Gardner had been unable to obtain a quotation from any
company except St. Regis. The other firms claimed to be sold out
totally. Further, the new contract with St. Regis was at a considerably
higher price than that secured in the previous agreement. Gardner
suspected that H. G. Craig had prevented the other companies from
entering into competitive bidding, opening the way for St. Regis to
jump prices as much as it wished.[37]

Representatives of many paper industry firms were called to testify.
In seeking to justify the increased price of paper, they addressed the
question of the cost of labor as an influential factor. The argument of
most manufacturers, as presented by the *Paper Trade Journal*, was that
wages had increased by nearly 50 percent following the changeover
to the three-tour system. This view was articulated at the hearings by
David S. Cowles, president of the American Paper and Pulp Association (APPA), who claimed that "the rate of labor in newsprint mills
has increased in ten years 30 to 70 percent . . . with a large part of this
increase taking place in the past two years."[38]

Norris, expressing the opposing view of the American Publishers
Association, contended that the price increases were excessive and not
justified. He insisted that labor cost "has not been increased, and that
the three-tour plan has not brought all this burden of increase and expense which has been attributed to it." He argued further that extra
running time and production more than paid for the extra labor. Since
rent and other fixed charges remained unchanged, he explained, the
three-tour system had not been a hardship on manufacturers and the
extra efficiency of the men working three tours offset the extra cost
of its products.[39] Although Norris argued his case persuasively, his
accusations lacked substance and depth.

George Sherman, representing St. Regis, refuted Norris's charges of
monopoly. Purely natural causes, he explained, had provoked the manufacturers to increase the price of newsprint. Yet, unlike most other
witnesses, Sherman doubted the assumption that price hikes could be
attributed to the three-tour system and the increase in wages. "The
labor cost increase," he said, "is not as great as you would think," and
he added that the greatest factor assigned to the increased cost of production was "the much higher cost of pulpwood."[40]

Sherman's testimony was a factor in the eventual vindication of the paper manufacturers. The House Investigative Committee concluded that although the cost of labor remained lower than claimed, the combined costs involved in higher wages and the adoption of the three-tour system constituted "a considerable and decided increase" both in size of employment and of wages paid out. These hearings also questioned the mill owners' assertion that they had been forced to raise prices because "their labor cost had thereby increased." The cause-and-effect relationship between price increases and the adoption of the three-tour system was easily refuted by the facts. There simply was not a general endorsement of this plan throughout the entire country. In both the western and southern mills few manufacturers had implemented the three-tour system.[41]

Sherman also responded to Gardner's testimony by clarifying his relationship with H. G. Craig. Sherman had abandoned his company sales office in New York City because it was too expensive, and he had returned to using selling agencies because they made good any losses incurred through a contract with a firm unable to pay its bills. This type of insurance, Sherman indicated, was indispensable for St. Regis. Sherman further pointed out that St. Regis made arrangements only with H. G. Craig and had not entered into a collusive agreement with other manufacturers to set a single high price for newsprint. Sherman did not, in the words of one of his inquisitors, have "any agreement in reference to the price of paper with other paper mills."[42] Finally, Sherman's testimony made it clear that he directed pricing strategies and that H. G. Craig did not in any way control St. Regis production.

The evidence seems to substantiate the contention that a price hike was justified by the adverse factors involved. There is every reason to accept the majority's report that the combination of items—the high cost of pulpwood, the value of spruce timberland, the upward movement in wages, the overall rise in the cost of materials, and the adoption of the three-tour system—forced paper manufacturers to raise the price of newsprint.[43]

Regarding the question of the tariff, the preliminary report of the committee majority offered both advice and a warning:

> It would seem that for the American publisher to be assured of low prices for his paper, it is essential to maintain paper mills in the United States. Any policy that would give the Canadian mill a preferential advantage over American mills in obtaining the raw

material at a lower price must inevitably result in the dismantling of American paper machines and the ultimate dependence of American publishers on Canadian mills.[44]

Over the next several years, the tariff issue would be briskly debated and eventually settled in favor of the publishers. Just as the committee had warned, Canada gained the preferential position to the detriment of American papermakers.

The findings of the investigative body supported the arguments of paper-manufacturing interests. Speaking for the APPA, David Cowles asserted that removal of the tariff would have a tendency to depress the price of paper and open the door to foreign competition, both Canadian and Scandinavian, to the detriment of an already "impoverished paper industry."[45] Once again differing with the conventional manufacturing view, Sherman presented St. Regis's position on the tariff. While acknowledging the harmful effects to the industry in general, he explained that immediate repeal of the duty would not "seriously affect me or those associated directly with me in business." He explained that by clear-cutting timber already owned by St. Regis, the company was assured a fifteen-year supply of pulpwood. When asked what St. Regis would do at the end of fifteen years, he replied, "Well, I hope I will not have to worry about that." He then responded seriously, saying, "I hope that within that period the state or the government will commence reforestation. I even hope that Quebec, or Canada, will do so."[46]

Further complicating the matter, politicians and industrialists in Canada gave strong support to their own growing paper industry. They resented tariff obstacles to the entry of Canadian pulp and paper into American markets, and some provinces retaliated by imposing bans on exportation of pulpwood to the United States.[47]

This dispute was concluded with passage of the Underwood Tariff Act in October 1913. Preceding this action, proponents of free trade had found legislative support in the Payne-Aldrich Tariff of 1909 and the Reciprocity Act of 1911. The latter act, had it been put into effect, would have removed the duty on newsprint imported from Canada and other countries. Similar provisions, though, were contained in the Underwood Tariff. As passed, the act admitted "free of duty newsprint paper and wood pulps from all parts of the world and without qualification of any sort." Ironically the Underwood Tariff did not immediately bring the low prices publishers had expected, since Canada was not able to produce enough pulp to dominate the market.[48]

In time, however, the infiltration of American capital into the Canadian paper industry became a significant development. The United States increasingly turned to Canada for its supply of newsprint. In 1909 the nation had produced almost all of its own, but by 1919 two-thirds came from Canada. This shift brought about overproduction of Canadian pulp, with the result that prices remained stable or declined.

A month after Sherman's appearance at the hearings, a crisis developed within the company when George W. Knowlton, Jr., decided to resign the presidency. Knowlton presented a reasoned statement, explaining his decision. His principal criticism was leveled at Sherman and Anderson, who, he claimed, made important company decisions without consulting him. Knowlton was also discouraged by the difficulties with which St. Regis had been confronted and the manner in which some problems had been addressed. For example, he felt that compensation paid by the Santa Clara Lumber Company for violating its timber contract was insufficient to offset the losses caused St. Regis. Furthermore Knowlton implied that the entire arrangement with Manufacturers Paper Company and the costly termination of that contract had been seriously mishandled. Knowlton conceded that St. Regis had overcome many problems and seemed ready to enter a period of steady financial gain. Since the company had attained a level of security, he felt that it was appropriate for him to leave office, especially because he was consulted on important decisions less and less. Knowlton's statement clarified his feelings: "I held the third largest interest in the company [and] I felt inclined to stay with it 'till I could feel that my investment was safe. I think that time has arrived, and I am now willing to step aside." Knowlton's resignation was accepted, and he receded into the background of company affairs, remaining on the board until 1916.[49]

St. Regis director Gordias Henry P. Gould became the company's third president. He was sixty years old and possessed considerable wealth, the result of a long and extremely successful business career. A native of the North Country, Gould earned a living in his younger years as a stage driver. In 1869, when he was twenty-one years old, he purchased a small lumber tract on the Moose River. From that original investment, he increased his holdings until he owned thousands of acres of virgin forest in the Adirondacks. Eventually his landholdings were extensive enough to allow him to form a partnership with Mary L. Fisher, Julia L. deCamp, and Florence L. Merrian, all daughters of Lyman R. Lyon. Under the name Lyon & Gould, the partnership purchased a sawmill and pulp mill in 1874 at the junction of the Moose and Black rivers.[50]

Gould built a wood pulp mill in 1880 with a capacity of 780 tons a year and in 1892 bought Fon-du-lac Paper Company, which had three northern New York mills. Three years later, he completed construction of a large paper mill on the west side of Lyons Falls. In 1906 he purchased the mills of the International Paper Company at Kosterville and formed the Gould Paper Company, which became one of the largest paper companies in the state.[51]

As one of New York's captains of industry, Gould was president of the Glenfield and Western Railroad Company, as well as vice-president and director of various trusts. His connection with St. Regis dated to the early days of the company. He considered St. Regis the best mill property in the North Country and had begun buying its stock shortly after its organization. Gould's first official involvement with management appears in the minutes of a board meeting held in January 1906. Four months later he was recorded in the annual report as a director.

Gould's personal qualities, suggested by contemporary newspaper accounts, included a willingness to work alongside mill laborers when mechanical difficulties developed. While such accounts emphasize Gould's industriousness and humility, others suggest he was a rugged individualist who brooked no disobedience.[52] What emerges from the various accounts is a picture of a man whose character traits contributed to a bitter management schism at St. Regis. Gould's intractability, for one thing, prolonged a difficult confrontation with organized labor. These events occurred late in Gould's career with the company, however; the early years of his tenure were tranquil and productive.

Still the first year of Gould's administration was not without problems and was a harbinger of difficulties to come. The year 1909 began with a high demand for paper, resulting from an increase in advertising and newspaper circulation. St. Regis could not take up its share in this demand because a serious drought hit the Watertown region. Sherman observed in February that "while I do not anticipate a paper famine, the condition is serious comparing the production with the demand."[53]

By mid-year, as the drought continued and the level of the Black River fell, St. Regis's mills either shut down or operated only part time. The problem was compounded by a sudden and large drop in demand.

But the trouble was soon turned to advantage. During the enforced closure, St. Regis repaired and rebuilt its plant and turned adversity into a long-term asset. By September, even with a continuing shortage of water, the company's fortunes began to improve as orders increased. When rainfall returned to normal, St. Regis went into full production with both revitalized machines and a resurgent market.[54]

To increase their holdings further, Sherman and Anderson purchased the properties of William P. Herring on the Black River in February 1912. These acquisitions included the Jefferson Paper Company, the Jefferson Power Company, the Jefferson Board Mills, and the Empire Wood Pulp Company. In October 1913, the Jefferson Company, a holding organization for the Herring interests, was sold by Sherman and Anderson for $100,000 to St. Regis, greatly increasing the latter's capacity.[55]

Herring had become interested in papermaking by chance. In 1887, he had left his western cattle ranch to establish a pulp mill at Poor's Island on the Black River. While in the West, Herring had established a friendship with Philip D. Armour, the meat-packer. After Herring became a papermaker, he turned to the manufacture of butcher's manila paper for sale to western meat-packers. Because of his western experience and his hardy nature, Herring was known in the North Country as "Buffalo Bill."[56]

Prior to purchase of the Herring interests by St. Regis, the Jefferson Paper Company mill at Black River produced manila butcher paper, while the plant at Herrings made groundwood, sulfite pulp, tagboard, and pulpboard. Acquisition of these properties boosted St. Regis's daily output of finished paper from 180 tons to 250 tons. St. Regis operated the Herrings mill until it was sold to Taggart Brothers Company in 1926, only to reacquire it again in 1949.[57]

The Northern New York Trust Company of Watertown was involved in this acquisition and was employed in raising funds for future purchase of real estate and water rights. Floyd Leslie Carlisle, a local attorney, had been instrumental in merging two local banks, the National Bank and Loan Company and the National Union Bank, into what became the Northern New York Trust Company in 1910.

George Sherman had been president of the National Bank prior to the organization of St. Regis. One purpose of Carlisle's enterprise was to infuse the North Country with new economic vitality.[58]

As St. Regis grew larger and more powerful, so too did the ambitions of its managers. Profits increased yearly, with the result that control of the company was sought after by some of the directors. David Anderson chose to sell his holdings—4,607 shares of preferred and common stock—to Gould in August 1914 and the following month resigned as general manager. This gave control of St. Regis to Sherman and Gould. (Anderson retained his holdings in the Taggarts Paper Company.)[59]

A week later, the other cofounder of St. Regis lost his position of power. On September 22 a special meeting of the board of directors was called by Gould, at which a motion was unanimously approved:

> Whereas the conduct of Mr. George C. Sherman, Treasurer and Secretary of the Company, has been such as to injure the credit of the Company and to impair the efficiency of its organization. ... Be it resolved that Mr. George C. Sherman be, and hereby is removed as Treasurer and Secretary of the Company.

The board selected Floyd Carlisle treasurer and Alvah Miller secretary.[60]

Some indication of the motivation behind this action is found in an earlier telegram to the board from Sherman:

> I understood you charged me with dishonesty and naturally became very angry. My plans as to Taggarts Paper Company will not directly or indirectly interfere with management of St. Regis Company. Mall and Baron will give their best services to St. Regis as long as desired. St. Regis owes Taggarts about fifteen thousand dollars. Am inclined to retire from active work if desired by full Board.[61]

Sherman's continuing relations with St. Regis are less clearly recorded. His resignation as a director is noted in the minutes of the board meeting of 9 March 1915, but his active presence at later board meetings is also recorded.[62] Sherman's subsequent activities in the paper industry are documented, however. He and Anderson had become sole owners of the Taggarts Paper Company by 1909. Following his expulsion from St. Regis, Sherman purchased Anderson's interest in Taggarts, managing that company until his death in 1920.

As a mill owner, Sherman demonstrated an enlightened paternalism; he introduced the three-tour system and a profit-sharing plan at Taggarts Paper Company. His idea of pensioning aged employees or giving them some kind of family protection was sincere, as illustrated by two actions. Upon retirement of Peter Clow, one of the oldest employees of the Great Bend mill, Sherman personally informed Clow that he would receive a pension of one dollar a day for the rest of his life and also collect $210 immediately. After Sherman's death it was learned that he had left a trust fund of $100,000 to provide pensions for elderly and infirm employees. The IBPM praised Sherman to his widow: "If the capitalists of this country were of the type of your beloved husband and our beloved employer, . . . there would not be the strife between capital and labor that predominates through the country today." Quite in contrast to its attitude toward "Old Man Gould," the union continued:

> It would be very hard to relate the extent of your husband's generosity at this mill; it would be still harder to convey the appreciation. To pass among the people here and see the advantages made possible by his wise judgment—contented people, happy homes, children being educated, all made possible by his unselfish consideration.[63]

The most important consequence of Sherman's and Anderson's departure from St. Regis was that power was now concentrated in the hands of G. H. P. Gould. Gould's tenure as head of the company offers a direct contrast to that of Sherman. Whereas Sherman reflected the ideas and attitudes of the Progressive era, Gould's methods harkened back to the nineteenth century. An old-fashioned entrepreneur, Gould rejected the modern corporation's separation of ownership and management, as well as the view that smooth relations between labor and management were essential. Gould was adamantly opposed to institution of the closed shop. Nowhere was his intractability on the labor question more apparent than in strikes that hit St. Regis and other northern New York paper mills between 1915 and 1917.

The struggle between labor and capital in the paper industry of the

Black River Valley focused on three issues: recognition of the International Brotherhood of Pulp, Sulphite and Paper Mill Workers (IBPSPMW) and the International Brotherhood of Pulp and Paper Makers, permanent establishment of the three-tour system, and resistance to wage reductions.[64] Paper manufacturers had been following a pattern of oscillation between the two-tour and the three-tour workday. The possibility that the Northern New York Paper Manufacturers Association would return to the two-tour system and reduce wages triggered the strike. Gould, as head of both St. Regis and the Gould Paper Company, typified the association's position when he indicated his intention to return to the two-tour system and refused to negotiate with IBPSPMW President John H. Malin.[65]

The strength of the manufacturers' association was balanced by that of labor, the latter deriving from growth of the union. The hold of the union is indicated by organizer Joseph Tylcoff, who wrote to Malin in spring 1915 that 98 percent of the workers at Deferiet were organized. The conflict between management and labor was heightened by a continued shortage of pulp supplies and increased competitiveness within the industry.[66] Manufacturers contended that removal of the duty on paper and increased freight rates had reduced profits to the point where wage increases were not possible. These factors combined to make what paper men believed was the most serious strike situation that had ever developed in the region's industry.[67]

An agreement was reached between J. T. Carey of the IBPM and George Sherman over adoption of the eight-hour workday by the Taggarts Paper Company. Continental Paper Company, however, refused to negotiate with the union in April 1915 and precipitated a strike that soon spread to St. Regis and other concerns.[68] Gould expressed the sentiment of many manufacturers when he stated that St. Regis welcomed the strike because business was light and it would be a good opportunity to close the mills for a time. His inflammatory rhetoric incurred the wrath of strikers: "We know we are right, and we are going right ahead. Let the other side make whatever statements they will, but we haven't anything to say further." His words were followed by eviction of strikers from the company town and importation of strikebreakers from New York City. The first strikebreakers were American citizens, but later imports were drawn from recently arrived immigrants. The ethnic composition of the latter group acted as a catalyst for violence, exacerbating the already explosive situation.[69] Gould's actions were endorsed by the St. Regis board of directors on 8 June 1915 and were emulated by other companies.[70]

St. Regis recruited ninety strikebreakers by the end of May, and paper was again being produced, although only two machines were running due to the inexperience of the new workers. Meanwhile the evicted strikers set up a tent colony, named Camp Tylcoff, across the river from the plant. While the number of inhabitants in the temporary town grew to four hundred or five hundred, conditions remained relatively calm and were marred only by minor incidents, such as a shot fired at the company hotel in Deferiet.[71]

The State Board of Mediation and Arbitration took steps to end the strike in mid-June but was rebuffed when St. Regis and the other operators refused to submit to arbitration. On 13 August an agreement was reached whereby the strikers would be rehired. Wages and working conditions were the same as before the strike. Union spokesmen conceded that the open shop would continue. The workers, according to the pact, agreed not to molest strikebreakers who continued to work at the mill.[72]

On these terms the strike ended in mid-August, but order was restored only temporarily. The strike began again on 2 September, this time with violence. The workers smashed lights and cut telephone lines at Deferiet, and they greeted the sheriff's deputies with gunfire when they arrived to quell the disturbance. The governor declared martial law and called out the National Guard to restore peace. Saloons within a mile of the St. Regis plant were ordered closed. Many strikers were arrested and charged with rioting. One man described the first night of the strike as having "all the excitement of an old-time western town being shot up by cowboys." Some managers feared for their safety; one drove to work with a club on the front seat of his automobile.[73]

The State Board of Mediation and Arbitration once again entered the scene. It appeared that both management and labor had misunderstood and in some cases violated the agreement. Deferiet management claimed that union men had chased strikebreakers out of the mill. Further, they contended, union workers had demanded the closed shop and union leaders had insisted upon wage increases. Labor charged that management had refused jobs to some returning strikers and that others had been demoted. Another charge was that workers returning to company housing were compelled to agree to eviction within three days if they stopped work for any reason. The truth of some charges is substantiated by a Gould scheme to draw strikers into the payroll office. There they were identified as riot participants and arrested.[74]

These charges and countercharges demonstrated the uncompromising position of each side and led to an escalation of the dispute. Gould publicly declared on 3 September that St. Regis would thenceforth be a nonunion mill. Although violence was ended by the presence of soldiers, Gould's announcement prevented settlement. John Malin expressed labor's equally rigid position: "We expect not only to defeat him [Gould] in this but we expect to bring about a satisfactory settlement of the strike as well." Gould's statement made him an easy target for the strikers. A member of the St. Regis Local 45 had this to say about his former employer:

> The St. Regis Paper Co., . . . have been able to secure a few "has-been paper makers," also a few jail birds [as strikebreakers], but has not succeeded in getting the mill running very successful [*sic*], and won't be until they come to their senses and settle with the Brothers who went out on strike. . . . Even we have Old Man Gould running, and before he is done with the I. B. of P. M. he will be all run out, and ready to quit and recognize the Union and give the boys a working agreement.[75]

Negotiations between the unions and other mill owners resulted in the signing of contracts in the spring of 1916. By that time most plants had converted to the eight-hour day. Labor relations at Deferiet, however, remained unsettled. Although production rarely reached full capacity during the year, Gould continued to be inflexible toward union recognition until his resignation as president on 1 December 1916. At the 14 December meeting of the board of directors, Floyd Carlisle was elected the company's fourth president.[76] There was an almost immediate change in management's attitude toward labor. In late December, St. Regis General Manager Celestine C. Burns announced a schedule of healthy bonuses for the New Year. This conciliatory gesture was followed by adoption of an agreement with the unions on 28 February 1917. Culmination of the long struggle came with Carlisle's signature on a new contract with the presidents of the IBPM, the IBPSPMW, and the International Brotherhood of Stationary Firemen on 1 March. The main terms of the settlement, which became effective 1 May, implemented the closed shop and established a procedure for collective bargaining.[77]

Gould's departure signaled the end of strife between labor and management, as well as the closing of the era of the old-fashioned entrepreneur. When Gould tendered his resignation, his nineteenth-century traits were praised by Carlisle as "distinguishing qualities of rugged honesty, force, and ability, which have so endeared him to us."[78] His departure cleared the way for changes in company policy. Late in 1916, Gould had begun negotiating sale of St. Regis to the Pulitzer-controlled *New York World*. Having failed in earlier efforts to acquire the Remington Paper and Power Company, the Pulitzers approached Gould with an offer to buy St. Regis. In October there appeared to be agreement, but the Pulitzers' lawyers asked for thirty-six hours to think about the terms. Gould tartly gave them thirty-six seconds, terminated the meeting, and boarded a train for Chicago.[79]

A month later, Gould sold St. Regis to a group of Watertown businessmen headed by Floyd Carlisle. This transaction, the largest of its kind in the history of the Black River Valley, included the Deferiet mill, the mills at Herrings and Black River, and fifty-eight thousand acres of timberland. The syndicate that assumed control of St. Regis included, in addition to Carlisle, David Anderson, who came out of retirement, Celestine Burns, Frank A. Empsall, and DeWitt C. Middleton. The fact that all were directors of the Northern New York Trust Company was an influential element in Gould's decision to sell. Gould explained the rationale for his choice of buyers: "They are all of our kind and they will run those mills in the interest of every one in northern New York, which is a very much better proposition than having a lot of foreigners come in our community to own, control, and operate our plants."[80]

By the time of the sale, St. Regis was established as a profitable and successful firm. Upon assuming control, Carlisle expressed satisfaction with the company and optimistically predicted that "the paper business is now bringing in tremendous profits to owners, and this condition is sure to continue for several years."[81]

4
Growing Up to Power

Floyd L. Carlisle had good reason to express optimism. St. Regis was entering a period of development that would foster expanded production of paper products and stimulate entrance into a new field, that of electric power. The emergence of St. Regis as a giant in the utilities industry is the most distinctive feature of Carlisle's years as president.

The interest displayed by Carlisle in waterpower had been foretold by earlier leaders. Farsighted men like B. B. Taggart, David Anderson, George Sherman, and G. H. P. Gould all recognized the potential of the rivers coursing through the North Country. Taggart's appreciation of electricity took form during construction of the St. Regis plant when he saw the potential value of the Indian River. Anderson had been chairman of a Watertown committee appearing before the New York State Flood Commission, which was interested in the relationship between waterpower and local industry. Anderson's group pressed for legislation establishing storage reservoirs to prevent damage during periods of high water. Gould, who was also a member of the committee, early on saw the necessity for adequate storage systems to combat the dual threat of flood and drought. His financial acumen led him to electrify his plants as a means of reducing production costs. But it was Sherman's voice that most clearly forecast the future:

> I honestly believe that inside of twenty years our modern paper plant will be absolutely abandoned at Deferiet and the water power sold for other purposes; that it will become so valuable

for water power purposes that we can afford to dismantle our
mill; I believe it implicitly . . . civilization and factories and railroads must grow to that water power.[1]

Control of the water essential to their industry had long been a primary concern of paper mill owners. Because the issue involved public
land and water, paper manufacturers recognized the need to act col-
lectively. The result was incorporation in September 1908 of the Black
River Power Association to protest diversion of water by the Black
River Canal at Boonville to the Erie Canal. Among the association
members were Gould, who was chairman, Anderson, Knowlton, and
B. B. Taggart.[2]

Seeking to maintain and increase the flow of the Black River, the
association took steps in 1910 to amend existing legislation that they
thought mandated "an unreasonable limitation on power to flow state
lands." Their program called for a survey of the area, formulation of
a water storage plan, and education of the public to the necessity of
storage.[3] These proposals brought to light a conflict over the proper
usage of water. Conservationists and large property owners in northern New York did not want dams built or river flow regulated and
voiced their opposition to the legislation. Labor organizations, on the
other hand, supported legislation promoting storage and control. Labor's alliance with industry was founded on the logic that floods force
mills to shut down and throw people out of work.[4]

The combined forces of the Northern New York Development
League and the Black River Power Association opposed a water storage bill proposed by the State Conservation Commission in 1912. Their
effort to gain control over the flow of the Black River aggravated the
federal government. In a report to President Taft, Commissioner of
Corporations Herbert Knox Smith listed three causes for the interest
of manufacturers: "the economy of operation; specialization in engineering enterprise; and the elimination of competition." Smith contended that the International Paper Company was a "trust . . . [with]
the largest amount of water power controlled by any industrial concern in the United States," and he warned that such monopoly could
be thwarted only if cognizance was given to the "close relation and
possible conflict between water power, navigation and irrigation."[5]

Electrification of the region's industry was dependent upon water as
an energy source. The transition to hydroelectricity was slow in com-

ing to northern New York mills. Based on the belief that steam power was cheaper, paper interests restricted their use of electric energy. Technical problems, moreover, hindered wide application of electricity. Although electric power was ultimately the most efficient source of energy, its complete acceptance was delayed. This was despite its advantages that included easy determination of costs through meter readings, longer machinery life, savings in floor space, and, not least importantly, product diversification made possible by the variable-speed factor. Electricity was more quickly implemented farther to the north. The S. D. Warren Company of Maine, for instance, shifted over completely to hydroelectric power by 1895, ushering in a period of expansion.[6]

Gould was one of the first papermakers in northern New York to install electric machinery, and over the years, other mills in the area adopted that form of power. But the real turning point for the region was construction of the Black River power plant in the early 1920s. That hydroelectric development provided St. Regis with six thousand additional horsepower for use in its three mills.[7]

The need to secure a reliable source of power was as essential to paper manufacturers as was the provision of adequate raw material. This quest for a stable reservoir of power was an important factor in St. Regis's entry into the utilities field. Testifying before the Commission on Revision of the Public Service Law of New York State in 1929, Floyd Carlisle reviewed the reasons for his decision:

> I got into the power business for a reason utterly unrelated to it. I was in the paper manufacturing business. I foresaw what literally came true, that the paper mills of northern New York would not hope to compete with the paper mills of Canada. The paper mills of northern New York had large water powers, which they were using in the manufacture of paper. I went into the power business more to be assured of a constant power supply and to be able, if we could not operate successfully as paper mills, to be able to sell power in some other way.[8]

The actual circumstances were complex. At the time, paper manufacturers had to confront the increased Canadian imports of newsprint made possible by the repeal of tariff duties in 1913. Thus American operators were looking for other product lines and for methods to cut production costs. Not to be ignored in this search was the impact of electricity on industry and on the country. As manufacturers came to recognize that hydroelectricity was the most economical source of power, the demand for power development grew.

A strong sense of regionalism had motivated formation of the Northern New York Development League in 1909. The league's express purpose was to promote the growth and progress of the area's industries. Its actions often centered on obtaining expanded private control of riparian rights.[9] This local activism had evolved from experiences of manufacturers that had led them to turn away from government regulation of water and timberland and to look toward private control of these resources.

Carlisle's motives have been the subject of much debate. The events were persuasive, but Carlisle's own remarks are informative. Roy K. Ferguson, Carlisle's successor, echoed his mentor some years later, although with a subtle shift of emphasis:

> Mr. Carlisle's interest was in riparian rights, in the water power of Northern New York's rivers as the untapped source for a vast new electric power network for the growing Empire State. He saw the paper industry at that time as potentially a great outlet for this power.[10]

As a native of Watertown, Carlisle's deep interest in the fortunes of the region was natural. Born in 1881, he received his early schooling in Watertown and in Dayton, Ohio, and later attended Cornell University. He returned to Watertown to study law in his older brother John's office, but he abandoned the practice of law to establish the Northern New York Trust Company in 1910. This career change directed Carlisle into the paper business and the power industry.[11]

One of Carlisle's first acts as president was to ask the stockholders to amend the company charter to permit directors to purchase the stocks, bonds, and evidences of indebtedness of other companies. An additional proposal would allow St. Regis officials to serve as directors and officers of other firms. Both requests were adopted.[12] These moves were vital to the establishment of a holding company, which would allow the company to amass large amounts of capital. Management of various investments by one central organization provided "engineering and managerial skill for making operations efficient in the highest degree."[13] Carlisle's application of the holding company concept enabled St. Regis to expand into the public utilities area.

In 1920 Carlisle consolidated the company's existing water rights on the Black, Beaver, and Raquette rivers with those of the Northern New York Utilities Company. St. Regis joined in the purchase of Northern New York Utilities with a group of paper manufacturers, including Harry S. Lewis of Beaver Falls, the Remington Paper and Power Company, the Harmon Paper Company, the Warren Parchment Company, the Champion Paper Company, and Taggart Brothers Company. The utilities company had been founded by John B. Taylor through consolidation of his Watertown holdings. In 1913, he incorporated under the name of Northern New York Utilities, Inc. At the time of its sale to Carlisle and his associates, Northern New York Utilities was the second largest owner of developed and undeveloped hydroelectric power in the eastern United States. Because Carlisle and the other manufacturers already owned extensive undeveloped power sites, control of the utilities company offered the best means of developing their power potential.[14]

The advantages of controlling one's own supply of electric power were manifest. Paper machines could be run at a variety of speeds, making production of a range of grades possible. Flexibility of output was desirable, especially since the American newsprint market had been seriously undercut by Canadian imports. General agreement existed that the market could be stabilized through the production of new grades. Beyond supplying the mills with their own source of power, the purchase of the Northern New York Utilities Company would advance the region's economy and attract new manufacturing interests.[15]

The region's paper and hydroelectric industries were mutually reliant upon both timber and water. St. Regis's policy of acquisition and control of water rights ensured provision of power and was in harmony with its approach to the problem of securing a continuous pulpwood supply. Faced with a dwindling pulpwood supply and its higher cost, however, the company was forced to consider alternative means of procurement. This concern led management to advocate scientific methods of forestry.[16]

Floyd Carlisle listened receptively to the arguments of the foresters. In 1920 he and his brother John initiated a large-scale replanting of St. Regis and Northern New York Utilities Company timberland. They hired F. L. Rogers, a graduate of the forestry school at the State University of New York at Syracuse, to provide professional guidance. Thus began a program of reforestation that eventually enabled Carlisle to tell stockholders: "1,500,000 trees were planted during 1927 on its pulpwood tracts located in the Adirondacks and it is expected that 2,250,000 trees will be set out during 1928 and increasing numbers in subsequent years." Throughout the decade these measures by the company and its affiliates were unsurpassed in New York State and were considered among the most advanced in the nation.[17]

Despite early successes and the interest of both Carlisles, St. Regis encountered serious problems with its nursery and replanting efforts. Difficulties arose for the most part from insufficient technical knowledge. Lacking specific direction, the company's policies were unevenly applied. As one employee connected with the program later remembered, "It varied with each location. You did one thing in one place and another thing at another place. . . . There was no real broad application." Monetary gain was not equal to expenses, especially under the economic circumstances of the 1930s, and so St. Regis abandoned its nursery and turned to the purchase of seedlings from the state.[18]

There were other inducements for phasing out the reforestation operations of the early 1920s. As a result of its established policy of timberland acquisition, the company had turned north to Canada. Timber resources in New York had continued to diminish, and the more plentiful and inexpensive Canadian timber provided a solution. In 1920 the directors agreed to purchase the Godbout timber tract, 36,000 acres of land in Saguenay, the easternmost tip of Quebec, at the mouth of the St. Lawrence River. That same year, Carlisle was authorized to purchase 17,642 acres of timberland in New York's Lewis and Herkimer counties from the estate of T. B. Basselin.[19]

St. Regis Company of Canada, Ltd., was organized in November 1920 to supply pulpwood to the New York mills. This operation rewarded the company's policy of conserving its U.S. timberland for future needs. Remarking on this approach in 1924, a spokesman for St. Regis commented, "We will never experience a shortage of pulpwood so long as we want to manufacture paper. . . . When this is in full operation they [the Godbout facility] will be able to unload 1,000 cords of pulpwood every 24 hours."[20]

In conjunction with the formation of St. Regis Company of Canada, Ltd., the Canadian Securities Corporation was organized to handle the sales of securities. From 1924 to 1927 there were indications that St. Regis would increase its Canadian operations with construction at Cap Rouge of a mill to produce pulp, paper, and cardboard products. Some of the Godbout tract consisted of crown-held land; this timber was required to be manufactured in Canada. Consequently Carlisle's attempt to circumvent the law by building a plant was resisted by the Canadian government and financial interests.[21]

Following his success in solving the labor difficulties of 1915-1917, Carlisle assumed the role of spokesman for a number of northern New York paper companies. Bargaining in the name of the regional industry as well as for his own company, Carlisle presented a less conciliatory attitude toward labor than he had during the first dispute of his administration. At the APPA convention in April 1921, manufacturers declared themselves prepared for a long struggle against labor's demands for pay hikes and other benefits. In fact, the manufacturers took the offensive by calling for a 30 percent reduction in wages for unskilled and semiskilled workers in any new working agreement. The unions, of course, unanimously rejected this ultimatum.[22]

Carlisle argued the case for the proposed cutback. He contended that while the purchasing power of the American dollar had increased and the cost of living had declined, the wages of paper employees had risen to a level higher than those of any other industry. Union leaders considered such argument to be pointless and stood opposed to any reduction in wages. With the lines drawn, the membership voted to stage an industry-wide strike in all unionized paper mills of northern New York in May.[23]

The unions walked out on 1 May, affecting about eight thousand men of the IBPSPMW. On 11 May, another thousand men struck the seven largest plants in the area. Together they represented 60 percent of the entire newsprint production of the United States and Canada.[24] While the strike was intended to paralyze the industry, no such condition materialized. Economic conditions were such that most of Carlisle's group viewed the strike favorably. The mills were stocked with inventories that would last for at least two months. The strike provided management with an excuse to shut down while the economy weathered a slump.[25] Within two months, the unions announced willingness to accept Carlisle's terms. In mid-August newsprint workers agreed to return to the lower rates in force during 1919, a cut of 10 percent in the wages of skilled employees and 25 percent in pay for the unskilled. Management also lowered salaried employees' pay by 10 percent.[26]

When management called for a further reduction in wages in 1922, the conflict was heightened by the operators' refusal to establish a standard schedule of wages for unskilled laborers. Attempts to revoke the closed shop were resumed, encouraged by recent successes of IP in this regard.[27] The position of the unions was weakened by economic, social, and political factors. Faced with hostile public opinion, an unsympathetic government attitude, and a decreased demand for paper, the unions were ill prepared for a prolonged strike. Equally important was the divisiveness within the membership itself, a schism that arose from a jurisdictional dispute and conflict over the differing pay scales of skilled and unskilled workers.[28]

Before a final agreement was reached in 1924, several developments modified the position of union leadership. An upturn in the economy brightened the employment picture and resulted in wage increases. Acting on the existing breach within the unions, management drove the wedge deeper by negotiating separate agreements with Carey's skilled IBPM membership and John Burke's IBPSPMW. And by adopting a paternalistic approach toward the employees' needs—providing pension plans, vacation packages, stock options, and other benefits—management weakened union arguments.[29]

As regional spokesman for the manufacturers, Carlisle proved an able negotiator. Recognizing the natural conflict between labor and management, he understood that common sense could defuse tension and misunderstanding. At a meeting of the northern New York division of the American Pulp and Paper Mill Superintendents' Association, he championed the principles of arbitration by noting: "Labor unions must hold themselves subservient to the laws of the land . . . [otherwise] the greatest conflict this country has ever seen is sure to come in the not far distant future." After more than two years of constant strife between labor and management, the contending parties —nine manufacturers and two unions—finally agreed to terms that exemplified the new conciliatory attitude of both sides.[30]

In this climate, labor-management relations improved while union membership declined and the issue of the closed shop became less urgent. Within this context, Carlisle represented the new breed of manager that historian Thomas Cochran sees as emerging from the modern, professional business class. In the years to come, Carlisle became "accustomed to computing in general effects the fairly remote future with a calculus that integrated long-run factors with immediate pecuniary gains." Part of that broader comprehension is reflected in his treatment of labor and his promotion of a better public image.[31]

During this period Carlisle recruited Roy K. Ferguson to assist him in various operations. Carlisle met Ferguson at the Lake Placid Club, where the young man was employed as assistant manager. Carlisle, as Ferguson later recollected,

> was a man of great vision [who] believed in the growth possibilities of the paper industry . . . [and who also had a] dream of a public utility empire. . . . I was approached by Mr. Carlisle to join with him, and being a kind of starry-eyed youngster looking for a chance to get ahead, I was greatly impressed with Mr. Carlisle and quickly accepted his offer to become his assistant in the St. Regis Paper Company and also in the investment banking business.[32]

Ferguson moved to Watertown in 1917 to manage the securities department of the Northern New York Trust Company and soon proved himself. Carlisle established an investment firm, F. L. Carlisle and Company, Incorporated, in 1921; and Ferguson was transferred to New York City to begin the new firm. This company was set up to deal in northern New York securities and to locate capital for Carlisle's ventures. Later it became the agent for purchasing and selling power and paper properties for St. Regis.[33]

The personal and business relationship between the two men would have profound consequences for St. Regis in the years to come. If indeed Carlisle was farsighted, Roy K. Ferguson shared that visionary quality. Harold S. Sutton, longtime associate of both men, observed their interaction:

> Roy was always very careful never to do anything which would in any way detract from Mr. Carlisle's obvious leadership qualities. . . . That is not to say that Roy didn't give him a great deal of good advice and many times, I know, changed his mind on things.[34]

Other talented businessmen also gravitated to Carlisle. To assist him in his investments, Carlisle hired H. Edmund Machold and Charles Norris. Machold was known for his varied and successful career as lawyer, farmer, legislator, and businessman. His dairy farm was the showplace of Jefferson County, and his achievements in the legislature of New York were striking. As a Republican legislator, he had worked successfully to benefit dairy and agricultural interests as well as utilities and had spurred passage of a bill establishing a storage reservoir, which later bore his name. Machold was elected a director of St. Regis in 1923 and three years later became vice-president of F. L. Carlisle and Company. Charles Norris was elected a St. Regis director in January 1925. Norris was a lawyer in Carthage and a Democrat of considerable influence. Establishing a power grid across upper New York involved a considerable amount of political maneuvering, and Carlisle drew heavily upon the talents and contacts of Machold and Norris.[35]

By assembling a talented staff, Carlisle hoped to achieve two principal objectives: creation of a power network and expansion of a paper company. Through the purchase of Hanna Paper Corporation common stock in 1921, he advanced the paper interests of St. Regis. The acquisition made St. Regis the third largest paper manufacturing firm in the United States, with production reaching five hundred tons of newsprint daily. Although the agreement allowed the two companies to operate independently, management of Hanna was assumed by St. Regis.[36]

The Hanna interests included mills and newsprint plants at Raymondville, Norfolk, East Norfolk, Norwood, and Carthage. Charles H. Remington had built or purchased four of the mills early in the century. The Hanna interests acquired them in 1916, converted them to production of newsprint and directory paper, and then bought the Carthage mill from the Champion Paper Company. Carlisle purchased the preferred stock of the Hanna Corporation in April 1925, raising the necessary funds through sale of the Herrings mill to the recently reorganized Taggart Brothers Company, which was expanding production of bag paper. Shortly after acquiring the Herrings plant, Taggart Brothers converted it to production of lightweight paper for cement bags.[37]

Acquisition of the Hanna properties enhanced St. Regis's position in papermaking, and Carlisle's next move consolidated his control over the region's power resources. He organized the Power Corporation of

New York as a holding firm for the power rights of St. Regis, Hanna, the Raquette River Power Company, and undeveloped properties owned jointly by Carlisle and H. F. Furman. The contract, formalized in October 1922, stipulated that in payment the Power Corporation would issue three hundred thousand shares of common stock and ten thousand shares of preferred stock. A few days later, Carlisle outlined the role the holding company would play in the industrial development of the region:

> The transfer of the paper companies' water power plants into the new power company will facilitate working out water storage upon the rivers and hasten their being changed into hydraulic plants, when their energy will be available for all general uses as well as making paper.[38]

Carlisle's success in consolidating his influence is demonstrated by the interlocking directorships of several companies. By 1924 the offices and directorships of St. Regis, Hanna Corporation, Norwood & St. Lawrence Railroad Company, and the Power Corporation were held by business leaders long associated with Carlisle: John Carlisle, Celestine Burns, Frank Empsall, Alvah Miller, and H. E. Machold.[39]

St. Regis extended its scope in early 1926 with organization of the Northeastern Power Corporation. This was accomplished by the exchange of St. Regis-held common shares of the Power Corporation of New York for common shares of the Northeastern Power Corporation. An additional six hundred thousand shares of Northeastern stock purchased in 1927 gave St. Regis a majority holding of 1,452,660 shares.[40]

In 1922 St. Regis began a full transition to the making of catalog, directory, and magazine papers. This change resulted primarily from the lifting of tariff protection in 1913. Not until the recession of 1921-1922, with its drop in newsprint prices, did manufacturers give up the struggle to restore tariff duties. Their failure to secure the desired aid from the Fordney-McCumber tariff was the last gasp of manufacturers to protect themselves against foreign competition.[41]

Concurrently with their tariff efforts, paper executives took steps to secure their investments. The need to develop alternative product lines was apparent, as were the directions in which they might go. Just as booming population and improved living conditions had increased the demand for newsprint in the early 1900s, so also did social advances in the second decade initiate demand for diversified paper products. The accelerated development of science and technology, especially in the fields of chemistry and electricity, enabled manufacturers to produce a variety of new commodities.

St. Regis adapted itself by turning to the production of specialty papers. Canada's inability to supply the entire demand for newsprint following removal of the tariff duties gave the firm time to restructure its plants. Also, its growing income from utility investments provided both an additional cushion and an adequate supply of power. Finally the gradual electrification of the company's mills and plants during the 1920s permitted installation of machinery equipped to run at varying speeds, allowing the production of a diversity of paper grades.[42]

In December 1925 the New York Telephone Company awarded St. Regis a one-year contract to supply between twenty-three thousand and twenty-four thousand tons of paper. This was the firm's first large-scale production of directory paper. Entry into the catalog market was obtained through acquisition of the Carthage mill, which manufactured catalog paper for Montgomery Ward. St. Regis inherited this contract and kept it by maintaining high-quality production. The mail-order house sought one mill that could produce all of its catalog paper and, in 1926, opened bidding for a long-term contract to all large producers in the United States and Canada. St. Regis was the successful bidder for a ten-year contract calling for thirty thousand tons of catalog paper annually.[43]

Early in 1927 Carlisle reported to stockholders that St. Regis had "added materially to its American pulpwood reserves" through purchase of a two-thirds interest in the New Hampshire-Vermont Lumber Company. (The remaining one-third of this property was acquired by International Paper.) With this transaction came valuable waterpower and storage reservoirs, which were retained by the New England Power Association, an affiliate of the Northeastern Power Corporation. The more than three hundred thousand acres of timberlands were managed by St. Regis and provided a source of wood for the Deferiet mill as the supply from the Godbout tract lessened.[44]

That same year, the firm organized two subsidiaries that provided facilities for the development of a specialty line of papers. The Harrisville Paper Corporation was formed to acquire the assets of the bankrupt Diana Paper Company of Harrisville, New York, which had produced catalog and magazine grades. The property consisted of two mills with an annual capacity of eighteen thousand tons of paper and fifteen thousand tons of groundwood. In September 1927 St. Regis organized the Oswego Board Corporation and constructed a mill at Oswego, New York, to produce all-wood fiber roofing, sheeting, and insulation board. The board was processed from waste pulpwood and other shredded wood materials shipped from the Deferiet plant, and it was sold by Johns-Manville under the latter's own trade name.[45]

The most striking step toward diversification was the entrance into the plastics field. St. Regis purchased Panelyte Corporation of Trenton, New Jersey, in 1928, an action of considerable consequence in future years. Panelyte plastic was a mixture of phenolic resins and wood flour, paper, canvas, or linen and was originally used as electrical insulation. Later St. Regis developed its own system of combining kraft paper and the resins. Recalling the farsightedness of St. Regis's leadership in this venture, Roy Ferguson remarked, "We looked upon plastics, even then, as a logical and potentially valuable complement to the paper industry. This has certainly proved to be."[46]

Access into the multiwall bag field was a second major development that greatly enhanced the trend toward diversification. A significant undertaking in this process was the formation by Carlisle in 1928 of the Taggart Corporation, a holding company that included the entire stock of Taggart Brothers Company, Taggart Oswego Paper and Bag Company, and the Champion Paper Company. (The last firm controlled all of the capital stock of the Carthage Power Corporation.) Three bag manufacturing plants located at Oswego, Herrings, and Watertown were acquired as part of the transaction. Taggart Brothers had become a licensee in 1924 of the Bates Valve Bag Company, which held the patents on multiwall valve bags and had built a mill at Oswego to manufacture kraft paper for use in production of the bag.[47]

When Bates was put up for sale in 1929, Carlisle bought it for slightly over $14 million, a price that included a large sum for customer goodwill. This sum became a source of disagreement between Ferguson and Carlisle, since Ferguson felt that goodwill could be overvalued. Another point of dissension was that the Bates patent was due to expire in 1947. In the short run the price paid for Bates appeared to be quite high, but in the long run the acquisition of the multiwall bag patent

proved highly important. Years later Ferguson paid tribute to the genius of Adelmer M. Bates and the effect his invention had on the
company:

> We are talking about uncelebrated events that not only shaped
> St. Regis and assured its leadership role in industrial packaging
> but in fact marked a new era in packaging and a technological
> breakthrough for kraft paper.[48]

The Bates Valve Bag Company had been created by Adelmer M.
Bates and John E. Cornell. Bates was a salt salesman who developed
an idea for a valve bag to facilitate the packing and handling of salt and
aggregate products. Cornell managed the Hyde Park Hotel in Chicago
and financed Bates while he developed a machine to fill valve bags.
Together they created a thriving multiwall bag business in Chicago
and added plants at Nazareth, Pennsylvania; East Pepperell, Massachusetts; Covington, Kentucky; Los Angeles, California; and Menominee, Michigan. Other plants were located in Birmingham, Alabama;
Toledo, Ohio; Oakmont, Pennsylvania; Dryden, Ontario; and Three
Rivers, Quebec. When Bates died in 1926, the company was reorganized and subsequently sold to Carlisle.[49]

St. Regis expanded its multiwall bag business into the international
market with the acquisition of the Bates International Bag Company
in 1930. The firm had issued licenses to thirty companies in forty foreign countries, with Bates International holding stock in thirteen of the
concerns. The foreign bag producers were licensed to sell and lease
filling machines and to sell machinery parts and wire ties.[50]

Two additional purchases in 1930 substantially increased the company's resources for multiwall production: the acquisition of the Cornell Multiwall Valve Bag Company of Delaware and the Pacific Pulp
Mill Company of Tacoma. The Cornell Company owned patents for
multiwall paper bags and filling machines. The Tacoma mill provided
a major source of kraft pulp and became the St. Regis Kraft Company,
a wholly owned subsidiary capable of producing forty-six thousand
tons of kraft pulp a year. St. Regis's position in the bag market was
further enhanced in 1930 by acquisition of an interest in the Western
Valve Bag Company of Nevada. A new factory for the manufacture
of packers and bag-making machines at Oswego and a modern plant
for the manufacture of multiwall paper bags in Los Angeles were also
completed in 1930. Plans were drawn for additional Pacific Coast bag
plants to be built at Oakland and Seattle.[51]

By 1930, the production of St. Regis bore little resemblance to what it had been ten years previously. The best-selling items were catalog and directory papers, but the company also produced manila, kraft, mottled wrapping paper, waxed paper for the baking industry, and small amounts of newsprint. In his 1930 annual report to the stockholders, Carlisle emphasized the changes that had occurred. No more than 10 percent of the company's operating revenue derived from newsprint sales, whereas "ten years ago 90% of the entire business consisted of newsprint."[52] By the onset of the Great Depression, the company had completed its transformation from a producer of newsprint at a single mill into a diversified manufacturer with a growing list of profitable plants.

As the 1920s drew to a close, Carlisle continued to expand his electric power investments. In 1929 he organized the Niagara Hudson Power Corporation, a combination of the Northeastern Power Corporation, the Buffalo, Niagara and Eastern Power Company, and the Mohawk-Hudson Power Corporation. Initially the organization was controlled by four principal groups: Carlisle and St. Regis, J. P. Morgan and Company, the Schoelkopf family interests, and the Aluminum Company of America. St. Regis exchanged its Northeastern shares for common shares of Niagara Hudson; later in 1929, additional shares of Niagara Hudson were purchased, bringing St. Regis's interest to a market value of $55,650,000.[53] By this strategem Carlisle came close to realizing his goal of using the logging streams of the Adirondacks to turn electric generators and to build a power grid across the state.

Approximately one-half of St. Regis's total assets were invested in utility holdings by 1929. In the preceding five years, the value of the company's power investments had soared from $5.9 million to $55.65 million. The market crash and the depression abruptly halted this trend and ended the power and paper alliance that Carlisle had conceived. In early 1931, Carlisle restructured his firm's utility investments by exchanging its Niagara Hudson common stock for 15 percent of the United Corporation's outstanding common shares. United was a holding company headed by F. L. Carlisle and Company, Inc., but it also represented the interests of J. P. Morgan and Company, Drexel and Company, Thorne Loomis and Company, and the American Superpower Corporation. United's holdings penetrated vast congeries of public utilities systems throughout the East.[54]

As the effects of the depression began to be felt at St. Regis in 1931, the firm's formerly profitable investment dividends now served to reduce its nonoperating income. In 1932 United Corporation reduced its annual dividends from common stock from seventy-five to ten cents a share. The result for St. Regis was a $831,000 drop in income. The company began to reduce its holding of 2,046,466 United shares in 1932 and continued to do so for the next several years, at substantial book loss.[55]

As was true of most other businesses during the depression, the financial problems of St. Regis were compounded by a steep decline in sales. Existing contracts for the purchase of kraft and pulp had to be honored although there was no demand for those supplies. In an effort to adjust to conditions, the company began to retrench. In addition to disposing gradually of its United Corporation stock, the company closed the two remaining newsprint mills at Norfolk and Raymondville and some additional operations. Stringent economic measures were imposed in every office and at every mill. Nonetheless, the company maintained confidence in the economy's ability to recover and in the paper industry's eventual resurgence by proceeding with research and development.[56]

Carlisle resigned as president of St. Regis in June 1934 and became board chairman of Consolidated Edison. He remained as chairman of the St. Regis board. Ferguson was recommended by Carlisle to succeed him as president. Over the years, while managing F. L. Carlisle and Company, Ferguson had developed expertise in the paper business. He was elected assistant secretary and assistant treasurer of St. Regis in 1925; two years later he attained a directorship. In 1928 he was made a vice-president, and in 1930 he joined the newly formed executive committee. Ferguson had grown measurably under the tutelage of Carlisle and had come a long way from the "starry-eyed youngster" who first met Carlisle in 1917.[57]

As Ferguson took office, St. Regis was slowly separating its utility and papermaking concerns. Carlisle's fascination with electrical power had strengthened the company's papermaking abilities. Electrification had permitted diversification of production, and facilities such as the Hanna mills offered as great a potential in paper production as they did sources of hydroelectric power. The timberland of the New Hampshire-Vermont Lumber Company, valuable for water rights and storage reservoirs, was also an obvious source of much-needed pulpwood. Panelyte plastics proved valuable as electrical insulation, and the idea of impregnating kraft paper with resins represented a new and exciting application of paper. Added to these aspects of the business was the great inherent strength of the new line of multiwall valve bag products.

Thus in 1934, as the company started to show signs of recovering from its losses, a new era began. Under the direction of Floyd Carlisle, the character of the firm had changed. Roy Ferguson, with his financial expertise and his experience as an officer over the previous nine years, seemed the ideal candidate to build on the foundation Carlisle had established.

5
Surviving Depression and War

The paper industry was among the first to show signs of recovery from the blows struck the world economy during the Great Depression. St. Regis, although sharing to some extent in this recovery, still reported a net loss when Roy K. Ferguson assumed the presidency in June 1934. Floyd Carlisle continued to serve as chairman of the board and as a member of the executive committee until his death in 1942, but it was clear that St. Regis had entered an era that would bear Ferguson's stamp. The first measures Ferguson enacted set the tone and style that would extend for more than two decades. Ferguson's own words, from a 1948 speech, best summarize the new era:

> When the depression had had its severe effect on us as well as other companies, we moved into what is the current era. If we think of the first step as the newsprint era, the second as predominantly the power phase, the third I should like to see rededicated as the pulp and paper development. . . . It became evident St. Regis had a place and a name in the pulp and paper industry which should be developed into an active, aggressive, forthright organization that could do an enlarged job, and so that was the effort.[1]

Ferguson's administrative ability and financial skill played a large part in the company's economic resurgence. The New York banking community, especially the powerful First National City Bank, respected his financial acumen. William R. Adams, later a president of St. Regis, recalled one quality that made Ferguson such an effective administrator:

> When one of us, take myself as an example, was having troubles . . . he'd simply say, "What are you going to be able to do? And when?" And you'd tell him. That's all he expected. . . . There are people who make too much of an issue of the fact that you are in trouble. They don't have a quiet talk with you and find out what can be done, what the new program is. Ferguson had a great capacity to do that.[2]

During the twenty-three years Ferguson served as president, he demonstrated an unusual capacity for selecting able assistants. His willingness to delegate authority to subordinates was praised by associates. Hugh W. Sloan recalls that Ferguson let his top aides fight out their differences in conference, often over lunch. "He was so clever," Sloan admits, "he never got himself aligned. That's why he was such a fine head of a company; he gave himself latitude to move in the direction that he felt was in the best interest."[3] Thus Ferguson established his position as a charming and forceful administrator. And he freed himself to concentrate on the difficult financial problems facing the company in the 1930s and 1940s, while experienced subordinates took care of production and sales.

Prominent among his staff was Vice-President Edward R. Gay, a former Bates employee who supervised the company's divisions. Gay was a dynamic force in the subsequent growth of St. Regis and later assumed many promotional responsibilities. Willard J. Dixon, secretary of St. Regis, served on the executive committee and supervised the multiwall bag licensees. William H. Versfelt, Sr., became treasurer in 1936 and assisted Ferguson in the finance area.[4] Other seasoned officers managed the manufacturing divisions. Carl B. Martin, hired in 1912 to manage company timberland, took charge of the northern New York groundwood and kraft mills in 1935. Joseph Harnit looked after bag manufacturing for both St. Regis and the Taggart Corporation. Ralph Maltby, who had joined St. Regis in 1921, handled the international division. Maltby was president of the Champion Paper Company before its purchase by the Hanna Corporation and subsequent assimilation by St. Regis.[5] These men emerge from the record as the principal individuals who helped Ferguson pull St. Regis out of the depression. Their ideas and programs were also vital in the postwar period.

The immediate problem facing Ferguson was financial. St. Regis and its subsidiaries were heavily obligated as a result of the expansion program of the 1920s, and they were overcapitalized as well. Ferguson pared capitalization down to hard assets and wrote off the goodwill of investments. Losses were severe but did not affect manufacturing capacity.

One of Ferguson's first acts was to cancel $2.4 million in debts owed St. Regis by the subsidiaries, an action that solidified the financial condition of the subsidiaries, which were overburdened by other obligations. Next he scaled down the capitalization of both St. Regis and the subsidiaries. With the approval of the stockholders in 1936, he reduced the capital stock of St. Regis from $85 million to $47.5 million by halving—from $10 to $5—the par value of 7.5 million shares of common stock; the 100,000 preferred shares remained at a par value of $100.[6]

St. Regis also lessened by slightly over $7 million the value of investments in its subsidiaries: St. Regis Securities Corporation, Harrisville Paper Corporation, Oswego Board Corporation, Cornell Bag Corporation, Panelyte Corporation, St. Regis Kraft Company, and St. Regis, Limited of Canada. The largest reduction involved the Bates Valve Bag Company; its capital was lowered from $14.2 million to $1 million. Written off were goodwill, valued at over $11 million, and patents and licenses. Ferguson also reduced Bates International's capital by $906,100, of which $830,646 consisted of goodwill.[7]

These efforts were part of an austerity program that permeated every part of the company. Further economy measures were taken between 1937 and 1943. Subsidiaries were absorbed by the parent company, and the St. Regis Sales Corporation consolidated all sales efforts. The business of Bates International was continued by the new St. Regis International Division.[8]

While seeking the answers to its own financial problems, St. Regis was caught up in the push and pull of New Deal efforts to stimulate the economy. Amid the activity of the new federal agencies, the paper industry maintained its traditional pattern of lagging behind other industries in feeling the effect and severity of depression. Part of this lag resulted from the nature of the product and its uses. With the occurrence of major events, good or bad, demand for news increased demand for paper.[9]

The paper industry also tended to recover more rapidly than the general economy, and this was the case during the 1930s.[10] The most negative aspect of the industry was the chronic instability of prices and profits, which industry analysts blamed on distribution methods and costs. The *Paper Trade Journal*'s 1933 annual review called for improved management and marketing: "An important factor for the paper industry is the necessity of adjusting production to demand." The same appeal had been made a month earlier by John A. C. Kavanaugh, director of the Statistical Department of the APPA:

> A more complete knowledge of the market and the adaptability of the product to the needs of the market, along with adherence to a reasonable set of trade customs which will put competition on a more honest basis—are indispensable to profitable marketing.[11]

Papermakers persisted in meeting decreases in consumption by increasing manufacturing capacity, despite growing recognition that this practice depressed profits. A statistician for the G. H. Mead Company of New York concluded:

> Only a comparatively few concerns have successfully solved their distribution problems. A fundamental difficulty is that most mills are dominated by production-minded instead of sales-minded executives. . . . Production continues to be in excess of market demands and selling below cost is widely prevalent.[12]

Thus the experts were advocating continued efforts in areas of planning and market analysis and praising cooperative attempts by industry to solve common problems. Consolidation appeared to be the answer for many producers, and rumors of mergers were heard frequently.[13]

Positive conditions for the adoption of the ideas of the New Deal existed. Meanwhile the projects of the Public Works Administration and the Civil Works Administration increased the business of cement companies by nearly 30 percent in 1934, and St. Regis was able to capitalize on the new opportunity in the bag market. In addition, mail-order houses began to sell more goods and subsequently bought more catalog paper. These were among the first encouraging signs of recovery.

Enactment of the National Recovery Administration was greeted with general enthusiasm by paper manufacturers, as is colorfully and

humorously illustrated by a poem appearing in February 1934 in the
Paper Trade Journal:

> *Ding Dong Bell!*
> *Business went to hell.*
> *Who put it in?*
> *Old Man Depression.*
> *What overcame it?*
> *N.R.A.—and we acclaim it.*
> *What a noble act was that*
> *Of a lowly Democrat*
> *Who restored prosperity*
> *All Hail to Franklin D.!*[14]

The major impetus to economic recovery came from the NRA. Under
its program, leaders in the pulp and paper industry were responsible
for drafting codes to stabilize prices and wages and improve the conditions of labor. Edward R. "Ted" Gay took an optimistic view of the
codes despite his antipathy to governmental intervention in business:

> Unfair trade practices will be violations of the law, punishable
> through the courts. The day of the price-cutter and the chiseler
> will be over . . . much as we dislike to see the Government taking
> a hand in business, it [NRA regulation] is pretty good news.[15]

The codes brought order and stability to the industry. Zonal pricing,
open-price filing, standards for billing and sales, and union recognition
were features that helped end unfair competition. Of great importance
to the newsprint manufacturers was a rapprochement between publishers and papermakers. Ground was laid for discussion of mutual
problems, and cooperation replaced distrust.

The leading trade journal credited the NRA with the most significant changes of the recovery years. APPA President S. L. Willson
summarized its positive effects in 1934:

> It has enabled the industry to build up an association that was
> disintegrating, and which now represents nearly every mill in the
> country, and to prompt their support in financing it. . . . It had
> developed cooperation between competitors and eliminated jungle

competition. It prevents selling below cost, and it has resulted in the standardization of grades and prices.[16]

Although the Supreme Court declared the NRA unconstitutional in May 1935, leaders of the American Paper and Pulp Association, the Association of Newsprint Manufacturers, and the National Paper Trade Association favored continued adherence to code provisions. To such leaders the program had been a definite advantage, and they wished to salvage the wage and price schedules and the rules of fair practice.

Whatever faults businessmen saw in the New Deal, it convinced them of the need to break the destructive economic cycle characteristic of the preceding decades. Industrial codes had exposed industry to a brief measure of self-government. When federal programs began to stimulate new demands for paper, the industry quickly increased production to 88 percent of capacity. Experience had tempered, at least for a time, the temptation to risk heavy capital investment in new plants or to accept high overhead for the sake of obtaining a higher volume of production. After the industry's considerable expansion in the 1920s, it operated close to capacity and met the demands of the market. In 1935, the *St. Regis-Bates Monthly News* made this statement about the NRA and its impact:

> After a couple of years of ruinous prices and shrunken markets, the members of the industry came to recognize the necessity for cooperative action. The NRA afforded the means by which such action could be effective. And, regardless of what Congress may do with NRA, there is every reason to believe that this group of [paper] manufacturers will continue to work together, for their mutual benefit.[17]

As sales rose in 1936, St. Regis realized its first profit in five years. The kraft and bag industries led the recovery. The kraft industry prospered throughout the depression, especially in the South, as kraft paper supplanted wood, textiles, glass, and metal in the production of containers. As the principal manufacturer of multiwall bags, St. Regis benefited from the market surge; its sales reached 200 million bags in 1937.[18]

To supply its profitable bag plants, St. Regis had entered into a contract in 1931 to purchase thirty thousand tons of kraft pulp annually from the National Paper Products Company, a Zellerbach operation.

During the hardest years of the depression, this turned out to be more than St. Regis needed, but Zellerbach showed no inclination to reduce the contract amount or price. As a result, St. Regis's surplus paper was sold at a loss to the Brooklyn Standard Bag Company. But with the surge in the bag business in 1935, Ferguson renegotiated the contract with National Paper Products so as to limit the amount to between ten thousand and twenty thousand tons.[19]

The improved economic situation set Ferguson to mapping a program of modernization and expansion. The cost of rehabilitation efforts between 1935 and 1939 was over $5 million. In a 1937 letter to the stockholders, Ferguson outlined the expenditures and the reasoning behind them: "to improve our products and enable the Corporation to reach broader sales markets."[20]

One of his first moves was to explore the potential for achieving self-sufficiency in kraft. Thus in 1936 the Tacoma kraft mill, closed for the previous four years because of depressed prices, was reopened. Old machines were rehabilitated and new machinery and equipment were installed. The additions included a new bleaching plant and a new type of furnace to recover chemicals and to control gases. The furnace was supposed to eliminate the emission of offensive odors and thereby mitigate the objections lodged against the plant by surrounding communities. Criticism of pulp plant odor had retarded growth of the industry in both Washington and Oregon. Further expansion at Tacoma came in 1940 with the addition of two digesters.[21]

Multiwall bag production continued to increase during the late 1930s as usage spread beyond the industries that had pioneered this form of container. The sugar industry, for one, came to realize the advantages of St. Regis bags:

> Back in 1936, the corporation had a Sales Promotion Department whose function was to develop other new markets. . . . The sugar industry was one of the early ones we went after, diverting manufacturers away from . . . cotton bags to more sanitary . . . paper bags. The packaging systems that Bates had developed—the packers themselves—also provided an opportunity for St. Regis to show the sugar industry how it could modernize and pack with automation.[22]

To meet this new demand for bags, St. Regis purchased the Modern Valve Bag Company of Allentown, Pennsylvania, in 1941. The Taggart Corporation, managed by St. Regis, purchased the machinery, equipment, and office fixtures of the Modern Valve Bag Company for installation in a plant under construction in Franklin, Virginia. Taggart erected this plant adjacent to the Chesapeake-Camp Corporation's paper mills, for which it had a contract to supply kraft. The loblolly pine of Virginia and North Carolina yielded the long fibers essential for the special kraft paper preferred by Taggart.[23]

St. Regis printing paper operations were improved by various means. NRA codes included formal recognition of different grades of groundwood paper, and St. Regis executive Charles McMillen urged the development of capacity for supplying clearly defined grades of paper. In 1936 the company installed a bleached sulfite mill at Deferiet, permitting the manufacture of higher grades of paper from the mill's own pulp supply. Four years later it added a chemi-pulp process, allowing more economical production of chemical pulp. A 25 percent increase in production was achieved by replacing an old machine with a rebuilt fourdrinier paper machine used in the Raymondville mill, which had closed in 1935.[24]

On the eve of America's entry into World War II, St. Regis was on its way to catching up with the financial strength of its competitors and to establishing the prestige of its growing list of products. But as George J. Kneeland, chief executive officer during the 1970s, remembered, "I think we may have been behind quite a few of them. . . . We never got into the South in large measure until the mid-forties. . . . Our delay was purely a matter of money." Attributing the company's weak financial condition to the costly purchase of the Bates Valve Bag Corporation and the subsequent onset of the depression, Kneeland stated, "We were lucky we were keeping our head above water."[25]

Still, the combination of Roy Ferguson's financial wizardry and the astute leadership of his able associates brought St. Regis solvency. By 1937 the company was experiencing a substantial increase in sales and net earnings despite poor markets. Concurrently, stable prices were achieved through increased efficiency. In spite of a loss in 1938 caused by lower prices, by 1940 St. Regis sufficiently regained its earlier advantage to report its best year ever as a paper manufacturer. The massive stimulus provided business by the war was launched in 1940 by the national defense program, which brought a high demand for all grades of paper. Kneeland said of the impact of the war upon St. Regis: "The coming of World War II in 1939 produced a great upsurge in business, but also a great upsurge in regulations with which we had to cope."[26]

World War II forced important changes upon the pulp and paper industry. Ferguson saw the war as bringing the industry to maturity and greater integration. He believed the War Production Board had a healthy impact and generated "a new self-reliance, a new faith in our own resources and an acceleration in our research." For Ferguson the fact that during the war St. Regis maintained operations at full capacity and even improved the efficiency attested to the positive influence of the nation's defense effort.[27]

For a short period after Pearl Harbor, the pulp and paper industry stood in uncertain position with respect to priorities and allocation of raw materials. At first paper was not regarded as an important contributor to the war effort. William R. Adams later recalled how the paper industry proved its usefulness:

> The first year of the war, the officials in Washington thought that paper was a dispensable commodity. . . . But then the phenomenal job that the paper industry did in packaging things for shipment right up to the front reversed that feeling rather markedly. By the end of the war, paper was pretty high up on the priority list. . . . I remember we had to make bags for food and for cement . . . that could stand being thrown overboard from the landing boat and pulled ashore through the water.[28]

The value of paper was evident in its wide applicability to war production. Various grades of paper were used in producing maps, blueprints, and training manuals. Millions of paperback books were published for distribution to servicemen. Massive amounts of pulp were employed as cellulose base for explosives. The output of paper products indispensable for military and civilian uses soared, while manufacture of certain luxury grades was discontinued. The war years brought a sharp increase in both production and income as the defense program stimulated industrial and business activity. By 1942 most of the company's production was devoted to the war effort. Aware of the future significance of these developments, Ferguson made plans to continue many of the new lines after the war. Unlike many others, he foresaw the condition of the postwar economy in an optimistic light and "felt confident that the demand for paper would be very high, kraft products particularly."[29]

St. Regis, along with most of American business, was forced to cope with wartime shortages. Its timber operations were seriously hampered by a loss of skilled woodworkers to the draft. There were other problems to be overcome in moving raw material to the mill and then to thousands of different places. Lack of such equipment as trucks, tires, gasoline, oil, and railcars were among the more obvious problems. The shortage of chlorine needed for the bleaching of pulp was especially acute. But wartime scarcity also benefited St. Regis and other operators. The demand for scarce burlap, steel, and solid wood products opened markets for pulp and paper products.[30]

The Panelyte Division, one of the first to convert to war production, produced a profit in 1941 for the first time in its history. Throughout the 1930s this division had expanded its output, producing laminated phenolic compositions in sheets, rods, tubes, washers, discs, and gear blanks for use in refrigerator door panels, radios, automotive fenders and doors, and in the electrical industry. But such peacetime products were abandoned in 1942 when Panelyte turned to making baffles, push-rod housings, and other airplane parts. It also produced laminated sheets for use in tanks, ships, and submarines for the American armed forces as well as those of the Allies. By war's end, Panelyte was devoting its entire production to military applications.[31]

Under the impetus of the war, St. Regis moved to diversify by acquiring majority interest in the Skenandoa Rayon Corporation, which produced high-quality yarn by the viscose process. Rayon was widely used during the war, especially in the manufacture of parachutes and various shrouds and cables. Long-term projections for the use of rayon in peacetime encouraged the purchase, but in 1945 a decision was made to sell St. Regis's common shares in Skenandoa to Beaunit Mills, Inc., of New York. The sale announcement explained that it was "in line with the St. Regis plans to devote its entire attention to its pulp, paper, multiwall paper bag, packing machine and plastics divisions."[32] Ferguson's desire to make St. Regis primarily a paper company was thus reasserted.

The war's impact on the growth of St. Regis is nowhere more clearly seen than in the field of packaging. Former President William Adams regarded the war as "very likely the most important stimulus the packaging industry ever had."[33] One element that led to the wider employment of paper bags was the shortage of such packaging materials as solid wood and wood shook, burlap, jute, glass, metals, and cotton cloth. No less important was the effort made by paper manufacturers to convince government agencies of the many uses of paper packaging. Advertising executives of St. Regis and other paper companies made gains for their industry by convincing government officials of the virtues of paper. Gardiner Lane of St. Regis recalls the industry's wartime concern: "We have got to go to Washington to convince these people that paper bags and paper are essential." Lane, who worked under Kenneth D. Lozier in the St. Regis advertising department during the war, recalls that in advising the government on paper, he constantly held that the benefits of paper usage "were all tied into the cost factor—the total packaging cost." This concept of "selling all the way through," as it came to be known, stemmed from the necessity of having to sell not only the government on the value of paper bags but also the supplier of the various commodities to be packaged.[34]

To expand multiwall bag use further, St. Regis organized the Technical Development Department in 1942. Its first goal was to assist the government in developing special-use bags. Clayton Bush managed the new department, assisted by Charles Woodcock.[35] Woodcock helped design a bag for shipment of synthetic rubber. He and his associates also worked with the Chemical Warfare Service in promoting a special bag for decontamination of gassed clothing. Numerous other bags were developed for use in the shipment of food products.

In 1944 St. Regis sold over one billion paper bags for the packaging of more than three hundred different products. To fill this growing demand, the company built an additional bag plant in North Kansas City, Missouri. Kenneth Lozier was involved in securing governmental approval for the new plant, not an easy accomplishment in the face of wartime building restrictions.

> I got thrown out of every office at the War Production Board. I realized one day that there was a man named Harry Truman, a Senator from Missouri who was riding herd on the . . . Board. . . . I went to see him. He said, "Can you stay in Washington for awhile?" I said, "I will stay here just as long as I need to." In ten days he called me and said, "Your plant is approved."

Not long after, Truman became president, and Lozier was invited to a White House reception. He thanked Truman for his assistance, telling him of its importance to St. Regis and to the war effort. Truman responded briefly and in characteristic language: "Well . . . I'm damned glad that something came out right."[36]

The Oswego Machine Division also responded to the increased opportunity by accelerating its output of packaging and filling machines. The War Production Board had initially converted the division to the production of parts for recoil mechanisms, bombsights, and other items. But once the board realized the savings in manpower and material made possible by packaging systems, it directed the Machine Division to concentrate on the production of mechanical packers.[37]

While the war years increased bag and kraft production, severe limitations were also imposed. In addition to shortages of chlorine and fibrous materials, discontinuation of pulp imports from Scandinavia exacerbated manufacturing problems. Imposition of wood pulp blockades and cartels as early as 1940 resulted in a critical reduction in wood pulp inventories. Restrictions on the importation of logs from British Columbia and a manpower shortage in the Pacific Northwest forced closure of the Tacoma plant in late 1942. This action by the War Production Board was based on an evaluation of the Puget Sound District as a "critical wood area."[38]

Caught between shortages of wood and chemicals and a fluctuating demand for paper, St. Regis produced catalog, directory, and groundwood book paper by combining sulfite and groundwood pulp. The shortage of wood put a premium on the use of groundwood, since groundwood pulp yielded more volume than did chemical pulp. Publishers turned to the lightweight groundwood book paper because it enabled them to produce the same number of pages and conserve wood.

In 1944 St. Regis introduced a new method to produce bleached groundwood paper through a sodium peroxide bleaching process developed with the aid of Du Pont scientists. This technique added brightness, permanence, and color to the excellent printing quality of groundwood paper. Installed in 1945 along with a fourth digester, the system completely integrated the Deferiet mill's wood supply and pulp and papermaking capacity.[39]

The strictures placed on the Pacific Northwest during the war made it clear that the Tacoma kraft operation needed its own supply of wood. Consequently St. Regis purchased a 60 percent interest in the Lake Logging Company of British Columbia in 1943, anticipating reopening of the Tacoma mill when import restrictions were lifted. Also acquired in 1943 were perpetual cutting rights on 109,000 acres of timberland near Tacoma. This timberland, owned by the West Fork Timber Company, enabled St. Regis to reopen the mill in April 1944.[40]

It was recognized that the demands of war would cut heavily into the wood resources of northern New York and New England and Canada. To compensate for this anticipated drain, St. Regis organized the Moose River Lumber Company in partnership with the J. P. Lewis Company of New York. The new firm was authorized to acquire timberland and standing timber and to manage land for other purposes. Its first action in 1941 was to buy cutting rights on two parcels of land owned by the Adirondack League Club in Herkimer and Hamilton counties, New York.[41] Heavy cutting in the North Country by St. Regis and other companies depleted the area's wood supply, and the resulting timber shortage would have profound effects upon the paper industry.

The years of domestic and international crisis wrought major changes in the American economy and society. Historians define World War II as the catalyst lifting the economy out of the depression. Between 1934 and 1944, St. Regis became very distinctly a paper company, one of the country's largest producers of kraft paper products.[42] During this period, its net sales rose from roughly $9 million to approximately $48 million. It operated at a loss in 1934, 1935, and 1938, but net income for the 1941-1944 period averaged slightly over $2 million a year. By 1941 St. Regis had expended $6.7 million on plant improvements and reduced its funded debt from $6 million to $2.5 million.

On 1 January 1944, St. Regis sold $10 million worth of fifteen-year debentures to finance its expansion of manufacturing facilities to meet anticipated postwar demand and provide additional working capital. Three months later, the stockholders approved a recapitalization plan that eliminated the payment of $70 per share in arrears on outstanding shares of the company's 7 percent cumulative preferred stock. Under the plan, holders of this preferred stock exchanged each share for 3.6 shares of a new 5 percent cumulative prior preferred stock.

Significant strides were made in other areas as well. Royal Kellogg summed up labor-management relations during the late 1930s and the war years: "They've been excellent. . . . [Union] leaders had the paper manufacturers' respect and there has been no labor trouble since then [1920-1921], except one or two sporadic cases." The same attitude was reflected on the labor side by Matthew Burns, president of the International Brotherhood of Paper Makers. He noted in 1936 that manufacturers had had a profound change in their outlook toward unions in recent years. Pay increases had been granted even though few "companies are earning a worthwhile profit," and opposition to unions had become the exception rather than the rule.[43]

The paternalistic policies in the field of labor relations adopted in the early years of Carlisle's administration were continued by Ferguson. Health, accident, and life insurance programs were implemented by St. Regis and Taggart in 1935. Financed by corporation and employee contributions, such plans provided comparable coverage and benefits to those in use by other major industrial concerns.[44]

Three years after the war's end, Archibald Carswell, chairman of the first annual meeting of the Multiwall Bag Division, looked back upon the recent history of St. Regis with a mixture of levity and seriousness:

> Mr. Ferguson came uptown from Wall Street [to head St. Regis in 1934], and it was quite a question whether he was the new president or whether he was the head undertaker. . . . For several years it was truly hard. We had no money. The stockholders . . . were getting no dividends, and were more than a little vocal about it. But when there was something which required doing, Mr. Ferguson found the money somehow with which to do it. Indeed, it was in those dark days that the foundation for much of our present expansion of business was laid.[45]

Ferguson's financial genius and talent for molding a loyal and competent management team had put St. Regis into a stronger position than it had ever before held.

Adelmer M. Bates and John E. Cornell incorporated
Bates Valve Bag Company in 1901, which was
acquired by St. Regis in 1929. *Photo courtesy of
St. Regis Paper Company*

George W. Knowlton, Jr. President 1900–1908

Gordias H. P. Gould, who started his career as a logger, guided the company's destiny between 1908 and 1916. *Photo courtesy of Lewis County Historical Society*

H. Edmund Machold, ca. 1930. Vice-president, 1924–1934. Executive Committee, 1930–1965. *Photo courtesy of Marine Midland Banks, Inc.*

Floyd L. Carlisle, ca. 1930. President, 1916–1934. Chairman of the Board, 1934–1943. *Photo courtesy of Marine Midland Banks, Inc.*

A logging crew poses at Camp #3, St. Paul & Tacoma Lumber Company, circa 1918. Decades before it merged with St. Regis in 1957, St. Paul & Tacoma's output—for many years over one million board feet daily—helped make Tacoma the "Lumber Capital of the World."

"Are the men more careful ... or are these *bags* better?"

"YOU'VE noticed that, Chief! I checked up on it a few days ago. I think the men are a little more careful of *everything*, because they're all trying their best. But I *do* know that the bags are very much improved!

"I have a friend in one of the Kraft paper mills supplying the stock for these bags. I understand from him that there's no comparison between the paper they produced three years ago and now ... it's so much better now.

"And, when the Multi-Wall *Sewn* Paper Bag factories worked out of their 'semi-hand' stage, and *mechanized* all the way through, they insured their jobs just as we have ours ... with machines-that-can't-miss instead of 'variable' human hands.

"Besides, in the cement mills, packing machines and handling methods have all been ... Chief, am I making a public speech or something?"

A series of timely bulletins is being mailed to Highway Officials and Contractors. To insure that yours come to you promptly, send your name and address to The Associated Manufacturers of Multi-Wall Sewn Paper Bags, 60 E. 42nd St., New York, N.Y.

Public speech or not, engineers-in-charge appreciate assistants checking up. The check-up, by the way, usually results in a decision to make the Multi-Wall Sewn Paper Bag the container for the delivery-to-job of cement ... and particularly in the case of the latter-day special, fine-ground, high-early-strength cements.

The Associated Manufacturers of

MULTI-WALL *SEWN* PAPER BAGS

60 East 42nd Street, New York, N.Y.

ARKELL AND SMITHS Canajoharie, N.Y.	THE JAITE COMPANY Jaite, Ohio	TAGGART BROS. CO., INC. 60 E. 42nd St., New York, N.Y.
BATES VALVE BAG CORP. 60 E. 42nd St., New York, N.Y.	THE THOS. PHILLIPS CO. Akron, Ohio	UNIVERSAL PAPER BAG CO. New Hope, Pa.
BEMIS BRO. BAG CO. Peoria, Ill.	THE RAYMOND BAG CO. Middletown, Ohio	THE VALVE BAG CO. 60 E. 42nd St., New York, N.Y.

Advertisement addressed to Highway Officials and Contractors ... appearing in the June, 1932, issue of "Roads and Streets."

A 1932 advertisement for Multi-Wall Sewn Paper Bags, the product on which St. Regis's Bag Packaging Division was originally established. St. Regis remains the world leader in multi-wall bag technology, with licensees in more than twenty countries.

R. K. FERGUSON HEADS ST. REGIS

Former Watertown Banker Named President of Paper Corporation

FLOYD L. CARLISLE, FORMER PRESIDENT, NAMED CHAIRMAN

MR. FERGUSON HAS BEEN VICE PRESIDENT AND SECTARY OF THE COMPANY

BUSINESS OUTLOOK FAVORABLE

Mr. Ferguson, Former Accountant at Lake Placid Club, Was Given Position With Northern New York Trust Company and Later Went to New York When F. L. Carlisle & Co. Was Formed.

(Special to The Times.)

New York, June 25.—Roy K. Ferguson, for some time vice president of the St. Regis Paper company, of the Taggart Corporation and also of the Bates Valve Bag Corporation, has been chosen president of the St. Regis to succeed Floyd L. Carlisle.

Roy K. Ferguson.

Mr. Carlisle, who has headed the company from the time of its purchase by a syndicate of local capitalists organized by him in the fall of 1916, becomes chairman of the board. M. Edmund Machold will continue chairman of the executive committee, a position he has held for some time.

Aside from the elevation of Mr. Ferguson to the presidency and the conferring of the board chairmanship on Mr. Carlisle, the only other change is the promotion of William H. Versfelt, New York, from the assistant secretaryship to the office of secretary held by Mr. Ferguson, Harold C. Sutton is made assistant secretary in place of Mr. Versfelt. The change in officers occurred at a meeting of the directors.

The other officers remain as they have been, C. R. MacMillan, first vice president; Ralph B. Maltby, second vice president; Carl B. Martin, treasurer; Albert Robinson and W. C. Hull, assistant treasurers.

For some time Mr. Carlisle has felt overburdened and expressed a desire to be relieved of some of his responsibilities, it is said, focussing his attention on the power industry.

"Business is running under somewhat increased orders, and the outlook for the balance of the year is favorable," said President Ferguson. "We are looking for improved buying due to increased demand for cement. There is improvement in the catalogue grades and there is prospect of certain developments which may result in opening up some of our idle mills.

Until his elevation to the presidency Mr. Ferguson held the position of secretary along with a vice presidency. He has been a member of the board of directors for several years.

Mr. Ferguson's rise to prominence in the financial and industrial world dates back about 20 years to his discovery by Mr. Carlisle at the Lake Placid club, where young Ferguson was employed in an accounting position. Mr. Carlisle was at that time a young banker, the Northern New York Trust Company, which he headed and which he formed a few years before at Watertown, having become a flourishing institution looking for thriving industries in which to invest its surplus money.

From the Lake Placid club Mr. Ferguson was brought to the Northern New York Trust Company and eventually became an assistant secretary. When the Northern New York Securities, Inc., was founded to handle the securities business of the trust company, Mr. Ferguson was chosen a vice president.

On June 25, 1934, *The New York Times* noted the appointment of Roy K. Ferguson as St. Regis's fifth president.

The former St. Regis mill at Rhinelander, Wisconsin, in 1961. Before its sale in 1979, Rhinelander produced glassine (waxed paper) and other specialized packaging grades. *Photo courtesy St. Regis Paper Company*

The pulp and paper mill at Deferiet, New York, about 1945. This mill, the company's first, began operation in 1899. Originally designed to manufacture newsprint, the Deferiet mill today produces specialty groundwood paper for use in directories and catalogues. *Photo courtesy of Niagara Mohawk Power Corporation*

A driver watches for snags during a log drive on the Machias River, Washington County, Maine, 1948.
Photo courtesy of U.S. Forest Service

The company's pulp and paper mill at Bucksport, Maine, in 1966. Installation of the $85 million #5 machine here in 1977 made Bucksport the nation's single largest producer of lightweight coated publication paper. Time Inc. and other leading publishers are major Bucksport customers.

Roy K. Ferguson, ca. 1950. President, 1934–1957. Chief Executive Officer, 1957–1963. Chairman of the Board, 1948–1971. *Photo courtesy of St. Regis Paper Company*

The bleached sulfate pulp mill at Hinton, Alberta, under construction in 1956. Most of the pulp produced here is exported to the United States, where it is used to manufacture a wide variety of products requiring bright, clean, long-fibered pulp.

The printing paper mill at Sartell, Minnesota, in 1956. Built in 1905 to manufacture newsprint, the Sartell mill was acquired by St. Regis in 1946. A $250 million expansion due for completion in 1982 will add a pulp mill and a coated paper machine, strengthening St. Regis's position as a leading maker of lightweight coated publication papers.

Rewinding paper at the dry end of the machine, Jacksonville, Florida, kraft mill. *Photo courtesy of St. Regis Paper Company*

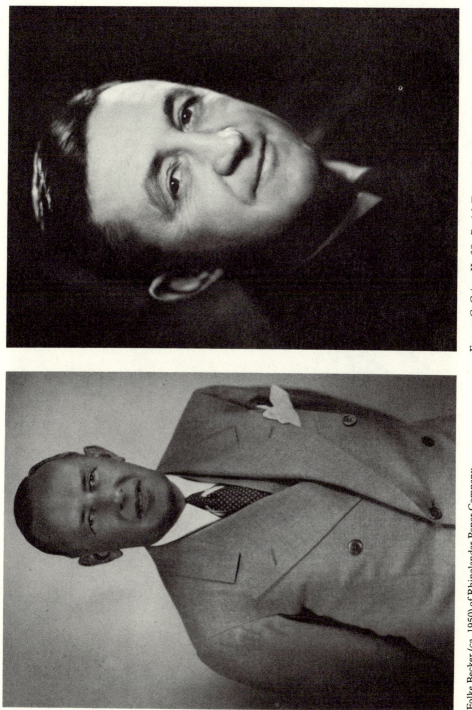

Folke Becker (ca. 1950) of Rhinelander Paper Company.

Everett G. Griggs II of St. Paul & Tacoma Lumber Company.

Paul Neils of J. Neils Lumber Company.

Roy K. Ferguson and William R. Adams in the early 1960s. *Photo courtesy McGhie Associates, Inc.*

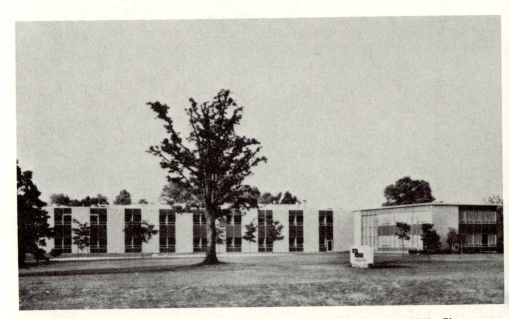

View of the Roy K. Ferguson Technical Center in West Nyack, New York, in the early 1960s. *Photo courtesy McGhie Associates, Inc.*

St. Regis's kraft-making facility at Tacoma, Washington, in 1967. Mt. Ranier provides a dramatic backdrop.

The Roy K. Ferguson Mill in Monticello, Mississippi, under construction in 1967.

The "Little Chief" paper machine, located at the company's Roy K. Ferguson Technical Center, West Nyack, New York. Researchers at West Nyack can simulate all the operations of a full-scale paper machine with this equipment. *Photo courtesy of McGhie Associates, Inc.*

The *William R. Adams*, christened in 1968, was designed for export of kraft production from Jacksonville to Europe. *Photo courtesy St. Regis Paper Company*

Planting seedlings on a pine plantation operated by the Southern Timberlands Division, circa 1955.

William R. Adams. President, 1957–1971. Chief Executive Officer, 1963–1972. Chairman of the Board, 1971–1972.

William R. Caldwell. President, 1971–1973.

George J. Kneeland. Chairman of the Board, 1972 - date. Chief Executive Officer, 1972–1979.

William R. Haselton. President, 1973 - date. Chief Executive Officer, 1979 - date.

6
Coming of Age

The years following World War II saw unprecedented growth in the American economy. An expanding population demanded services and commodities in greater quantity and variety than ever before. The war created not only an appetite for both familiar and new products but also provided the means for their acquisition. Optimism was expressed by the editors of the new St. Regis *International Division Monthly Bulletin* in January 1947: "At the beginning of this second postwar year the world looks forward with increasing hope to an era of new opportunity for unimpeded industrial progress which will make easier the lives of the men, women, and children of all countries."[1]

Years later William Adams took stock of a pertinent factor for his industry. Because the paper industry "was one of the few basic industries that was not allowed to expand during the war, paper was in high demand at a high ratio to capacity from 1946 to 1955." In spite of restrictions on capacity, industry developed novel applications for the use of paper during the war, and these were enhanced in the postwar era. Paper production soared in order to keep pace with demand. In the period between 1941 and 1966, output increased nearly threefold, and annual domestic use of all paper products rose from 250 to 530 pounds per capita.[2]

The wartime global struggle had stretched industrial capacity beyond previously known limits. The packaging revolution was the catalytic agent of a profound change in the paper industry during these years. Among the more dramatic changes was the successful application of polyethylene to kraft paper. Paper receptacles and folding cartons opened myriad new markets, and containers became more widely used in the agricultural and the industrial sectors.

Packaging supplemented the role of the sales representative. Convenience, low cost, disposability, and attractiveness were major advantages offered by the packaging revolution. The postwar boom made possible the greatest shopping spree in history, and paper companies competed with other manufacturers in the rush to market attractive and efficient containers. Marshall McLuhan has observed that American-European culture became "intensely visual" in this time and gave widespread credence to his thesis that "the medium is the message."[3] The media have indeed shaped history; advertising has been very influential in the development of the paper package.

The paper industry prosperity during these years was not limited to the packaging field. Because the paper industry is a service industry, the ebb and flow of its fortunes closely reflected political and economic developments. Consequently during the late 1940s, all grades of paper products reached all-time highs; overall production increased to 21 million tons in 1947, and during the first six months of 1948 the total sales value of all industry products exceeded $3 billion.[4]

Attractively designed and colorfully printed packages had a major impact on the rise of the supermarket, discount store, and large department store chain. Provided spacious metal shopping carts, postwar shoppers moved among open shelves and tables more swiftly and with a wider range of selection than had been possible in small stores of the past. Leisure time thus gained gave millions of people more time for recreational activities. The postwar thrust toward a visual culture was accompanied by the exodus from the inner city to the suburbs, where Americans lived in larger homes and dined out more often, especially at drive-ins, where economies afforded by direct take-out service and the use of paper cups, plates, bags, barrels, and boxes were passed on to the customers. Social change presented difficult problems to the pulp and paper industry, especially the need to adopt new manufacturing methods and to procure adequate supplies of wood pulp, chemicals, machinery, and, to a lesser extent, skilled labor.[5]

By late 1949 these difficulties appeared to be largely overcome, and the business spiral continued upward during the 1950s. Even a recession beginning in 1956 was not as detrimental to paper and board manufacturers as it was to other industries; production declines were lower than those of other major industries. Excess pulp and paper production contributed to the general economic downturn, but industry and government experts were optimistic that the difficulties would soon be overcome. One cheerful prediction made by the U.S. Department of Commerce in 1958 foresaw continued growth and diversification for both pulp and paper producers resulting from new "uses and applications of various grades of paper and board." Other influential factors seen by experts were the lowering of production costs and the raising of quality as a result of research and development, the design and installation of new equipment, and the adoption of new operating methods.[6]

The postwar expansion program of St. Regis reinforced and built upon efforts to modernize the company begun in 1935. Over the years of depression and war, Ferguson had reinvested earnings of 7 percent on net sales to modernize plants and improve operational techniques. As a result, St. Regis had grown into its capitalization. Throughout the 1930s, St. Regis had been a small paper company with disproportionately large capitalization and investments. With 4.1 million common shares, St. Regis had a larger capitalization but smaller capacity than International Paper. But by 1947 St. Regis had assets valued at $130 million—doubled since 1939—and net earnings in excess of $14 million, which permitted resumed payment of dividends on common stock after a sixteen-year lapse.[7]

Growth was the key word for the nation and the dominant impetus at St. Regis. Between 1945 and 1960, quantum leaps were made in sales and income: 1945's net sales of $52.5 million rose to $536.2 million in 1960, and net income was boosted from $2.2 million to $21.9 million. Employment more than doubled—from 11,900 in 1946 to 28,250 in 1960. Growth came through the acquisition and expansion of existing plant and through the construction of new mills and facilities. Acquisition was the means of dramatic entry into the South. Expansion made Tacoma an integrated operation, and construction of new plants was undertaken in an area extending from Alberta in the Canadian Rockies to Pensacola and Jacksonville in Florida.[8] Accompanying this increase in size was a substantial diversification of the product line. St. Regis focused its attention primarily upon printing paper, kraft paper, and multiwall bags. Involvement in plastics, packaging machinery, and kraft pulp followed. The company moved into many new product areas, including corrugated boxes, glassine, bread wrap, folding cartons, gummed and laminated products, lumber and plywood, pulpboard, school supplies, and folding boxboard.

The perennial nemesis of paper manufacturers—maintaining an adequate supply of raw materials—was overcome during these years. Timberland acquisition bolstered the company's raw material supply from 1.4 million acres managed or owned in fee in 1945 to 3.7 million acres in 1960. These holdings were a principal factor in total integration of the company's operations.[9]

Growth, diversification, and integration were simultaneously cause and consequence of expanding markets. The shift from a regionally centered operation to one of national proportion characterized this change as it applied to St. Regis. New products and markets required different organizational forms. The organization that had well served a regional corporation was not able to meet the needs of a multidivisional concern. In these years St. Regis came of age as a modern industrial enterprise.

Although the heaviest period of acquisition occurred between 1955 and 1961, the firm began to increase its production capacity by purchasing additional facilities during the mid-1940s. Acquisition of the Watab Paper Company mill in Sartell, Minnesota, initiated what became a major expansion of the Printing, Publication, and Converting Paper Division. This purchase increased the output of catalog, directory, and publication paper. Three mills were purchased from Time Inc.: the Maine Seaboard Paper Company at Bucksport, Maine; the Hennepin Paper Company at Little Falls, Minnesota; and the Bryant Paper Company at Kalamazoo, Michigan. Time had bought these mills during the war to guarantee its paper supply and later engaged St. Regis to manage them. Negotiated by Ferguson, this arrangement included a provision that St. Regis be given option to buy the mills. Time officials indicated their disinterest in operations at the end of the war, and the option was exercised by St. Regis in December 1946. As a long-time marketing and sales executive observed, these mills provided "facilities that were far broader than those existing at the Deferiet mill," which had been the major printing paper mill during World War II. Together with the Sartell mill, acquisition of the Time Inc. properties doubled production capacity to 180,000 tons.[10]

The Bucksport facility was expanded over the years, but the mills at Little Falls and Kalamazoo were eventually eliminated. The former was sold in 1951, and the latter was leased with a purchase option to the Allied Paper Division of the Thor Corporation in 1956. Bucksport, Deferiet, and Sartell became the crux of the Printing Paper Division, and improvements made at these mills between 1956 and 1958 increased yearly capacity by forty thousand tons.[11] Advancement of the Printing, Publication, and Converting Paper Division was furthered by development of the sodium peroxide bleaching process. Large-scale application of the process for bleaching groundwood had been introduced in 1944. Jack W. Hartung, who was originally affiliated with the Bryant operation and later became St. Regis vice-president for purchasing, described the immediate impact of sodium peroxide bleaching on printing paper production and its later effect on the manufacture of recycled papers:

> Deferiet was a groundwood mill, and conventional bleaching methods didn't work. These methods degraded the fiber and, as a matter of fact, had a tendency to turn [it] gray. Sodium peroxide . . . generally did not damage the fiber, and did a pretty good job of bleaching. . . . Fiber retention of wastepaper suffered greatly when de-inked and bleached by conventional methods. The retention, in fact, got so bad that it was in the range of 50 percent by weight of the total product. . . . But by using the peroxide process, we were able to increase our retention to approximately 65 percent.[12]

The dimensions of the Kraft Pulp and Paper Division were also changed through acquisition. At the cessation of hostilities in 1945, St. Regis owned the kraft pulp mill in Tacoma and kraft paper mills in Oswego, Herrings, Carthage, and Watertown. Tacoma shipped some pulp to these four eastern plants and sold the balance on the open market. The eastern mills mixed pulp from Tacoma and Scandinavia and were thereby able to meet much of the kraft paper demand of St. Regis bag plants in the East. The company's bag factories in the West, however, lacked paper manufacturing facilities of their own and were compelled to purchase kraft paper from local suppliers.

This situation changed with the purchase of the Nashua River Paper Company of East Pepperell, Massachusetts, in 1946. Nashua, in addition to supplying the multiwall bag plants with kraft paper, also made high-grade specialty papers, including gummed tape, plasticized paper, crepe paper, and coin wrap.[13]

Thus St. Regis acquired the plant in which Adelmer Bates and his brother R. M. Bates had developed paper for use in making valve bags in the 1920s. In 1919 R. M. Bates discovered a paper sack of unique construction, in Norway, a tube made up of four or five walls of kraft paper and tied at both ends. Several years passed before Adelmer Bates recognized the full significance of how kraft paper could be used in packaging by designing and building high-speed filling machines. His invention of a gusset-sided bag with a leak-proof valve proved of great benefit to the health of workers. Cement, grain, and flour dusts had long plagued workers with respiratory illnesses, often causing premature death. The invention and acceptance of the Bates multiwall valve bag was a safety breakthrough that has received less recognition than it deserves.[14]

While kraft bags made an important contribution to worker safety and while their production grew at a prodigious rate, it became apparent to St. Regis management that dependence on the transcontinental haul from Tacoma and the long voyage from Scandinavia put the company at a cost disadvantage. An early effort to correct this came in 1950 with purchase of the pulp mill of the Atlas Plywood Corporation in Howland, Maine. Ferguson arranged the purchase, assigning George Kneeland as his emissary. Kneeland's account of his meeting with representatives of Atlas sheds light on Ferguson's methods of acquisition and how he tested those being groomed for top management roles:

He [Ferguson] said, "I want you to go to the Bangor House and you'll find George Bearce there at a meeting." So I said, "What did you wish me to do?" He said, "Get there and listen." I didn't know what the meeting was about. . . . I realized before long that we were negotiating to buy a pulp mill, the old Howland mill. It got to be about five minutes to twelve, and this meeting had started at eight-thirty. Everybody seemed to be in agreement as to what should be done, what we were going to pay for the mill, and how it was all going to work out. George Bearce said at that point, "Fine; Mr. Kneeland is here from New York. I'm sure he has the money." Of course, I didn't have a damned thing. So it was just about twelve at this point and I said, "As long as we are agreed on what we are doing, why, we'll have lunch. It's all ready." As lunch was being served I quickly got Roy Ferguson on the phone and asked him, "What the hell do you want me to do? I don't have any money." He just laughed and said, "Go down to the bank on the corner. I'll call them and they will give you a certified check." That's the way he was. He wanted to see what you'd do.[15]

The Howland mill purchase soon proved to be no answer to cutting pulp delivery costs. The mill's antiquated machinery produced more costly pulp than that bought on the open market, and in 1952 the mill was closed.

This attempt to solve the pulp supply problem met with failure, but Ferguson's bolder move into the South paid off. It provided a temporary solution to the pulp problem and propelled St. Regis into a more competitive position in the industry. It also set in motion processes of thought within management that would bring significant changes in the corporate structure. The move to the South stands out as a turning point of signal importance in the history of St. Regis, perhaps the most important one of all.[16]

Development of the southern paper industry had begun several decades earlier by such companies as the Great Southern Lumber Company of Bogalusa, Louisiana, and the Southern Kraft Corporation of Camden, Arkansas. This development was facilitated by new processes that permitted the use of southern pine in the manufacture of paper pulp and by the growing uses of paper, which stimulated expansion and relocation of paper companies.[17] Charles H. Herty's pioneering work during the 1930s resulted in a chemical process for production of strong paper from soft southern pine. The economic benefits were evident in production of a fair-quality multiwall kraft, which was competitive with northern kraft. In line with the dominant strategy of the postwar years—acquisition and rehabilitation of facilities leading to integrated production—St. Regis moved to the South, where usable trees could be grown in eighteen to twenty years as opposed to seventy-five years in the North.

St. Regis's southern operation was initiated in 1946 with the purchase of the outstanding stock of the Florida Pulp and Paper Company of Pensacola from James H. Allen, a self-taught expert in forestry who early saw the financial advantages available to the South through careful use of its timberland. With R. J. Cullen, he had established mills in Louisiana, Arkansas, Alabama, and Georgia, and in 1939 he had formed a partnership with the Pace family, owners of ninety thousand acres of longleaf yellow pine in Florida. By the time of the sale to St. Regis, Allen had built the Florida Pulp and Paper Company into an impressive example of the development of southern industry. His role as a principal architect of the southern forest products industry was widely acknowledged.[18]

Both the Florida Pulp and Paper Company and the Alabama Pulp and Paper Company had been financed by Reconstruction Finance Corporation loans and by eastern and southern banks. The forest land owned by the Pace family, plus twenty thousand acres owned by the MacMillan family of Brewton, Alabama, served as collateral for this funding. Of no less importance in the launching of both enterprises was the financial acumen of Ferguson and Allen. Of significance as well was Allen's reputation as a successful mill builder and conservation-minded manager of timberland. He had been second in command in construction and operation of the Louisiana Pulp and Paper Company at Bass Rock, Louisiana. He had served the International Paper Company in its Mobile plant and had worked out the economic formula for the Southern Kraft Mill at Panama City, Florida. Allen was also credited with the expansion of the Union Bag and Paper Corporation at Savannah, Georgia.[19]

When the Florida Pulp and Paper Company and the Alabama Pulp and Paper Company, both wholly owned St. Regis subsidiaries, were formally merged with the parent company in December 1948, Allen wrote a final report pointing out that the two subsidiaries had a total earned surplus of $8.2 million, which made up a major part of the total assets of $17.6 million conveyed in the merger. He wrote with pride of his two companies:

> It is a thing worthy of note that whilst we have made a lot of money and have put to use a great supply of materials, the improvement that has been made in the affairs of our men, women and children is the thing of which we are most proud. We want our stockholders to realize that we have built this business for permanence. There is enough timber available in this area that those working with us may feel secure about work far into the future.[20]

St. Regis's move into the South was built upon this foundation during the 1940s. Allen's devotion to the economic and cultural health of his native South was a passionate part of his character. According to his executor, Allen cared little about money and was most openhanded in dispensing his wealth to persons and institutions appealing for help. He became a St. Regis vice-chairman and member of its board of directors and continued to run the Pensacola operations until four days before his death in December 1950.[21]

Integration of new facilities with those already in place in Florida was worked out by Ferguson, Allen, and their associates during the merger negotiations. These included the kraft paper mill and adjacent multiwall bag plant under construction at Cantonment, Florida, sixteen miles north of Pensacola. The new plants were constructed under the direction of Russell G. Seip, a protégé of Hardy S. Ferguson, the well-known designer of pulp and paper mills. The kraft mill was especially designed to manufacture a heavy-duty multiwall bag paper for sale to St. Regis. St. Regis assisted in the financing, receiving a 60 percent equity in Alabama Pulp and Paper Company.[22]

The anticipated expansion at the Pensacola plant and construction of a new facility in Jacksonville increased the raw material needs of St. Regis in the South. New holdings and cutting rights were obtained under the direction of Albert Ernest. After acquisition in 1947 of harvesting rights to 208,000 acres of the Suwanee Forest owned by the Superior Pine Products Company, Ernest joined St. Regis. His vigorous forestry policies were enhanced by the fact that he was, as George Kneeland observed, "a typical Southern gentleman. . . . He knew where the wood was, and he knew all the families and would talk to them as a compatriot, a peer, because he was a Southerner. He wasn't some fellow coming down from the North."[23]

St. Regis agreed to continue scientific management of the Suwanee tract, which had been under the able supervision of William M. Ottmeier. The firm also adopted Allen's forestry practices in management of newly acquired longleaf pine acreage, including cutting rights on 47,500 acres purchased from the J. W. Gibson Company in 1952. The firm started tree nurseries on this tract and at Pensacola. It was planned to plant six million seedlings per year for distribution to landowners affiliated with the St. Regis operation.[24]

A slump in the construction industry resulted in a sharp decrease in bag sales in 1949 and set St. Regis to searching for new uses for kraft paper. St. Regis created in that year the Kraft Paper and Board Division with the clear purpose of developing new markets. The move proved successful and was linked to the start-up of a new $6 million kraft paper machine at the Tacoma mill. These accomplishments, together with completion of the Pensacola plant and the end of dependency on Canadian and Scandinavian imports, placed St. Regis in a major position as a producer of kraft paper and board.[25]

St. Regis now moved to secure leadership of the high-quality kraft pulp market. Ferguson announced in June 1954 plans for constructing a new bleached sulfate pulp mill at Hinton, Alberta. The new plant was to have a daily capacity of four hundred tons, and costs were to be shared with North Canadian Oils, Limited, of Calgary. Frank Reuben, president of New Pacific Coal and Oils, Limited, had conceived the project and found Ferguson an enthusiastic supporter. The North Western Pulp and Power Company was organized to build the mill. Equity capital of $10 million was provided equally by the two companies, while loans were arranged from the Royal Bank of Canada and the Bank of Nova Scotia to meet construction costs. St. Regis assumed responsibility for designing and constructing the mill and for managing its output upon completion. Part of the output, it was agreed, would be purchased by St. Regis for use in its paper mills. The balance was to be sold on the open market. The venture was guaranteed a perpetual supply of white spruce and lodgepole pine under terms of a long-term timber grant from the province of Alberta. The wood was to be drawn from two million acres on the back slope of the Canadian Rockies.

St. Regis entered this partnership because a ready market existed in the United States for a high-brightness, high-quality bleached kraft pulp, much of which had to be imported from Scandinavia. St. Regis officials spent several months in Scandinavia investigating the Kamyr system, a continuous pulping process that produced uniform quality. Installed at Hinton, the Kamyr process consisted of six-stage bleaching with chlorine dioxide and was supposed to yield a capacity of five hundred tons a day. The result was the brightest bleached pulp known at the time, a product that showed little deterioration of strength. Hinton received wide attention for initiating continuous kraft pulp production in North America.

But operations at Hinton, begun in 1957, were not perfected overnight. Difficulties arose, both with the novel system and with management of the mill. Andrew Storer recounts some of the early problems:

> Weather was a big problem. We had put water lines only six feet below the ground instead of ten feet below, and they would

> freeze. Labor was a factor in that area. . . . I can recall some very
> serious power plant requirements and some big generators that
> had to be sent back after they were installed.

By 1963 these various impediments had been overcome, and Hinton
set a production record of 583 short tons of pulp in a twenty-four-
hour day.[26]

The postwar years also had a considerable impact on the Multiwall
Bag Division. Expiration of the bag patents in 1947 and increased competition resulted in adaptive measures. With most of its bag operations
in the South and on the West Coast, St. Regis decided in the late 1940s
on a new strategy to serve its customers from Pensacola; Franklin,
Virginia; and Tacoma. The basic patents on multiwall valve bags had
expired, bringing new competition into the converter field. Many competitors were located closer to the principal markets than St. Regis
was. To remedy this situation, St. Regis bought a new bag plant at
Franklin, reopened service bag plants in Kansas City, and in 1959 purchased the Chemical Packaging Corporation, a multiwall bag manufacturing company in Savannah, Georgia. As an outlet for Southwest
markets, St. Regis purchased the Lone Star Bag and Bagging Company
of Lubbock, Texas, and the Wagner Bag Company of Salt Lake City.
Lone Star produced burlap and textile bags and cotton bale coverings
at plants in Houston and Lubbock. Wagner's operations were similar.
St. Regis had produced multiwall bags for the two companies before
acquiring them and subsequently substituted multiwall paper bags for
the production of textile bags.

Internationally St. Regis responded with additional capacity. St.
Regis of Canada expanded its facilities at Dryden, Ontario, and Three
Rivers, Quebec. To these was added a new plant at Vancouver, British
Columbia. In 1952, the company reorganized the St. Regis Paper and
Bag Corporation of Puerto Rico, which had been established in 1949,
and entered a partnership with the Ponce Cement Corporation. St.
Regis also reorganized the Oriental Bag Company, Limited, a former
Japanese subsidiary, under the direction of the alien property custo-
dian. Compensation for damage to the company during the war, plus
provision of technical assistance and a reconditioned bag machine, gave
St. Regis a one-third interest in Oriental.[27]

The crisis in the multiwall bag business provided the incentive for
reorganizing the system of sales, as the need to develop a new selling
method had been made clear. Previously St. Regis sales had been de-

centralized with no real overall guidance. In 1948 the first annual sales meeting of the Bag Division was held. Its influence was both immediately apparent and long lasting. Charles Woodcock, involved in the division in those years, commented on its broad meaning: "The 1948 meeting grew out of a need to bring about a total, unified selling effort on a national basis." B. W. Recknagel expanded on this statement, noting that "it was out of that meeting that the stage was truly set for a market-oriented company (or a market-oriented division at that stage of time)."[28]

Recknagel described the situation that widely obtained prior to the 1950s throughout the paper and container industries:

> In the earlier years the production people were frequently insulated from the customer. . . . The idea was that the salesman was supposed to do it all. . . . If anybody was at fault for a lack of orders, it was that so-and-so dumb salesman or the equally dumb sales manager.[29]

A new national sales effort, directed by Archibald Carswell, regrouped management, sales, and technical personnel in an improved organization to coordinate efforts at all levels. Ably assisted by such men as Willard Hahn and Kenneth Lozier, the division was instrumental in locating and exploiting new markets.

The idea of "selling all the way through" had been introduced during the war years and was continued into the postwar period by Lozier's "flying squads." The successful campaign of selling the customer's customers was conducted by sales teams composed of young war veterans. The technique, widely promoted in trade magazines and publicity brochures, was first applied to the baking industry. Bakers were approached and persuaded to request that their shipments of flour from millers be made in multiwall bags. The millers agreed and were pleased with the results when the paper bag provided greater protection against weevil infestation and contamination during transit and storage. The millers were also impressed with a new packer that the Engineering and Machine Division at Oswego developed for high-speed packaging of flour. The packing machine and the bags constituted a system that was one key to St. Regis's continuing success in the bag business.[30]

Selling all the way through was a concept that guided the national organization at all levels. It was an effort to sell a system, not merely a product. Andrew Storer described this multilevel selling as one that "can be interpreted as a horizontal kind of selling approach in which you are anxious to develop a rapport, to sell our capabilities to any area of influence in the customer company that has a bearing on the sale of multiwall bags."[31]

Technological developments mounted rapidly in these years, and two events with influence on the multiwall bag field could not have come at a better time. In 1949 Kenneth Arnold, director of St. Regis research and development in the 1950s, successfully extruded polyethylene on kraft paper in collaboration with Du Pont scientists. Polyethylene, with its resistance to moisture and chemicals, and kraft paper, with its strength and low cost, had an immediate effect on packaging. The multiwall bag with a ply of polyethylene-coated kraft paper soon had a national market. One user was the Oscar Mayer Company, which adopted the bag and an automatic filling machine of stainless steel to package meat trimmings. Storer elucidated the far-reaching significance of this packaging breakthrough:

> Combining it [polyethylene] with paper, as we were successfully doing, offered a very definite advantage to paper to move into areas of packaging where paper alone did not provide adequate protection. . . . A longer-range objective that we saw for polyethylene was as the replacement for the old asphalt-laminated sheet as the moisture barrier in bags, which was dirty and messy but the only thing available. . . . There was a very definite need for an improved . . . barrier, and the qualities of polyethylene provided this. . . . The objective was to utilize these qualities . . . to broaden the markets for paper as a packaging medium in the multiwall bag field.[32]

A radical alteration in construction of the bag itself—the stepped-end pasted multiwall bag—was also implemented in 1949. Edgar Hoppe, St. Regis European manager, developed the stepped-end bag and also proved its superiority over the sewn bag in the early 1940s. When exclusive patent rights on an Italian design for a stepped-end pasted bag were acquired in 1949, it was put into production at Pensacola.[33]

New and improved products were only one aspect of the research program undertaken by St. Regis. Technical laboratories, pilot plants,

market studies, and increased involvement with manufacturing and
sales brought organizational changes. Integration of research and development within the manufacturing and administrative processes gave
evidence of the company's growth into a truly modern business enterprise. The establishment of the Manufacturing Development Department in 1949 to serve as liaison between sales and manufacturing was
the first real indication of this trend. In 1952 the pattern was continued
by consolidating the three main research divisions into one central
operation at Deferiet. Small facilities continued independent experiments at other plants.[34]

The Product Development Department, organized in 1953, took the
union of research and manufacturing further. The St. Regis annual
report for 1955 explained the department's function:

> [It] coordinates all activities relating to new or improved prod-
> ucts. . . . [It] studies the needs of customers, conducts market
> research and economic studies to predetermine the sales and profit
> possibilities in proposed developments, directs field testing, and
> guides promotion work to the point where the manufacturing
> and sales departments can take over.

The concept of an integral marketing and manufacturing process,
dependent on contemporary social, political, and business conditions
as well as on future projections, received a strong commitment from
management in the late 1950s. Formation of the advance planning
executive committee in 1955 and the St. Regis development committee in 1957 demonstrated a deepening concern with coordination of
the company's multiple functions.[35]

Not only did St. Regis build upon its traditional field of paper products—printing paper, kraft products, and multiwall bags—but it also
moved into new fields. The container business was the cutting edge of
the packaging revolution, and Ferguson realized that St. Regis needed
to move aggressively into that area. As with bags, the defense effort
and postwar social and economic changes created new markets for
containers. The kraft industry had begun to capture the container
market during the 1930s, and the use of paperboard and fiber boxes
by the military during the war provided the impetus for increased use
of this new packaging. Automatic machines and new containers reduced labor costs and made container packaging attractive to manufacturers and processors.

Box makers had originally purchased linerboard for conversion and until the mid-1950s enjoyed a strong market. However, producers of linerboard began integrating their operations from forest to finished product, at the expense of independent converters. A brief recession, coupled with increased competition from newcomers, convinced many in the converting industry to sell out. The converter desired a sale that would bring a quick and satisfactory profit, while the producer sought to buy a lucrative converting operation that filled a geographic gap in its marketing structure.

"We set out to create our container business, not only in the United States, but abroad as well." Reginald Vayo summarized the strategy that St. Regis followed:

> So the acquisition route was selected . . . because we did not have the know-how or the market to build a container business from scratch . . . the first arrangement [was made] with Superior Paper Products, and a year later General Container. . . . We acquired Pollock . . . and the next acquisition we made, which was the key to the whole thing, was the F. J. Kress Box Company. . . . To make us national, we merged with Grower's Container, which had container plants on both the West Coast and the East Coast.[36]

Although Superior Paper Products, General Container, and F. J. Kress were among the pivotal elements in the development of the container field, numerous acquisitions between 1954 and 1958 formed the nucleus of the operation. Superior's box plants at Pittsburgh and Mt. Wolf, Pennsylvania, manufactured and sold corrugated boxes and fiberboard for shipping containers. Superior supplied manufacturers of glass containers, cans, and household appliances. General Container Corporation, purchased in 1955, operated several plants that manufactured corrugated fiber boxes and built-up inner packing, folding boxes, set-up boxes, corrugating medium, and container chipboard. St. Regis therefore obtained both a folding carton business and a container business.

Competition among the leading pulp and paper companies to achieve a larger share of container and specialty paper markets built steadily through the mid-1950s. Control of box and container companies was sought by various means—exchange of stock, outright purchase, contracts to purchase plant output, and options to buy the properties—all with the aim of achieving greater integration and establishing closer geographic links to the buyers of end products. Other companies joined to St. Regis during this period included the Ajax Box Company of Chicago, a provider of corrugated fiber boxes and corrugated and embossed wrapping and display material. Acquired in 1956 were the Growers' Container Corporation of Salinas, California, which manufactured fiberboard containers and converted flexible packaging materials, and the Cambridge Corrugated Box Company of Cambridge, Ohio, which fabricated boxes from corrugated sheets. In 1957 the St. Regis Container Corporation, which had been a subsidiary since 1955, was merged with St. Regis. Superior Paper and Ajax Box were included in the move.[37]

In this fashion St. Regis put in place what was described by those moving up in management ranks as "the full wagon." Bernard W. Recknagel has described the process strategy:

> Predominantly by service [our licensees] had moved in on the bag market, and strategically located multiple plants. They had the entree of what we later called "the full wagon." One of the things we did in the late fifties and early sixties was to give St. Regis a full wagon: so when we went in to key customers, they would no longer say to us, "We would like to buy from you, but we buy from Bemis because they supply all of our needs—if we need paper, they have that; if we need burlap, they have that; if we need cotton, they have that."[38]

While building a container business, Ferguson simultaneously developed a new Flexible Packaging Division. In 1955 he made the Pollock Paper Company acquisition and placed Laurence S. Pollock of Dallas on the St. Regis board of directors. Pollock had twelve plants in the Southwest and Midwest, producing folding boxes and cartons, corrugated containers, and paraffin cartons used in packaging food. It had net sales of $34.8 million in 1955. A prime item manufactured by Pollock was bread wrappers; in addition the company produced waxed paper and frozen food wrappers. A less critical purchase in 1955, but one that complemented packaging operations, was the Gummed Products Company of Troy, Ohio. It produced box and sealing tape, gummed printing paper, and foil and film laminations.

To support Pollock's output of waxed paper and bread and frozen food wrappers, St. Regis acquired in 1956 the Rhinelander Paper Company of Wisconsin, which provided base stock for Pollock. The Rhinelander plant also produced glassine and greaseproof papers, lumber, and other forest products. Although the market for glassine paper was declining, Ferguson saw potential in the overall Rhinelander operation. Along with its paper output, Rhinelander produced torula yeast, used in animal foods and later in items for human consumption. It salvaged other chemical by-products from sulfite waste liquor. In addition, acquisition of the Wisconsin operation brought St. Regis a 50 percent interest in the R. W. Paper Company of Longview, Washington, a joint enterprise of Rhinelander and the Weyerhaeuser Timber Company for the production of glassine paper.[39]

In April 1956, St. Regis acquired the Pacific Waxed Paper Company of Seattle, a manufacturer of frozen food and bread wrappers, overwraps, and waxed paper. This merger provided Pollock with a West Coast market outlet.[40] But shortly after St. Regis acquired Pollock and Pacific Waxed Paper, polyethylene began to supplant waxed paper. Flexible packaging began a meteoric rise in food wrapping, as recalled by Joseph Rosenstein, regional general manager of the Flexible Packaging Division in Dallas:

> When Crown [Zellerbach] made the 1958 announcement that polyethylene film would be substituted for cellophane, this represented business potential for Crown and, as it developed, for St. Regis. . . . By the end of 1958, we were extruding film in Dallas competitively with Crown—which was from a technological standpoint, a tremendous feat. . . . This proved to be, from the standpoint of the division's profits, a lifesaver. Within a short period of time, we had an operation in Dallas that was extruding film; and we took the plant in Birmingham, where waxed paper production had been abandoned about a year before, and transformed it into an extrusion plant.[41]

St. Regis participation in the development of polyethylene had begun in 1949 with its pioneering work in the polyethylene-coated ply in multiwall bags. Growers' Container produced polyethylene bags in addition to its container output. The Chester Packaging Products Company of Yonkers, New York, acquired in 1956, manufactured polyethylene film. Chester also coated or laminated polyethylene on cellophane, foil, and kraft paper and manufactured extruded polyethylene pipe used in home plumbing, irrigation, and in the piping of chemicals.[42]

While St. Regis created a domestic container business, the international market also expanded under the direction of Reginald Vayo, vice-president of the Kraft Division. The foreign expansion began with shipment of linerboard to Europe, where the company sought possible acquisitions. Looking south, St. Regis recognized opportunities in the Central American banana box industry and built container plants in Panama, Costa Rica, Guatemala, Ecuador, and Surinam.

"The next big move," Vayo recalled, "was in South Africa, when we joined forces with Oscar Fruman and we put together the biggest overseas operation that St. Regis had at that time—in fact, for quite some time it was St. Regis's major international operation."[43] The South African acquisitions consisted of an interest in Transvaal Box Manufacturing, Limited; Millfields Cardboard Box Manufacturers; Solid Cardboard Box Manufacturing, Limited; National Containers, Limited; Atlas Box Company, Limited; and Fruman's Properties, Limited. These firms produced corrugated, folding, and set-up boxes. Joining with these companies, St. Regis acquired a half-interest in Herzberg Mullone Automatic Products, Limited, of Capetown. Herzberg had three plants producing corrugated, folding, and set-up boxes and small specialty bags of paper and other material.[44]

The rapid expansion of St. Regis and other companies in the container field glutted the market for paper products and by 1958 caused a general slowdown of growth in the industry. Integration and diversification had often been accomplished through mergers; between 1956 and 1958, there were seventy-seven major mergers in the paper industry. Some concerns, such as Georgia-Pacific and Weyerhaeuser, found that logs and waste from manufacture of solid wood products offered highly profitable opportunities to expand paper and pulp production. Traditional lumber companies entered the paper business through mergers, adding box, bag, or converting lines in order to make the maximum profits from the raw materials in their own forests. Competition was further intensified when metal- and glass-packaging companies, including Continental Can, American Can, and Owens Illinois Glass, ventured into the paper business. The total effect of expansion and mergers was to create a saturated market. The immediate impact on St. Regis thrust it into conflict with the Federal Trade Commission.

In 1956 the FTC began a long investigation to determine whether

St. Regis's growth pattern had substantially reduced competition. Confirmation of the charges would be seen as an antitrust violation. The FTC concluded its investigation in 1963 and ruled that St. Regis must sell seven of the corrugated container companies purchased during the years of the inquiry. An additional ruling stipulated that if St. Regis wished to acquire paperboard producers or container plants within the next ten years, it would have to receive prior approval from the FTC.[45] The antitrust ruling by the U.S. Supreme Court, however, did not undo the fact that the company had established a firm position in the container field.

On another front, wartime operations of the Panelyte Division had been reconverted to the manufacture of parts for refrigerators, electrical appliances, and items for freezers. Panelyte made an insulated door for freezers and ice-cream boxes, using a technique learned during production of bomb-bay doors for B-26 aircraft. For postwar refrigerators, Panelyte engineers also developed insulating snap-on frames, which broke the thermal flow from the inside to the outside of the unit, and dripless baffle plates for freezer compartments.

In 1947 Panelyte began marketing a decorative laminated sheet developed by C. Russell Mahaney and Westinghouse. It had a hard, stainproof surface that cabinet and furniture manufacturers used for counters and tabletops. But Panelyte faced a difficult competitive struggle with heavily advertised Formica, which by 1955 had secured firm command of the market.

Consumer demand and a technological breakthrough, meanwhile, permanently altered the refrigeration industry and challenged Panelyte's position. Refrigerator makers, using plastic injection molding techniques, were able to feature deep-draft refrigerator doors with shelves and compartments. Because the Panelyte plastic-kraft sheet was not sufficiently pliable for this design, St. Regis erected a pilot plant at Trenton to test molded plastics, but the venture was unsuccessful. A primary difficulty was that molded doors were fragile and could not be transported to refrigerator manufacturers in Ohio, Indiana, and Michigan without substantial breakage. To remedy this problem, St. Regis purchased the Cambridge Molded Plastics Company of Ohio and the Richmond Molded Plastics Company of Richmond, Indiana, in 1953. The Richmond plant produced refrigerator inner-door panels, television tube mounts, picture viewer housings, furniture drawers, carrying cases, trays, advertising signs, and novelties.

To fortify itself further in the plastics field, St. Regis acquired the Kline Manufacturing Company of Galena, Ohio, in 1955 and moved its vacuum-forming and extrusion equipment to the recently acquired Richmond plant. In the same year, Michigan Molded Plastics of Dexter was acquired, and St. Regis began producing compression and injection molded plastics for the automotive, appliance, ordnance, and industrial fields.

Strong opposition would develop within the ranks of St. Regis management, however, against a major move into the chemical industry, a necessary adjunct to continued expansion in plastics products.[46]

Between 1945 and 1958, St. Regis engaged in a struggle to produce substitutes for paper and solid wood products. Its marked success in acquiring properties during this period of national economic growth made St. Regis a diversified operation. The critical element in achieving this change in corporate character was guarantee of a plentiful and constant supply of raw material. Persistent search for timberland led the company into the lumber and plywood business through its acquisition of the J. Neils Lumber Company of Portland, Oregon, and Libby, Montana, in 1957. This one deal, made with one of the oldest and most respected families in the lumber industry, gained St. Regis three hundred thousand acres of timber in western Montana and southern Washington. Three sawmills at Libby and Troy, Montana, and Klickitat, Washington marketed such by-products of regular lumber operations as lath, pressed-wood logs, wooden boxes, and railroad grain-car doors. St. Regis began immediately to produce chips from the slabs and edgings. A plywood mill was added in 1960.[47]

Within a few months of the merger with Neils, St. Regis purchased the St. Paul & Tacoma Lumber Company of Tacoma, another lumber industry veteran. This brought an additional source of timber: 133,700 acres of Douglas fir and hemlock within forty miles of St. Regis's Tacoma pulp plant. The St. Paul & Tacoma acquisition added a large sawmill, dry kiln facilities, and log storage area to St. Regis holdings in Tacoma. Additional timber in Washington was acquired through purchase of the Northwest Door Company of Tacoma in 1958, which owned or controlled cutting rights on 4,665 acres and manufactured panel, flush, screen, combination, and garage doors, as well as fir, mahogany, birch, oak, and knotty pine plywood.[48]

The Neils, St. Paul & Tacoma, and Northwest Door Company purchases were among the final components of the postwar acquisition policy. Prior to World War II, the company had pursued a rather conservative land purchase policy, based in part on the belief that land ownership was expense with no income attached. The pressure created by increasing annual demand for paper helped overcome these reservations. Also advancements in industrial forestry prompted the realization that company foresters could manage and develop land efficiently and profitably.[49]

From 1944 onward, the company's landholdings increased greatly. In that year St. Regis controlled or owned outright 650,000 acres in the United States and Canada. The large gains made with purchases in the South and in Maine in 1946 added another 659,000 acres. More than 350,000 acres were acquired in 1947, and by 1951 St. Regis's total holdings exceeded two million acres. At the time of the various additions in the Northwest, approximately three and one-half million acres were owned or controlled by the company.[50]

Under the influence of such foresters as William Greeley and David Mason and facing the threat of federal regulation, the forest products industry took steps in the 1940s to implement forestry on their lands and to educate private woodlot owners to do the same. St. Regis was slow to take an active part in this movement. When the American Forest Products Industries, Inc., an industry agency, initiated the American tree farm movement in the early 1940s, St. Regis moved hesitantly toward acceptance of the program. Not until the hiring of A. B. Recknagel as technical director of forestry in 1948 did management apply technical forestry fully. Recknagel's background was in academic forestry, with special emphasis on improvement of timber and pulpwood production in the North Central and Northeastern states. His assignment encouraged Pete Hart and Albert Ernest, who until this time had been more responsible for procurement than for land management. Recknagel recalled the circumstances of his employment:

> In my report to Roy Ferguson . . . I made certain recommendations and was literally flabbergasted when he asked me to become technical director of forestry for the company. . . . I accepted and in the spring of 1948 I entered what I still consider the most unusual task of a somewhat checkered career.

One of Recknagel's most significant contributions was assisting other foresters in making known the current status of forestry to the industry and to the public. A frequent speaker at industry conferences, Recknagel stressed adoption of multiple product recovery, a new concept in forest management involving use of the total tree.[51]

St. Regis amassed timberland in the postwar period. Despite its enlarged raw material source, usage of these lands followed the firm's historical pattern: conservation of company woodland and purchase of cutting rights to provide wood for manufacture. In 1953, for example, 70 percent of the yearly requirement of 1.1 million cords of pulpwood was purchased. The extent to which outside supplies were acquired was determined by market prices.[52]

Particularly during the southern expansion, timber was secured under contract. The company assumed full responsibility for management of a tract. Included was agreement that the property "would be left in as good or better condition than it was received," explained Paul M. Dunn, who succeeded Recknagel in 1953 as technical director of forestry. This approach allowed the company to procure timber without expending capital for land purchase and professional management.[53]

The drive to acquire timberlands, additional plants, and new product lines had taken St. Regis to other regions of the country and to other parts of the world, shifting its base of operation away from the upper Northeast. A primary cause was the diminishing supply of pulpwood in upper New York, a concern even in the time of George Sherman. The scarcity of raw material, which had motivated American firms to look to Canada, was further depleted by heavy harvesting during World War II. In the postwar era there was no comparison between the limited timber resources of the North Country and those of the relatively unexploited states of the South and Northwest. The papermakers of upper New York realized early in the twentieth century that the cut-out-and-get-out policy of earlier lumbermen was inherently ruinous. But early efforts to perpetuate timber suffered from lack of technical knowledge and from an absence of widespread support.

Early experimental reforestation conducted by New York State was ineffectual. The emergence of professional foresters in North America came too late to make a significant contribution to reforesting the North Country. Only since the mid-1950s has concerted forestry been applied by private landowners in the Northeast. The natural climatic conditions of the area, moreover, meant that natural reforestation was too slow to keep pace with the saw.

The urge to halt the relocation process continued to be sounded as late as 1952. St. Regis forester A. B. Recknagel, in a report to the Empire State Section of the Technical Association of the Pulp and Paper Industry, addressed what he saw as the devastating economic effects of the paper migration. Comparing the stagnant wood pulp capacity of northern New York with that of the rest of the country, as both cause and consequence of the movement to other areas, he advised against the migration and recommended the intensive management of northern New York forests as an alternative. Cooperation with small timber owners to facilitate their production was also urged by Recknagel. In addition, he criticized the New York tax system for features that encouraged flight from the region.[54]

The St. Regis North Country operation also suffered from an obsolete physical plant. Great market changes, linked with St. Regis's program of acquisition and diversification, also ended the primacy of the North Country. In 1939 the North-Central operations of St. Regis produced 100 percent of the company's kraft paper; in 1950 the same area represented only 40 percent of capacity, whereas 39.3 percent was in the South and 20.7 percent in the Northwest. In 1946 the combined Tacoma and Pensacola production made up 16.4 percent of St. Regis kraft paper output, but by 1950 it had soared to 60 percent.

As St. Regis acquired and built new kraft and printing paper facilities, management shifted several older mills to specialty papers. For example, in 1949 when demand for the type of bag product at Carthage declined, production was altered to that of toweling and creped paper. Other New York mills were shifted to kraft specialty papers, including a neoprene-impregnated paper used in production of linoleum and a special interleaving used in manufacture of stainless steel.

Other plants were sold. In July 1950 Ferguson announced the sale of the Norfolk paper mill to the National Paper Corporation. A year later, Marathon Corporation, which manufactured paper for the protective packaging of food, purchased the Oswego mill. Oswego had produced kraft paper for years from a mixture of Canadian and Scandinavian pulp. Marathon, producing high-grade bleached sulfate pulp from its Ontario woodland, could more economically supply raw material needs at Oswego than could St. Regis. The production of towel paper and converting operations were transferred from Harrisville to Carthage, and the Harrisville mill was sold to the Harrisville Paper Corporation in 1953. The following year, Abe Cooper of Watertown bought the historic Watertown paper mill.

Gradually, and in retrospect inevitably, St. Regis's hold on the North Country yielded to the incessant pressures of modern times. Historic sites were closed, and recollections of the old days grew vague. As the years passed, few people remembered individuals like "Buffalo Bill" Herring, who was reputed to have responded to a minor labor problem by throwing a workman off a roof and completing the job himself. Few people recalled the stir created in Watertown when the Sherman family introduced the city's first hot-water shower, nor did they remember the company that Sherman ran after leaving St. Regis, which fell into decline after his death in 1920. "Old Man" Gould had been one of the last nineteenth-century papermakers, and he had given way to the up-to-date wizardry of Floyd Carlisle. Later, during the depression, the elaborate holding-company structure designed by Carlisle was permanently dismantled. A new generation represented by Roy Ferguson entered the scene, men engaged in technologically advanced production of paper.

"An awareness of opportunity" was the principle that guided Roy Ferguson's business life. His talent and personal dynamism resulted in a more varied and complex level of operation. Although the company might be described as a one-man operation during this period, in actuality Ferguson was supported by highly qualified men.

Chief among his lieutenants in the later years was Edward R. "Ted" Gay, named executive vice-president in 1957. His foresight in the field of market analysis and his ability to motivate others were among the qualities that made him valuable. His perception of sales trends was instrumental in the move to more sophisticated marketing methods. One associate remembered Gay as a key figure during the 1950s:

> Ted Gay was more the marketing thinker in the company—the strategist—and Mr. Ferguson was the financial side of the picture, together with Bill Versfelt, who was then vice-president and treasurer. But . . . Ted Gay made the greatest input in terms of where St. Regis ought to be and the direction in which we were moving. He probably had much influence on Mr. Ferguson's moving in certain directions that best fulfilled our long-range growth goals.[55]

Another aide of great importance was Joseph A. Quinlan, who had worked his way up from the ranks to vice president. Widely known among railroad and government figures, Quinlan was adept at getting things done despite bureaucratic obstacles. He was relied upon by Ferguson to secure quick results when, for instance, speedy delivery of a particular shipment was required. His role indicates that even in a tightly organized modern corporation, there is a need for a person able to bend the rules when certain matters need to be expedited.

The ability of Ferguson and his aides to seize opportunity in post-war America accelerated the company's growth. That growth in turn created a more complex and therefore more problematic corporate structure. Acquisition and diversification yielded new products, and divisions multiplied to encompass the new functions. The lines of command demanded redefinition, and the corporate body required coordination of its burgeoning activities. Success brought prosperity, and it also pointed to the end of the one-man enterprise.

Ferguson moved to consolidate areas of operation that had taken shape haphazardly during the years of development. He established new vice-presidencies to supervise timber reserves, pulpwood procurement, production, and sales. Because the South was the major area of expansion, Ferguson and the board of directors named Albert Ernest vice-president in charge of southern timberland and pulpwood procurement. Along with southern counsel J. McHenry Jones, Ernest played a vital role in securing wood in the region. William R. Adams was put in charge of the manufacture of pulp and paper. Robert P. Bushman was selected to head the manufacture and leasing of bag making, filling, and closing machines. Willard E. Hahn was assigned the responsibility of overseeing the manufacture of bags in the United States. C. Russell Mahaney continued to manage the production and sale of Panelyte. Arch Carswell handled the sale of bags, Edward G. Murray the sale of printing and publication papers, and Reginald L. Vayo the sale of kraft pulp and paper. To coordinate advertising the board named Kenneth D. Lozier vice-president in charge of advertising and public relations in 1953. In 1946 the company had organized the St. Regis Sales Corporation, which handled sales and purchase invoicing for all operations, including subsidiaries.[56]

Recognition of the difficulties inherent in the growth process came from an additional corporate level. The middle management committee, formed in 1955, began as a casual group of young men, among them George Kneeland, Gardiner Lane, and Bernard W. Recknagel. "We were unhappy with the state of affairs, as young persons usually are if they are energetic and want to get ahead," recalled Recknagel about the group's origins. In addition to providing a forum for the airing of mutual problems, the committee became a vehicle for upward mobility. Upper-echelon encouragement came from the office of Ted Gay. Lane, who worked for Gay, offers a view of the executive vice-president:

> I guess that he [Gay] felt that we were going to wind up with a tremendous gap in our corporate structure unless some of the people in my age bracket were brought into the management picture. . . . Thus he encouraged a group of us to get together to discuss the problems of the corporation with our superiors. . . . Of course the proof of the pudding is in the eating, and out of the . . . group came Bill Caldwell, who became president. [B. W.] Recknagel came along as executive vice-president, and George Kneeland is chairman of the board.[57]

Inauguration of an orientation program in 1953 evolved out of the shared concern of upper and middle management. Designed to introduce younger executives to the broad scope of operations in which the company was involved, the program indicated top management's awareness of the younger group's needs. Meetings and retreats were set up to acquaint the growing number of men coming into St. Regis with the company's senior officials, divisional managers, and plant managers. It was recognized that many of the middle-level group were familiar only with the particular problems and responsibilities of the divisions in which they worked. Another purpose of the orientation program was to expose participants to the company's past experience and its present policies and plans.

The basic theme introduced at the first orientation meeting in 1953 was, appropriately enough, "the awareness of opportunity." At the second meeting, Ferguson outlined the importance of orientation in St. Regis's new approach to young executives.

> Formerly, personnel selection was considered the end of management's duty and then the individuals wrestled through the maze of corporate events until they finally found an appropriate niche or moved to a higher level, but in this day of specialization where each of [the young executives] is a specialist in his own field, a

broader range is arrived at by association and by sharing experiences of management with each other. That seems to me to be
one of the basic factors contributing to the success of the . . .
program.[58]

The aims and programs of the group were institutionalized in later
years in the Strymen, a larger and more formal organization that paralleled the changing nature of the company itself.[59]

William R. Adams was elected president of St. Regis in April 1957,
and Ted Gay, Arch Carswell, and Benton Cancell were named executive vice-presidents. Ferguson remained as chairman of the board and
chief executive officer. Adams's background offered both depth and
breadth of experience. A liberal arts graduate of Union College in
Schenectady, New York, Adams experimented with various manufacturing jobs in the Midwest and in upper New York before coming
to work for St. Regis in 1937. He accumulated paper manufacturing
experience as resident manager of the Herrings mill and, during the
war, spent two years working for the Office of Price Administration
in Washington, D.C. Returning to the company in 1943, Adams continued to take on increasing responsibility, becoming manager of the
kraft paper mills at Carthage, Herrings, Watertown, and Oswego. He
was elected to a vice-presidency in 1948. The company's presidential
change began a new phase, one that would be marked by greater decentralization of power and more intensive planning. The ability, skill,
and strength of Bill Adams were well suited to the demands of a
modern business enterprise during the turbulent 1960s.

7
Prosperity and Turbulence

St. Regis came of age in the years between 1945 and 1958. The period immediately following was one of increased corporate consolidation, industrial maturation, and international expansion. It was also a time for reappraisal and realignment, if not retrenchment. National economic growth had been tempered by recessions in 1957-1958 and again in 1960-1961, but the greatest uninterrupted boom in American history began in 1961 and continued through 1969. The gross national product grew from $518.7 to $931.4 billion, and unemployment fell from 6.5 to 3.5 percent. The paper industry closely followed national economic trends. During the first five years of the 1960s, pulp and paper industry growth reached 21 percent, nearly equaling the GNP's 29 percent expansion. Total paper consumption approached 47 million tons, while per-capita consumption rate climbed to 480 pounds.[1]

These prosperous conditions were offset by the fact that increased sales and per-capita consumption were not matched by profits and net earnings. St. Regis, for example, began the decade with a 24.3 percent drop in earnings in the first nine months of 1960. Analysts pinpointed several causes: insufficient research, concentration on production rather than on sales, poor pricing policies, and inattention to net profits. In addition, advanced marketing techniques were ignored. But the most damaging cause was the disparity between cost and price. While the cost of production had increased markedly, prices had not kept pace.[2]

This mixed economic environment emphasized the paper industry's need to gain a larger control over its growth. Unchecked expansion, carried on more for its own sake than as a rational means to a defined end, created massive problems of organization and communication. Trade journals and associations cautioned against overexpansion. Manufacturers heard the message, but the problems persisted.[3]

Social and political conditions were also uncertain during these years. The Kennedy administration inspired a new era of social consciousness and activism. Yet, by the decade's end, social concern had devolved into social protest. The violence of the times was intensified by the assassinations of John and Robert Kennedy and Martin Luther King, Jr. The hopeful promise so evident in the early 1960s was metamorphosed into despair and revolt.

Minority groups seized upon the new social consciousness to seek legislative remedies for civil rights abuses. Their focus was not merely upon gaining a greater economic share but more particularly upon the recognition of human rights. Outrage over legal and social discrimination produced the Civil Rights Act of 1964 and subsequent social legislation. The initial response of the business community was reflected in the 1963 St. Regis annual report:

> Late in 1962, St. Regis signed with the President's Committee a Plan for Progress, committing itself to an employment program that provides equal opportunity and promotion to the individual, without regard to race, creed or color. In 1963, the company implemented this program, eliminating discrimination wherever it was found to exist.[4]

Other activists turned their attention to preserving the environment. They saw population explosion, urban sprawl, and pollution of soil, water, and air as seriously impairing the quality of life and, even more seriously, threatening the welfare of future generations. This environmental concern was not new to the United States; it had been expounded earlier by George Perkins Marsh, John Muir, Gifford Pinchot, and other conservationists. What was distinct about the environmentalists of the 1960s was their strength. They demanded that technological development be controlled; pollution of air and water had demonstrated that modern technology often had disastrous side effects. Major antipollution legislation was enacted in the Water Quality Act of 1961, which was aimed at industrial and commercial wastes produced in the manufacture of primary metals, chemicals, pesticides, and wood pulp. St. Regis's response to the environmentalists was articulated by James E. Kussmann, vice-president of public affairs, in the late 1970s:

> There was a greater need to communicate what was being done, and what should be done, in all of the environmental areas. The matters of water pollution, air pollution, forest land management, timber harvesting, solid waste disposal and use, have built up to a crescendo of requirements for communication so that people understand what you are doing.[5]

The establishment of better channels of communication was reinforced by substantial research programs designed to solve the problems created by the company's manufacturing processes. Concern for establishing better communications with the public was also shown by the launching in 1965 of a forest-oriented advertising campaign. William Bunn, St. Regis's advertising director at the time, was supported in this effort by Recknagel and Dunn, among others. Still further evidence of concern for the company's image was establishment in the same year of a long-range planning and policy committee.[6]

In taking such steps, St. Regis responded to the pressure imposed by different special-interest groups and also to the growing influence of management science studies being conducted in schools of business administration. The historical swings from runaway growth to sharp economic dips forced consideration of the need for informed planning in both the private and the public sectors. More effective management became the critical factor in the struggle to understand and control production better and to reduce radical swings in supply and demand. During the 1960s management and planning achieved the status of a true discipline in the corporate offices of the nation.[7]

At St. Regis the seeds of corporate consolidation had been planted during the latter part of the era of major acquisitions. During the early 1960s the impetus to achieve more effective management was encouraged both by general business trends and by the views of senior executives. The attitudinal changes of St. Regis managers were clearly reflected in moves to integrate the acquisitions of the 1950s into the corporate structure.

William R. Haselton speaks for several of his colleagues in his assessment of earlier acquisition policy:

> The original apparent philosophy of St. Regis in the late fifties,

on a *de facto* basis at least, was to permit those who had run a company before its acquisition to continue afterward. The interference was minimal and coordination . . . was solicited but not particularly pushed. It was not really and truly until either someone died and a need arose, or problems multiplied to the point of being serious, that anything was done until 1963. . . . You had a bit of a feudal concept—as long as things went reasonably well and frictions were at a minimum you were permitted to run your particular fiefdom without any undue interference from the corporate sector.[8]

George Kneeland saw the policy of maintaining the autonomy of recent acquisitions as evolving from several factors, among them the rapid and sometimes chaotic conditions of their purchase:

When you go through what this company went through in acquisition and expansion, it obviously produces rough spots. . . . When one acquires many companies, you acquire also some rather strong-thinking individuals, and I think that period was one of trying to get more people to understand the growing complexity of the business.[9]

Another continuing factor has been pointed out by Robert F. Searle, who came to St. Regis from Arkell & Smiths, one of the oldest paper bag manufacturers in the United States. Searle contends that Roy Ferguson employed a business style that tended to permit owners and top managers of acquired companies to continue running them under the new relationship to St. Regis. Kussmann elaborates this policy:

Mr. Ferguson felt strongly that these people had run their companies and unless there was proven, adequate reason for us to do it differently, or a desire on their part to get out, that we weren't going to disrupt the management of those operations immediately.[10]

Searle, on the other hand, saw some less positive aspects:

In effect, the only thing that St. Regis did was to acquire the company by name, but left the operation of that company for a number of years entirely with the original owner. In this way a number of advantages that could have been achieved through those acquisitions weren't obtained. The security of many of these acquired operations was very, very closely guarded for a number of years. People from the corporation weren't even allowed to visit with these companies and were told to stay away from them, despite their good reasons for wishing to establish a closer link. I think that was merely the normal manner of acquisitions back in those days; today we certainly don't follow that trend at all.[11]

Various factors thus affected the degree to which newly acquired companies were integrated within the corporate body of St. Regis. The disadvantages of self-management included duplication of basic administrative facilities, poor communication and coordination, and failure by the acquisitions to perceive an overall sense of the corporation's problems, strengths, and long-range goals.

But such negative aspects were outweighed by positive accomplishments during the period of consolidation in the 1960s. The Ferguson method of acquisition brought with it a large measure of goodwill among the employees and the local communities involved. Another benefit was the influx of new blood into the ranks of top and middle corporate management.[12]

During the period of acquisition, the company's internal management structure was in a state of development, and it was not until the last half of the 1960s that sufficient maturation was achieved. Consequently St. Regis itself was not prepared to integrate its acquisitions. Also some of the acquisitions involved St. Regis with new areas of production, and it was some time before technical and operational knowledge could be obtained. Viewed in this way, acquisition practices can be seen as distinctly advantageous, for they gave St. Regis time to develop the managerial, operational, and technical base for later assimilation.[13]

The company's need to develop new strategies is made more apparent by a review of its growth program. Between 1956 and 1961, St. Regis acquired thirty-two companies, making diversification a vivid reality. In 1956 the company derived 24 percent of its net sales from products not even manufactured by St. Regis in 1947. Forty percent of net sales in 1958 stemmed from production of materials not manufactured in 1949. Nearly half of net sales in 1961 came from items not produced nine years previously.

Growth through construction of new plants had continued until 1957 when Hinton was completed at a cost exceeding $40 million. Plant expansion also increased the size of St. Regis. Jacksonville output was increased between 1955 and 1957 by addition of the Seminole Chief machine. The Western Star was part of a $30 million modernization program at Tacoma completed in 1961.

The convergence of economic, technological, and social conditions called for a deceleration in this pattern of growth. During 1961 and 1962 there were no major acquisitions, capital expenditures were tapered off, and St. Regis began channeling only half as many dollars into growth as it had expended two years earlier. Consolidation replaced growth, diversification, and integration as the dominant theme, and more accurately represented the conservative philosophy required to reorganize the various resources St. Regis had gained in the period of growth.[14]

The technical field was the first area to be revised by St. Regis management. In 1959 the company divided its technological operations into three units, based on the realization that fundamental research and technical services related to daily mill operations were functionally distinct. Research and Development, headed by Kenneth A. Arnold, had ultimate responsibility for programs in pulping, papermaking, coating, polymers, packaging materials, engineering, physics, by-products, and graphic science. Robert W. Reed, director of the Technical Services and Quality Control Department, supervised his unit's dealings with internal manufacturing, sales, and outside customers. The areas of responsibility of this department extended to printing papers, kraft papers, multiwall bags, and packaging materials. Quality control consisted of production testing to assure uniformity in all lines. Technical Planning, the third unit created, guided operations research, technical and economic project assessment, and technical budgeting. Directed by Thomas A. Hewson, the department also acted as liaison between the company's financial and scientific operations.

Closely related to the major technology departments was the Product Development Department, which determined what new products were needed and directed their development from theoretical conception to final production. The Engineering Division was also subdivided into theoretical research and practical application units.

Following the reorganization, the various fundamental research elements were consolidated geographically. Such research had frequently been conducted in each division of St. Regis, often at the mills, resulting in duplication of investigations.

> We certainly shouldn't overlook the fact that earlier there were a number of technical functions elsewhere in the company. One of these was the outstanding research and development laboratory of the Pollock Division at Dallas. The Rhinelander organization had an outstanding research and development organization. . . . [Howard Paper Mills, Creamery Package, Gummed Products, American Sisalkraft at Attleboro also had substantial technical operations.] So there was a lot of technology and divisions. . . . The major idea behind the Technical Center was to consolidate technology.[15]

Jack Wilber, technical director of the Printing and Packaging Papers Division in the late 1970s, thus described the company's technical research prior to construction of the research center at West Nyack, New York. The center had been developed at the urging of Ted Gay and William Adams. Gardiner Lane's comments represent management's view:

> We needed more sophistication in our technical image. . . . St. Regis definitely needed a sophisticated technical center. It needed one if it was going to acquire companies and if it was going to have the right relationships with the other major corporations.[16]

The Ferguson Technical Center was built in the early 1960s. Proximity to corporate headquarters in Manhattan was an attractive feature in recruiting scientists and in relocating researchers from other St. Regis laboratories.

Investigation at the center focused upon the development of pulping methods to produce higher yields and greater strength and brightness. Researchers began to examine more closely the mechanics of bonding fibers in a sheet of paper. They considered new uses for noncellulose portions of trees, and they developed computerized methods of controlling pulping and papermaking. Work was completed on a small pilot paper plant at the technical center in 1963. Laboratory experi-

ments now could be carried out at West Nyack under realistic conditions. Encouraged by these efforts, in 1964 management began
construction of a large and costly addition to the Ferguson Center.[17]

The heightened tempo of decision making was made further evident
in 1961 with the establishment of the Marketing Analysis Department.
Concern for finding better marketing methods had been under discussion among a middle-management group since the late 1950s. This discussion had now matured to the point where the corporation was ready
to consolidate marketing research, much as it had already begun to do
so in technical research. Andrew Storer recalls that it was Hugh W.
"Pete" Sloan and B. W. Recknagel who were chiefly responsible for
this step forward:

> The word "marketing" until 1961 was really an unknown term at
> St. Regis. I think Pete Sloan's feeling was that we needed market
> analysis on which we could base good long-term planning efforts.
> The marketing concept was very dramatically picked up when
> Reck [Bernard W. Recknagel] came on the scene at the corpo-
> rate level about 1964, with the retirement of Mr. Carswell. The
> division that began to reflect marketing thinking first was, I think,
> the Bag Packaging Division, principally because Reck was then
> running it. In my recollection, the first director of marketing that
> we had in any of our divisions was in the Bag Packaging Division.
> Mickey [Michael T. Biondo] was director of marketing in that
> division in the early sixties.[18]

In no other area of the company's operation was there more pressure than in the bag market. As Recknagel has explained, "Systems
selling, which is very much a part of today's Bag Packaging Division,
was one of the main keys to the marketing success." Consequently it
was that division which was the first to name a director of marketing
and came to enjoy some reputation as "a rather outstanding divisional
marketing organization."[19]

Robert Searle recalled that St. Regis's move into marketing analysis
laid a strong foundation for the gains of the 1970s:

> Until you had really marketed a product and satisfied customer
> needs, you really hadn't accomplished anything in business. Many
> of the older concepts were narrow to the point that many activi-

ties were pursued for the sake of pursuing the project, rather than for the sake of creating a marketable product that we were going to sell in the marketplace. . . . You really don't accomplish anything by developing a fine product that nobody wants to buy or that doesn't satisfy a market need.[20]

St. Regis continued to take measures to redirect its lines of authority. The most meaningful and far-reaching of these actions came in 1963 when the board of directors approved a major divisional reorganization. William R. Haselton, soon to head one of the new groups, gave the basis for the plan: "In 1963 we set up seven divisions by products and not by locations. . . . The regional concept had to go by the board." Prior to this realignment based on product similarity and marketing requirements, sales and production had reported separately to the chief executive officer. Haselton continues:

They [sales and production] didn't come together until they got to the chairman or the president. But the company had grown to the point where this was a practical impossibility. And while divisionalization had been done in certain areas . . . it was not done broadly until this organization change was formalized.[21]

This strategy made the executive and managing heads of each operating division totally accountable, the general manager for his specific division and the vice-president for his divisional grouping. The concept of a general manager had originated with Recknagel in his work with the Bag Division and, as Searle explained:

[It] was the first division within St. Regis to develop that type of vertical organization, by which the general manager had complete authority over the sales and manufacturing of the whole product line.[22]

This development decentralized certain key corporate functions. Refined during the 1960s, it became St. Regis's standard method of management at this level. Searle later assessed its overall value to the company:

The team concept has led to much better decision making. It gives a much broader type of base to work from . . . in the final analysis, a decision (whether related to production, marketing, research, or engineering) was a better balanced decision because it took into consideration all the aspects of putting a given product on the market.[23]

The importance of this reorganization was that it decentralized and reassigned procedures and services within the new divisional groupings. At the same time, it consolidated operations in a logical system. Accordingly seven group vice-presidents were given responsibility for the major company divisions: P. B. Duffy, Containers; W. R. Haselton, Lumber and Plywood; L. S. Pollock, Flexible Packaging; B. W. Recknagel, Bags; Alex Smalley, Food Processing Equipment; H. W. Sloan, Printing and Specialty Papers; and R. L. Vayo, Kraft Division.[24]

Long-lasting benefits derived from these decisions, according to Haselton:

> I have to say for the record that the most intelligent, sensible, and practical move this company made in the sixties was that move because it gave to the vice-president and manager the responsibility for sales, production and profits. Prior to that time such responsibility was not evident in many areas of the company.[25]

Other more subtle events were also important in the reorganization. The departure of Benton R. Cancell in 1962 to become president of Potlatch was of more than casual concern in realigning management responsibility. So too was the resignation of Archibald Carswell in 1964. The organizational actions of 1963 became the foundation for further structural consolidation throughout the decade.

In this same period, a decision of the Federal Trade Commission went against St. Regis because of its rapid horizontal concentration in the field of corrugated and solid fiber products. The plants ordered divested included those at Salinas and Fullerton, California; part of the acquisition of Growers' Container Corporation; the Jersey City and Jacksonville plants acquired through purchase of the National Kraft Container Corporation; the Birmingham plant acquired through the purchase of Birmingham Paper Company; and corrugated board and solid fiber plants at Tacoma and Emeryville, California.[26]

Some insight can be drawn from those who took part in these events. Corporate Secretary Homer Crawford, for example, credits Philip B.

Duffy with being the real architect of the new Container Division and "probably the most professional and soundest businessman I had known." Crawford gives Duffy credit for assessing the problem with the FTC:

> It was really on his recommendation that we were, for some reason, given the opportunity to name the plants we would divest. His decision, on the basis of business, economics and transportation, was to get rid of those western plants.[27]

Duffy had come to St. Regis with the acquisition and merger of the F. J. Kress Box Company in January 1959.[28]

Reorganization had a profound effect on St. Regis's entry into the solid wood products field. Haselton assumed charge of the new Forest Products Division and led an ambitious expansion of manufacturing, which took full advantage of the growing demand for housing and building of all kinds, including public road and bridge construction programs.

Haselton came to St. Regis from the Rhinelander Paper Company, where he had worked under Ben Cancell and Folke Becker. The same qualities that marked both Becker and Cancell—a signal capacity for management, unflagging energy, compassion, and an unremitting demand for excellence—are recognized qualities of Haselton, who became president of St. Regis in May 1973. Haselton took naturally to the German work ethic that Becker instilled at Rhinelander and that was also the norm at the nearby Institute of Paper Chemistry where he earned graduate degrees.

Beginning in 1958, Haselton supervised all operations at Rhinelander. He was well acquainted with the conservation efforts of Becker and others in the Lake States region. Haselton was also impressed with Becker's leadership of the Sulphite Pulp Manufacturers Research League, which had established headquarters in Appleton. Out of this latter group came the postwar production of torula yeast, a by-product of sulfite liquor. Haselton recounts how this product became an extremely profitable aspect of the Rhinelander operation:

> The purpose was to find something to do with sulfite liquor. And the "something" they came up with, of course, was pirated from Mannheim—the technology of growing torula yeast. And so after

World War II, a team went over to Germany and as part of the authority of occupying powers found out this technology and brought it back and applied it in the United States. The idea was to prove the theory in practice; a pilot plant had to be constructed somewhere. The story goes that Becker offered to pay twice his share in the partnership if the pilot plant was installed at Rhinelander, which was ultimately agreed upon. This had to be a stroke of genius, because once the plant was built there and proved out, it was virtually valueless to anybody except to Rhinelander. So then, I believe, Becker made his associates a rather modest offer to take the remaining shares off their hands. Since it was kind of "Do you want twenty cents or nothing on the dollar?" they took the twenty cents. Becker established a rather low cost yeast plant which has subsequently been expanded over the years into lignin and further expanded in yeast. It is an extremely profitable aspect of the Rhinelander operation today, and has been over the years.[29]

Haselton moved from Rhinelander to the West Coast in 1961 and became general manager of St. Regis operations in the Puget Sound area. It was there that he learned the lumber business:

It was a very interesting assignment, especially because I had little or no knowledge about the lumber business or western logging or related items. But one learns fast if one has to. Things progressed reasonably well except for the fact that the market for lumber in the early sixties was dismal and the market for plywood was hardly any better. The door business was a little better than that, but not much. And it was extremely difficult to break even in the years 1961, 1962, and 1963. . . . Part and parcel of this [the 1963 reorganization of divisional groups by product and marketing] was bringing J. Neils into the Forest Products Division. Prior to that time J. Neils had been a separate division reporting directly to Ben Cancell and later to Bill Adams. So we combined all the lumber, plywood, and forestry in the West into this division; this presented another problem of amalgamation which gave us plenty to do for several years after 1963.[30]

Those who worked out the management consolidation recognized the importance of consolidating also the position in raw material supply. A. B. Recknagel had shaped a beginning in forestry, one on which a more scientific base of professional management could be erected. Following World War II, important steps in industrial forestry were taken by Albert Ernest, Ben Cancell, Marcus Rawls, James H. Allen, and others who came into St. Regis by the merger route. When Recknagel retired in 1955, he recommended the dean of Oregon State University's School of Forestry, Paul M. Dunn, as his successor, and the nomination was endorsed by the chief forester of the United States, Richard E. McArdle. Dunn had earned a reputation in his field by expanding the forestry school and for his work in establishing a school of forestry in Chile.[31]

Dunn represented St. Regis at scores of forestry conferences. He was the eyes and ears of the company as forest land management grew in sophistication and as the challenge of conservationists grew. Dunn was frequently invited to join the advisory committees and councils of forest-related groups. A single example typical of the service he rendered was his membership on the Northeast Forest Research Council, which had been set up in 1924 by Samuel T. Dana. Dunn served on this advisory council of public and private foresters and timberland owners for over twenty years.[32]

Much credit for building the St. Regis timberland base belongs to men like Ernest, Allen, Rawls, Hart, and Dunn. It was their knowledge of the timber resources of the United States and Canada, in addition to their talent in arranging pulpwood purchases or long-term cutting leases, that provided a solid foundation for the expanding investments in new manufacturing plants and the modernization of older properties.

Albert Ernest was perhaps the most colorful character in the company's southern operations. He was born in Alabama and grew up in a family of timber cruisers. Marcus Rawls, long associated with Ernest, described him as "quite the greatest salesman where timberland was concerned. . . . He acquired almost a million acres for Union Camp, which used to be known as Union Bag and Paper Company, and he was responsible for acquiring a good half of what St. Regis has now in the South—one million seven hundred thousand acres."[33] Rawls further describes Ernest:

> Albert was a dynamic person. He had a great love for the outdoors and he was a wonderful storyteller. He had no formal edu-

cation in forestry; he had acquired it through reading and having been brought up in the woods. Albert, I would say, was a very forceful person. He had a lot of humor, but when he got active on property, he was all business. Once he got his business aside, though, he liked to play pretty hard, too. You wouldn't say that Albert was a teetotaler. He was also a very social man. You would have thought that Albert was Lord Chesterfield. He was a very dignified person and he knew how to conduct a social affair. A lot of our executives from New York enjoyed Albert's social graciousness over the years.[34]

Like Ernest, Rawls had limited opportunity for formal college education. He did, however, find a career in forestry after completing a year of training at the University of Florida in 1932, by obtaining a position in the Forest Service. Between 1933 and 1935 Rawls acquired a great knowledge of the timberland of the South as a member of the Forest Service forest survey.[35]

The work of such men led to the willingness of management to invest more heavily in land purchase and leases. During the 1950s and 1960s St. Regis thus assured its place as one of the world's largest pulp and paper companies. The company's annual reports reveal the dramatic story. In 1945 its total of timberland and lease land contained only an estimated four million cords of wood. By 1950 it boasted a total of 1.5 million acres owned in fee and held cutting rights on 415,000 additional acres. In 1954 it announced that it was planting on more than 700,000 acres in the Deep South alone. It also gave three million seedlings to individual tree farmers as encouragement of the then fast-growing American tree farm movement. In the same year's annual report St. Regis claimed nearly 1.7 million acres owned in fee and cutting rights on 568,000 acres.[36]

In 1957, after some years of experimental seeding of cutover land by aircraft, the company applied this method of reforestation to 5,000 acres in the Suwanee Forest in Georgia and to 1,500 acres of its newly acquired St. Paul & Tacoma land in the Pacific Northwest. At the same time, its growing corps of foresters made use of sophisticated timber inventories of lands in Montana and southern Washington in making plans for an aerial survey of approximately 206,000 acres in the Puget Sound area. St. Regis claimed by the end of 1957 over 2.2 million acres in fee, and cutting rights on slightly over 1 million acres.[37]

An interesting commentary on the impact of technological develop-ments is offered by McHenry Jones. Until 1954 use of slabs from lumber mills had been uneconomical in the South because of the high cost of debarking and chipping equipment. After successful introduc-tion of the Andersson barker and Soderhamn chipper on the West Coast in the early 1950s, production of such machinery in the South reduced cost and eliminated a major problem that had prevented ex-tensive use of forest industry waste material.

Implementation of the Andersson and Soderhamn equipment in the southern lumber industry was slowed somewhat by the economic and social attitudes of one segment of that group. In the 1950s many of the lumber companies of the South and West were still closely held by individual families. Those in the sawmill business saw their holdings of prime timber declining at the same time their mills needed repair and modernization. Additionally the heads of these companies were advanced in years. George Kneeland linked this phenomenon to the problem of inheritance taxes faced by landed families. And he saw the impact of still another factor, the need for cash:

> You start a business and it grows; and the question becomes, have you got the ability to get the capital to go with growth? . . . Com-panies reach a point where they are making money but they ab-solutely have no cash—and they need money. . . . The more you sell, the bigger your receivables become. You need more inven-tory. It's all good, but where is the money?[38]

Consequently the advent of the Andersson barker and the Soder-hamn chipper provided pulp and papermakers a steady flow of less expensive chips and also extended the business life of the old-line fam-ilies. One such company was the W. T. Smith Lumber Company of Alabama, owned by the McGowin family. Jones recalls that a success-ful contract was worked out by Ernest and himself to buy chips from the McGowins. Jones also notes that in many cases paper companies offered to install chippers or at least share the installation costs but were rebuffed by owners who preferred to sell their lands and mills. The outcome, in Kneeland's words, was "more mergers than anything I can think of." This trend among southern lumbermen and timber-land owners led to the establishment of the pulp and paper industry in the region.[39]

St. Regis foresters, once preoccupied with fire prevention and logging engineering, now concentrated on productive forestry. New reclamation policies entailed removal of inferior vegetation and replacement with desirable tree species. Experimentation was conducted with public forestry agencies to improve the quality of new growth on cutover land. St. Regis also joined in the American tree farm movement at the urging of its professional foresters.

Harvesting practices included both clearcutting and selective logging, depending upon terrain, species, and the long-term management plan. Selective logging required harvesting mature and defective trees, a practice that provided space and light for younger trees to grow. Reforestation occurred naturally in some areas, but where nature failed to regenerate itself, technicians reseeded or planted seedlings grown in St. Regis nurseries.

St. Regis had early shown an interest in forest experimentation and improvement. In 1948 the company had acquired a 920-acre tract in Washington, which became known as the Hemlock Experimental Forest. This project was pursued with the aid of the Forest Service. In New York in 1953, St. Regis joined with state foresters in promoting reforestation of private woodlands, advising and assisting owners in good management practices. Two years later the company encouraged the study of forestry by awarding three scholarships to outstanding students in the South, Northeast, and Northwest. Later it established a graduate fellowship program to complement the undergraduate stipends.

In 1956 the company established a seed orchard near its Pensacola mill. Strong root stock, onto which cuttings from mature pines had been grafted, were planted and used to produce seed. The seeds were later used in company nurseries in the production of seedlings. Early in 1957, the company anticipated production of twenty million pine seedlings in its nurseries during the growing season. This supply met its own need and those of private landowners who agreed to sell their timber crops to the firm. The next year, the number of seedlings available was increased by 25 percent.

One of the innovative methods adopted was that of direct aerial seeding. Beginning in the 1957-1958 growing season, 8,000 acres were experimentally reforested by this method. By 1962 direct aerial seeding had covered over 17,000 acres. Another approach to enhancing the company's resources had been made in 1958 when St. Regis foresters began experimenting with the application of different fertilizers.

By the beginning of the 1960s, the company had substantially expanded reforestation in the South. The number of seedlings raised and planted had been increased by 40 percent since 1957. In 1964 more than 335,000 acres of land were reforested by St. Regis in the South. When Southland Paper Mills in Lufkin, Texas, was acquired in 1977, over a half-million acres of timberland was included, and these lands too are carefully managed on a sustained-yield basis.

To the north, the Rhinelander Division in 1960 planted more than a million trees in Wisconsin. This accomplishment reflected to some extent the continuing influence of reforestation practices that St. Regis had inherited from some of the companies acquired during the Ferguson era.[40]

A small number of acquisitions made in 1959 and 1960 were strategically advantageous. Among the most important was acquisition of the Cupples-Hesse Company, which added a new line of consumer products, including envelopes and shopping and merchandising tags. The purchase of the Cornell Paperboard Products Company of Milwaukee, Wisconsin, extended inroads into the folding carton field made earlier by the General Container acquisition.[41] St. Regis added converting plants to its Other Paper Products Division: Sherman Paper Products of Newton, Massachusetts, Chicago, and Los Angeles. Acquisition of the Birmingham Paper Company brought to the product line the Nifty brand paper tablets and school supplies.

The Printing Paper Division also experienced growth in 1960. The Bucksport facility underwent an $8.6 million improvement program, including installation of an off-machine coater, an on-machine precoater, and two supercalenders. At Deferiet a double-coating process was initiated. The division was further strengthened in 1960 by the acquisition of three mills from Howard Paper Mills, Incorporated, of Dayton, Ohio. These plants produced a wide variety of printing and fine business paper, sulfite bond, mimeo bond, duplicator ledger, opaque circular, offset, envelope, and map papers.

The Schmidt and Ault Paper Company of York, Pennsylvania, was purchased and later merged with St. Regis in 1960, augmenting the Boxboard Division. In the same year, the company obtained the Creamery Package Manufacturing Company. Its four plants in Illinois and Wisconsin manufactured stainless steel equipment for processing, refrigeration, and storage of milk and other foods. In 1964 the company was dissolved and merged with St. Regis, and the two Illinois plants were closed.[42]

The growth of the snack food industry in the early 1960s provided a new field for St. Regis's Flexible Packaging Division. The 1964 purchase of the Atlanta Film Converting Company, to quote Andrew Storer, "was probably the principal acquisition that helped us tremendously in our entree into the snack food business." The efficacy of this move is demonstrated by its success in the intervening years. In 1975 Storer assessed the impact of the snack packaging market: "The influence has been quite predominant on our Flexible Packaging Division. It's been one of our major new markets, and has enabled that division to move away from its formerly heavy dependence on the paper industry."[43]

In 1960 the Packaging Materials Division acquired two companies with values of varied significance: the Central Waxed Paper Company of Chicago and the American Sisalkraft Corporation. Central converted flexible packaging and protective papers, and treated fibers for conversion by other companies.[44] The purchase in September of American Sisalkraft Corporation of Attleboro, Massachusetts, expanded both domestic and international operations. The company produced reinforced kraft paper that was laminated with sisal and asphalt. The product was used for covering, wrapping, packaging, and construction purposes and for base stock in tape used on corrugated boxes. St. Regis's need for reinforced papers had risen concurrently with packaging production increases. The acquisition of American Sisalkraft, a dominant manufacturer in its field with plants in Massachusetts, Illinois, and California, proved to be a sound move.[45]

American Sisalkraft's excellent overseas connections included F. W. Williams (Holdings), Limited, of Sydney, Australia, and two other companies in New Zealand and Australia that made products similar to those of American Sisalkraft. St. Regis and Williams also jointly owned Bates, Limited, of Australia. In England, St. Regis held a majority interest in Sisalkraft Holdings, Limited, which in turn held 70 percent of J. H. Sankey and Sons, Limited, owner of British Sisalkraft, Limited. British Sisalkraft produced reinforced papers and related products for construction and packaging purposes, and Sankey manufactured and distributed building materials.[46]

Addition of American Sisalkraft was but the tip of a mighty foreign market iceberg developing for St. Regis in the 1950s and 1960s. Reginald L. Vayo had been the major architect of this expansion of the company. He came to St. Regis in 1945 after serving with the War Production Board during the war. Prior to that, Vayo had his apprenticeship in the paper industry with the Brown Company between 1928 and 1940. Ferguson recruited him after the war to take over Kraft Division sales for the Tacoma plant. He was also assigned the task of negotiating the purchase of Scandinavian pulp to meet the needs of the company's mills. In 1949 Vayo was put in charge of the Kraft Division and saw its total sales build from $385,000 in his first year to a mammoth $350 million. His success was based upon a deep knowledge of both the manufacture of kraft and the subtleties of buying and selling in international markets.[47]

Continued success in both foreign and domestic markets was enhanced by passage of the Trade Expansion Act of 1962, which was intended to promote economic growth by expanding American exports. Designed to enlarge the chief executive's powers in this realm, the act facilitated the importation of foreign items in anticipation of expanded foreign markets for American products.

St. Regis's involvement with international trade dated to its early years. In the mid-1950s the company owned four plants in foreign countries. Additionally, it was associated with a number of licensees producing Panelyte plastics and multiwall bags in Europe, Asia, Australia, and South America. In 1958 an interest was acquired in a number of South African firms.[48] Two years later St. Regis International was established to conduct export sales for St. Regis and its subsidiaries from a general office in the West Indies.[49]

Africa continued to offer St. Regis possibilities. In 1964 the company purchased an interest in Amalgamated Packaging Industries, a converter of paper and board in Johannesburg, Cape Town, Port Elizabeth, and Durban and at Salisbury, Rhodesia. Amalgamated produced multiwall and grocery bags, corrugated and folding boxes, paper milk cartons, conical containers, and flexible packaging materials. St. Regis increased its holdings, gaining a controlling interest in 1965. Additional overseas expansion in 1964 included the development of corrugated banana box plants in Nicaragua, Panama, and Ecuador.[50]

International economic and political instability acted as a temporary check to overseas growth. But despite continuing doubt of economic security, demand for kraft pulp, paper, and paperboard rose by 1964, and within a year the sales of these products nearly doubled in volume.

Ferguson and Adams were able to articulate an optimistic appraisal of international affairs in the annual report for 1964:

> Increasingly the United States paper industry must look upon paper and paperboard as a world business influenced by broad international trends. In this view the market opportunity stands out clearly. Only in North America is the paper industry in a position to undertake large-scale expansion to meet the rising demand, having adequate timber to produce the necessary pulp, combined with highly developed technical knowledge and ample financial resources.

This statement summarizes management's attitude toward foreign enterprise. The vigorous expansion of St. Regis's international operations during the next several years is testimony to successful implementation of policies based on that philosophy.

Consolidation of the company's operations, in addition to its reorganization and growth programs, included disposal of marginally effective properties. Prior to the structural changes, attention had been focused on Canada. St. Regis of Canada, unlike its parent company, purchased kraft paper in the open market, making it especially susceptible to changing market conditions. In 1959 the company was sold to the Consolidated Paper Corporation of Montreal. In the words of Hugh Sloan, who was then president of the subsidiary, the decision to sell was based on "the fact that there was so much pressure from Bemis and from International Paper. You see, we owned no paper production in Canada for our bags."[51] Charles Woodcock, at that time in the Bag Packaging Division, suggests another element involved in the sale to Consolidated:

> This was the advent of the all-plastic bag in Canada, which seriously cut into multiwall bags in Canada. I think the timing was like six or eight months after St. Regis had sold those bag plants to Consolidated that this move occurred. So the timing was very good.[52]

As Woodcock stated, within months of the sale, Canadian firms introduced plastic bags for use by their fertilizer subsidiaries, and the paper bag business faltered.

To some extent, management viewed divestiture of the Panelyte Division as symbolic of the company's new administrative orientation and emphasis on planning. As Andrew Storer put it:

> The move to divest ourselves of Panelyte was part of a decision that we made in the sixties to begin to dispose of properties that didn't fit. And that went back to the beginning of strategic thinking—part of the market analysis effort in analyzing what we had, where it was going, and if it contributed long-range to the overall company welfare.[53]

By 1960 St. Regis was engaged in the production of laminated, molded, extruded, and vacuum-formed plastic products for various industrial and military applications. But raw materials were needed to compete in the large-scale production of plastics, as well as the facilities to transform petrochemical products into finished plastic items. Because St. Regis at this time was not able to integrate production from oil to refrigerator inner-door panels, it eventually withdrew from this sector of the plastics field, selling its Trenton facilities to the Thiokol Corporation in 1961. Operations in Indiana and Michigan were sold in 1964, and the Panelyte Kalamazoo plant was sold a year later.[54]

With increasingly complex activities conducted by both private enterprise and the government, the need for communication between the two sectors grew during the second half of the twentieth century. The origins of a public relations department at St. Regis began with the postwar expansion, particularly into the South. The need to inform the financial institutions of the company's plans and goals was an imperative for further growth. The employment of Samuel Shane by Ferguson was an early example of this realization. For some years Ferguson had read and admired Shane's reporting, first in Montreal and later in the *Wall Street Journal*. Shane became a specialist on the paper industry. James Kussmann, later to succeed Shane as head of public relations, credits him with being one of Ferguson's closest associates and with building a strong communications base for the company, both in financial circles and also at the community level.[55]

Environmentalist pressure was building, and this was a major cause for increased interest in developing a public affairs office. Kussmann summarizes the emergence of a trend toward better communications in this area: "It wasn't until about fifteen years ago that many companies in our industry recognized the need to communicate with government at all levels—whether it was the federal, state, local, or regional government."[56] St. Regis's interest in public relations accelerated during the late 1960s, but the decisions of earlier years expedited the institutionalization of public affairs and programs within the management structure.

At the annual stockholders' meeting in April 1964, William Adams reviewed past performances and considered future possibilities of the paper industry:

> During 1963, a new vigor seemed to develop in the economy. Basic materials like copper, zinc, aluminum—and paper, started to come into a supply-demand ratio which gave some buoyancy to their prices for the first time in several years. . . . The world situation, too, seems a bit calmer. . . . World trade, both outside the Iron Curtain, and to a much lesser extent over the Iron Curtain, is showing vigorous growth. . . . The paper industry, which has had a poor earnings record . . . seems particularly well situated to share in this era of activity.[57]

Taking into account improved national and world conditions and the constant dangers of papermaking—intense competition, overproduction, and low prices—Adams and his staff opted for expansion in carefully selected areas. The first and ultimately most ambitious of these undertakings derived in part from the sharp upswing in foreign and domestic demand for kraft products in mid-decade. The groundwork was laid in 1963 when St. Regis directed its engineering, forestry, financial, and marketing personnel to examine the need for a new kraft paperboard mill near Monticello, Mississippi. Their efforts culminated in 1968 in the building of one of the largest manufacturing operations ever undertaken by a paper company anywhere in the world.

The subsequent period continued the strategies established in the late 1950s and reinforced in the early 1960s. Consolidation was stressed, and great importance was given to long-range planning. Decisions for future acquisitions and divestitures were determined after careful examination and analysis based on estimated profitability and compatibility with the overall enterprise.

8
The Move to Multinationalism

The disturbing events and changing cultural conditions present at the beginning of the 1960s accelerated during the second half of the decade. Protest—against injustice, growth of bureaucracy, and rapid expansion of the war in Southeast Asia—was expressed by an ever-widening sector of the public. Although the majority of the population did not embrace activism, the revolt of the young and minority groups touched a sensitive chord throughout the nation.

Juxtaposed with this threat to the social order was the continued increase of economic prosperity for most individuals and industries. Seemingly the abundance of material well-being for the majority of white Americans precipitated the protests. In a land so plentiful, the lives of the less fortunate were painful contrasts, inspiring idealism and activism in the young, and angry determination among minorities. There were additional contradictions in the attitudes and policies of the nation, not only toward the social, economic, and political status of a portion of its citizenry but toward the controversial issues surrounding the Vietnam war.

Not least among the efforts of the protesters was the movement to prevent further spoilage of the natural environment. Pollution of air and water and depletion of natural resources had been recognized as a by-product of progress since the early years of the decade. Public and government attention focused on industries that tapped the earth's resources, and new regulatory policies were mandated. Implementation of some of these policies proved to be difficult. America's thriving consumer culture was based on economic growth, and any imposition of limitations on growth was controversial.

Despite the turmoil of the late 1960s, American business remained stable, providing a solid foundation for the nation's economy. The paper industry reflected the upward economic surge between 1965 and 1969 and, as in the earlier part of the decade, production and capital expenditures increased substantially. American producers also responded to a swelling demand for paper products from the Common Market with a boost in exports at the end of the decade. While the industry continued to be plagued by low prices, increased production costs, and inflation, the 1960s witnessed record business activity.[1]

Prior to 1969 the paper industry had been consistently less profitable than other businesses, but its strong showing that year marked a distinct break with the past and a positive portent for the future. William Adams, assessing the 1969 situation, asserted that the industry's profit performance, while unspectacular since 1956, appeared to be entering upon a new era of consistent high earnings. This was related to what he saw as the end of industry growth initiated during the 1960s. "There are just a few scattered additions now building," he stated, "and nothing more could be added to present plans for start-up before about the middle of 1972." Adams felt that the balance between paper supply and demand would be tight and therefore profitable. Looking even further into the future, he predicted that growth in the industry would proceed in a more careful fashion.[2]

The beginning of another boom had been predicted in 1965. In July Adams told the New York Society of Security Analysts that the paper industry faced its best prospects in a decade. He explained that annual paper consumption in the United States had increased 15 percent since 1961 but that earnings had not reflected increased volume until late 1964. He contended that in coming years the industry would not make its traditional mistake of overproducing, glutting the market, and creating surplus supply.[3]

It would seem that all was well for papermakers, but in its fall investment guide, Merrill Lynch expressed concern about low paper prices. The paper industry, it pointed out, had again overexpanded, and despite increased demand, prices were low.[4]

Record-breaking St. Regis earnings characterized the remaining years of the decade. Even in 1967, when there was a decline from the previous year's record high, the company logged the third best earnings in its history. The rate and magnitude of St. Regis's progress during the late 1960s is demonstrated by investments in nonconsolidated affiliates, which had a book value of $90.3 million in 1970. The paper company also experienced an increase in total cash generated, from $66.8 million in 1965 to $89.2 million in 1969. However, while generated cash increased, the amount expended on capital investments decreased significantly. Excluding timberland purchases, about $87 million in capital investments were made in 1966, and only $26 million in 1970.[5]

Spectacular growth was also registered in timberland owned or controlled. In 1965 St. Regis held cutting rights or owned in fee 3.9 million acres of land. Five years later the company owned or controlled 8.2 million acres. The expansion in landholdings did not, however, alter the company's historic policy of buying wood on the open market. "Since market wood is normally plentiful in the mills' operating areas," explained the 1966 annual report, "the company does not need to draw heavily on its own timber stands although these reserves are always available."[6] Company-owned land continued to be viewed as a reserve, guaranteeing continuous operation in the future.

Expanded production and earnings were closely related to the tremendous success of the company's overseas operations. Acting upon opportunities presented by the international economy, St. Regis benefited from its expertise and solid reputation. The corporation's International Division expanded significantly to accommodate increased business activity. An integral part of the overseas success was production at the Ferguson Mill in Monticello, Mississippi. Its relationship to the foreign market had been a key aspect in its planning. Finally, the firm's corporate structure continued its revision and consolidation, in keeping with patterns established at the beginning of the decade.

The social pressures of the 1960s were not without impact upon the company. In an interview, William Adams recalled that those events provoked St. Regis into a more beneficial stance toward all sectors of society: stockholders, the general public, and government.[7] Reflecting the growing importance of public relations, St. Regis increased the scope of its Public Affairs Department.

A generational change brought new leadership when Samuel Shane retired in 1966. James E. Kussmann, an assistant vice-president, succeeded Shane. Additional evidence of the Public Affairs Department's importance is demonstrated by Kussmann's appointment to a vice-presidency in 1973.[8]

St. Regis had grown in the mid-1960s through plant enlargement, through new construction, and through entrance into, or creation of, new markets. In the latter half of the decade, international operations grew impressively. Prior to World War II, the company's foreign business had centered on exportation of wood pulp. But the worldwide increase in demand for kraft products expanded the potential of overseas markets, drawing St. Regis's attention to that arena. Because of its sprawling size, the need to restructure the international organization became apparent. In 1965 Reginald Vayo was appointed group vice-president of the revamped International Division. Vayo's experience as vice-president of the Kraft Division had involved him with foreign activities. (Vayo was succeeded as Kraft Division vice-president by William E. Caldwell.)[9] Under Vayo the division was organized into three areas of operation: "1. manufacturing and marketing through wholly owned subsidiaries and partially owned companies, 2. export sales, and 3. patent licensing of overseas manufacturers and rendering of technical aid."[10]

The Ferguson Mill at Monticello was highly instrumental in the growth and expansion of St. Regis's foreign business. Although its immense production supported all of the company's kraft operations, its impact upon the International Division was especially clear. Carefully planned, the plant's enormous material demands were assured by purchase of 152,000 acres of timberland, mostly in Mississippi. This addition increased paper company holdings in that state and Louisiana to about 350,000 acres.[11]

To supplement this source of wood, St. Regis set up a supply system in 1966 that promised to provide more than 800,000 cords of pulpwood a year. The system was based upon advanced methods of mechanized harvesting and wood preparation that the company had developed in the South. The Ferguson Mill was considered the axis for twenty-two concentration yards at outlying points in the supply territory. Contractors would deliver wood to the satellite-concentration yard and it would then be shipped to the mill. About one-half of the logs were debarked and chipped at plants set up in the forest, and the remainder were processed at the mill.[12]

This mill, named in honor of St. Regis's longtime chief executive, profoundly affected many company operations. It made possible a more extensive geographic distribution of the bag, kraft specialty paper, and container products. The company's smaller kraft mills, no longer burdened with the production responsibility assumed by Monticello, were freed to produce the specialized grades in which they best competed. Shipments from Jacksonville, a deepwater port, were now able to meet foreign demand for convenience packaging.

The development of the International Division is illustrative of Ferguson's underlying business philosophy to anticipate and capitalize upon opportunities. St. Regis had been involved in foreign markets as early as 1929, when Bates was acquired. By 1945 it owned a bag plant in Belgium and subsidiaries in Brazil, Argentina, and Colombia. "We had about a 32 percent interest in Colombia," Reginald Vayo explained,

> and through a Delaware corporation we owned the plants in Brazil and Argentina. Then there was the debacle when a certain amount of funds were stolen down in Brazil . . . and Jack Cowles was put in charge of getting that thing cleaned up. St. Regis didn't put any money at all in Latin America for a time because they didn't want to get burned again.[13]

Negative experience plus the state of the international economy caused a reduction in foreign investments until the mid-1960s, but they reached a crescendo between 1969 and 1974. "We thought that the use of paper in many of the foreign countries was considerably below that in the United States," the current Chairman of the Board George Kneeland, explained, "and we could see the changes that were going to come just as they had come earlier in this country."[14] It was apparent that the demand for paper would explode as developing countries made upward strides. Increased literacy and income meant increased demand for paper products.

International expansion in 1965 involved the replacement of F. W. Williams by Australian Consolidated as St. Regis's partner in Australia and brought the American company into production of glass and fiber containers and plastics. Europe also offered additional prospects for St. Regis, and the company gained an interest in a corrugated material plant in Barcelona, Spain.[15]

Growth continued in both Latin America and Europe during 1966. The company joined with Panamanian citizens in construction of a paper mill to produce corrugated material for Central American box producers. St. Regis supplied some of the funds for the erection of a box factory in Venezuela. A new company, Neopac, was organized by St. Regis in Randers, Denmark, to manufacture corrugated boxes.[16]

Africa had promised a huge growth potential, and St. Regis's rapid development there realized this projection. In the 1966 annual report, the company claimed to be "one of the principal factors in this [Republic of South Africa's] packaging industry." National Packaging Company Limited of Johannesburg, owned primarily by St. Regis and the Fruman group, had a profitable year, and Amalgamated Packaging of Durban was reorganized. Additional investments were made in Zambia.[17]

By the end of 1967, investments outside the United States and Canada had reached a book value of $26 million. St. Regis had at least 50 percent ownership in thirteen firms with sales that year an estimated $85 million. Also in 1967, the International Division earned $30 million from the sale of kraft pulp, paper, paperboard, and other products to foreign countries.[18]

The following year, St. Regis-controlled foreign companies had sales of $88 million, and the ten firms in which minority ownership was held recorded sales of $46 million. Shipment of more than a third of a million tons of kraft pulp, paper, and paperboard pushed St. Regis's total export sales to $35 million, figures that demonstrate the degree of overseas escalation.

To handle this increasing volume of exports, the corporation acquired a fourteen-thousand-ton ship especially designed to handle large paper rolls. Commissioned the *William R. Adams*, the vessel loaded at a new terminal near the St. Regis mill at Jacksonville. The cargo of the *William R. Adams* consisted of paper and paperboard produced in Jacksonville. Export pulp, meanwhile, came mainly from the Tacoma mill and was shipped from that Northwest port.[19]

Export demand for all products remained strong through the end of the decade. A softness developed in European demand and prices for kraft linerboard, but those items continued to do well in the Far and Near East, Latin America, Africa, Australia, and New Zealand.[20]

International operations thus completed the transformation of St. Regis into a global enterprise. The intensive effort devoted to foreign markets had been rewarded with substantial income from international activities. Based on its impressive success of the 1960s, St. Regis accelerated investments abroad in the early years of the succeeding decade.

Rapid growth of international investments and returns was supported by successful domestic activities. Expanding on earlier policies aimed at integration of operations, St. Regis moved into new areas, supplementing and strengthening existing functions. Plant improvement and new construction received generous budgets; capital expenditures in 1965 were $51.3 million, a new company high. In 1968 capital improvement exceeded $60 million, with $8 million going to the Rhinelander Division alone.[21]

Kraft production was increased in May 1966 when St. Regis bought 115,031 shares of the common stock of Southland Paper Mills, Incorporated, of Lufkin, Texas, from the Louis Calder Foundation. By January 1967 company purchases totaled a 38.6 percent interest in Southland, which had net sales of $44.1 million in 1966. Southland had a four-machine pulp and paper mill at Lufkin and was building a two-machine mill at Houston that was expected to begin production in 1967. Over the years, the division functioned with increased success and was merged with St. Regis in 1977.[22]

In contrast to the Kraft Division, which could expect a strong demand for its products, the Bag Division by 1965 had almost saturated its markets. Attempts to locate or create new fields for its products brought mixed results. One effort to capture a valuable market involved a plan to replace standard refuse receptacles with disposable, thirty-gallon, two-ply, wet-strength SOS bags, the jargon used for self-opening sacks of a style similar to grocery bags. By 1965 the Bag Division had developed a system of bags, bag-support frames, and a refuse collection truck known as the Kuka-Shark. Replacement parts for the special truck had to come from Germany, forcing the division to maintain a large and expensive inventory. This liability, coupled with failure to promote the system effectively, caused the division to give up the truck. However, it continued its other operations using SOS bags. This project too faced difficulties in penetrating the market and enjoyed only moderate success.[23]

Counterbalancing this disappointment was the Bag Division's breakthrough into the grocery bag market itself, accomplished in 1966 through the acquisition of the Great Western Bag Corporation and its sales affiliate, the Murray Bag and Paper Corporation of Los Angeles.

Established in 1952, the companies had grown substantially in the years prior to their purchase by St. Regis. The division also expanded production of the stepped-end bag through plant enlargements at Salt Lake City in 1969.[24]

With a foothold in the western bag business, St. Regis strengthened its position with construction of a multiwall bag plant at Union City, California, in 1966. The company hoped to recover the cost of this investment by increasing production 50 percent above the output of the older San Leandro plant. The Union City bag plant was designed to produce industrial and consumer-type multiwall bags and also to serve as the Bag Division's western area sales headquarters.[25]

Strong growth was also made by St. Regis in consumer markets, which demanded an ever-growing supply of folding carton, flexible packaging, and container products. In 1966 Louisville became the home of the St. Regis Consumer Packaging Center. This facility was designed to convert company kraft and special paper into small bags for use by the food products industry in such items as pancake mix. A year later two machines were installed to extrude plastic film for use either as plastic bags or with kraft in multiwall bags. Purchase of the Domtar Packaging Company of Morristown, New Jersey, in 1968, allowed St. Regis to manufacture vacuum-formed polyethylene trays and cups for use in the confectionery and food industries. In a two-year period, 1967-1968, the Container Division added new plants in Wisconsin, Michigan, Florida, and New York.[26]

To remain in the forefront of domestic production of lightweight coated paper, St. Regis in 1965 channeled $45 million into expansion of its Bucksport facility, already the most profitable in the Printing Paper Division. The program included installation of a number four machine designed to produce an eighteen-foot-wide sheet, precoated on both sides, at speeds of up to twenty-five hundred feet per minute.[27]

The merger with Southland Paper Mills in 1977 made St. Regis the nation's second largest producer of newsprint. Southland began producing newsprint from southern pine in 1940, as a result of Charles H. Herty's pioneering research, and bolstered the southern forest industry by finding a major use for its predominant species of tree. At Lufkin, Texas, four machines produce 1,150 tons of newsprint daily.

The Forest Products Division, which had been formed in 1963, increased productivity to meet the demand of the housing boom in the Tacoma area. To handle the upsurge, St. Regis expanded its converting capacity by building a veneer plant, studmill, and dry land log-handling facility. The trend in construction also pointed to the need for more effective distribution. In 1967 the company built a distribution center near Everett, Washington, to handle the movement of lumber, plywood, studs, and other forest products. The facility also had a component manufacturing department that made house and commercial roof trusses, precut lumber, and wall, floor, and roof panels.[28]

The accelerating demand for housing required efficient distribution methods. In its search for such a system, St. Regis acquired the Wheeler Lumber Bridge and Supply Company of Iowa in 1968. William Haselton details the rationale for this highly successful purchase:

> Any company who is a primary producer is always being solicited to avoid the wholesaler and sell more and more to the ultimate end user. . . . We learned of the availability of Wheeler and we met with them. We could not have been more impressed; they were extremely fine people with a built-in, well-managed multiplicity of outlets around the grain and farm belt. They were involved not only in distributing lumber products, but also in other exotic areas like engineering bridges and treating materials like posts and pilings—which we already were doing . . . and we wanted to get closer to the market. Wheeler provided that as a secondary benefit. . . . The price, the people, and the profitability were all attractive.[29]

Haselton and Andrew Storer also point to the anticipated demise of the plywood business in the Pacific Northwest as a factor in the situation. In part the result of technological developments enabling plywood to be produced more economically in the South, the decline of that industry in the Northwest compelled investigation of new products and wider distribution systems.[30] When the construction industry slumped in 1969, the company closed its Tacoma hardwood plywood plant and sold a similar facility at Pensacola.[31]

Storer also notes that as demand for wooden bridge timbers and plywood forms diminished, prestressed concrete moved in to take their place. Wheeler, sensitive to the trend, became a licensee for the production of Span-Deck through affiliation with the Iowa Prestressed Concrete Company. Thus acquisition of Wheeler confirmed management's awareness of the great opportunity offered by entry into the highway market. Wheeler, with total sales in excess of $20 million, was a major supplier of highway products in the upper Midwest.[32]

The late-1960s witnessed further development of two closely related goals of the corporation: acquisition of additional raw material sources and maintenance of existing timberland. By the end of 1967, St. Regis owned or controlled 5.9 million acres, much of it acquired in the preceding ten years. Company forest managers calculated that St. Regis had the right to cut 35 billion board feet of standing timber.

Approximately 90 percent of the company's total sales were derived from products made from trees. The company's mills consumed, as sawlogs, pulpwood, and chips, the equivalent of 1.6 billion board feet in 1967. Half of this wood was harvested by St. Regis from its own land or from land on which it held cutting rights. The other half was bought in the open market, either as logs or chips. By dividing its acquisition of raw material, the company was able to realize a goal of long-range timber management: the cutting of less wood each year from its own land than was added by annual growth.[33]

The acquisition of 152,000 acres in 1965 from the Crosby Lumber and Manufacturing Company expanded St. Regis ownership in Mississippi and Louisiana to 350,000 acres. An additional means of securing a firm raw material base involved land exchanges with other private owners or with the Forest Service. These exchanges in 1965 gave the company easier access to its land in the Puyallup River Valley of Washington and acreage closer to its Tacoma mill. Such transactions made for important savings in road building and other logging costs.

In 1966 St. Regis exchanged 7,900 acres of timberland with the state of Washington. The company gave up scattered tracts intermingled with state ownership in Grays Harbor and Willapa counties. St. Regis received in return land in the Mineral and Kapowsin regions, forested with old-growth timber and contiguous with land owned or controlled by the company. The exchange therefore consolidated holdings in a major operating area.

St. Regis invested $9.5 million in timberlands in 1968, with the addition of 95,000 acres. These included well-stocked slash pine plantations in north-central Florida and 33,000 acres in Maine. Of even greater importance was the obtaining of cutting rights on two million acres of crown land in Alberta, formerly held as a contingent reserve for the Hinton mill. Alberta Hi-Brite, produced at Hinton, had established a reputation as one of the world's finest market pulps. Closely attendant to this addition in western Canada was acquisition in January 1969 of the remaining common stock—slightly less than 50 percent—of North Western Pulp and Power Limited. The partnership of North Western, St. Regis, and North Canadian Oils had launched the pulp mill at Hinton in 1954. By such aggressive commitment of its assets, St. Regis management made clear its anticipation of soaring demand for quality pulp and its recognition of an increasing scarcity of raw materials.[34]

Aerial photography was combined with ground cruising in Maine to provide more reliable data on the volume, age class, and timber types on company land. Such data were essential in planning expansion of the Bucksport mill. At the same time, company foresters experimented with better methods of increasing the volume of pulpwood obtained from other owners. Their success, in the face of strong competition, followed a pattern already well advanced in the South. This pattern involved the use of new facilities for handling, storing, and debarking so as to provide a balanced flow of raw material for Bucksport.[35]

St. Regis increasingly turned its attention toward growing public concern over forest land. The growth of cities and towns, as well as highway systems, brought home the fact that land was becoming scarce and its value accelerating. Foresters were confronted with a more complex range of management decisions. Recognition of the need to coordinate these functions better resulted in establishment of the Shelter, Timber, and Land Management Division in 1969. William R. Haselton assumed leadership of the newly formed group.[36]

One practice continued by the division was to extend the use of company land for such other purposes as grazing and farming, wildlife development, water control, and recreational activities. Additionally company foresters worked with their counterparts in public forestry programs and professional societies to educate the public with regard to protecting forest resources. These practices were intensified by the firm commitment of management.

Foresters focused on the major part of the company's timberland, and a small percentage was not managed because of unsuitability for growth of merchantable trees. In an attempt to develop other uses for this marginal land, St. Regis assigned the newly formed Land Development Division to Haselton in 1969. Development of land for commercial, residential, and leisure use, however, remained a minor aspect of company operations. The dangers inherent in a new area of business were sufficiently perceived to restrain St. Regis from following some of its competitors into the real estate field. Haselton explains the prevailing attitude: "St. Regis resisted the temptation to go out and buy a development company and say, 'Boys, take it from there; we trust you.' . . . We were in land development, but we did it on a basis of reserve and constraint." This caution was well founded; similar ventures of other forest products companies proved unsuccessful. "Perhaps we didn't make so much money as the others in 1969 and 1970," Haselton notes, "but they lost all they made and much more in the seventies."[37]

The final year of the 1960s found St. Regis in a peculiar position. Although the company had expanded capacity during the decade by 32 percent and increased its debt by 125 percent, revenues had also climbed. Still, profits had been decreasing, and the company was getting bigger rather than more profitable.[38] The corporation ended the decade with a year of record earnings, but its stagnant profit picture was a serious factor for management to consider. Predictions of an economic downturn in the 1970s also caused somber reflection.

Future profitability made a strong impact on the ongoing process of reorganization. The result was a major compartmentalization of responsibilities in 1969 through creation of executive vice-presidents for Operations, Administration, and Marketing and Communications.[39] Haselton recalls the details:

> In 1969 there was a further amplification of that philosophy [the 1963 reorganization by product rather than by geographical location]. We continued the amalgamation by creating three groups from five to six divisions in 1969. One was for packaging and Duffy headed that. One was for food equipment and consumer products—which was a very, very small group—and that was under Alex Smalley. . . . The other group [Shelter, Timber and Land Management] was under my control. We had three domestic groups and one foreign group by late 1969 or early 1970—it had really been brought together.[40]

The restructuring of corporate staff included appointment of the new executive vice-presidents. William E. Caldwell was placed in charge of Operations, George Kneeland was named to head Administration, and Bernard Recknagel was appointed to Marketing and Communications. These men became the senior management. Six men were appointed senior vice-presidents, including John E. Cowles for Finance, Edward J. McMahon for Personnel and New Developments, and Reg-

inald L. Vayo for International. Duffy, Haselton, and Alexander
Smalley assumed responsibility for, respectively, Packaging; Shelter,
Timber, and Land Management; and Food Equipment and Consumer
Products. The five operating divisions—Kraft, Printing Paper, Container, Flexible Packaging, and Bag Packaging—were headed by
divisional vice-presidents, all reporting to Caldwell, executive vice-
president of Operations.[41] Further decentralization of management and
diffusion of divisional responsibility was one major result of these
changes. Tightening of divisional operations was a secondary impact.

The work of John Cowles in applying sophisticated accounting
methods was of immense importance to St. Regis, an importance not
obvious to casual observers. For the first time, cost-accounting procedures common to other enterprises were applied to St. Regis's operation, and decisions could be made on the basis of real costs. These
accounting tools are essential to modern management.[42]

In the years of rapid growth following World War II, Roy Ferguson had displayed an uncanny knowledge of merger mechanics. But
his attempt, begun in 1968, to merge with the Radio Corporation of
America was never consummated. Various reasons have been pro-
pounded as to why Ferguson sought a merger of the two companies
through an exchange of stock. Ferguson may have been influenced by
close friends in the New York banking community, as suggested by
corporate secretary Homer Crawford:

> Obviously, the people at RCA and the man who just retired from
> the bank—Meyer—had some discussions with Mr. Ferguson. I have
> no idea when they started, how long they lasted, or who initiated
> them. I imagine they were basically initiated by this banker.[43]

Another view is that Ferguson's feelings about St. Regis management
might have led him to consider the merger. Ferguson's advancing age
made him concerned over his own investments, as another associate,
Edward J. McMahon, explained:

> I think it is true that Mr. Ferguson, who was a great and wonder-
> ful gentleman, had gotten old and paid more attention to his own
> investments. He was frustrated with Mr. Adams, and Mr. Adams
> was frustrated with him. . . . He was a very brilliant man; there is
> no question about that. He had lived through a lot of cycles: he
> basically believed . . . that there is very little new. . . . He was an

unbelievable optimist in everything, which I found at odds with his getting discouraged with the management of the company. But we were highly criticized in financial circles, and those were the people he associated with—the bankers and so forth—and they might have gotten to him.[44]

George Kneeland takes a different approach. Kneeland, who in his own words "always had a rather unusual association with Roy Ferguson," was privy to many of Ferguson's opinions even though he was not yet a senior executive:

> He wanted a much greater value on the stock than that which it was selling for in the marketplace—and he did get a value put on the stock by that offer. His aim was to establish a value on the company; that is my opinion.[45]

The same line of thinking was expressed by James Kussmann in an interview:

> I think RCA was considered for a couple of reasons. One was RCA's ability to raise capital. Perhaps a feeling that they had a more sophisticated management than we did. Getting a good price for the stockholders. Roy Ferguson's concern for the stockholders has always been very important. He felt that the common shareholder had invested his money in the company and given management a lot of trust. . . . Mr. Ferguson might have felt that if a merger with RCA could give the stockholder 25 percent more, or 20 percent more for his stock, it might be a good deal.[46]

Whatever Ferguson's motivation, the merger appeared to many St. Regis executives to be more advantageous to RCA than to St. Regis. Andrew Storer observes, "I think the move on RCA's part was toward our forest lands; the move to get into a natural resource industry; diversification."[47] A stronger statement along this order is made by Hugh W. Sloan, whose actions placed him in direct conflict with Ferguson:

> Well, I think that was the only falling out I ever had with Roy Ferguson. I took a look at their [RCA's] statement, I took a look at ours, and I took a look at the whole deal. . . . it was a lousy deal,

as far as I was concerned. RCA's earnings were terrible, and the
swap was unfair to St. Regis stockholders.[48]

The extent to which RCA might have viewed St. Regis as a desirable
acquisition is suggested by Kussmann:

> I think that they recognized that our timberlands were on our
> books at $73 million, approximately. We owned, at that time,
> about 2.6 million acres which had a true value of about $150 per
> acre. So it's easy to see that the net worth of St. Regis was much
> greater than reported—which made it very attractive to RCA.[49]

Although Ferguson's thinking remains unclear, what is evident is
that he persuaded St. Regis directors of the benefits of such a course,
at least to the extent of gaining approval for initial negotiations on 8
January 1969.[50] The preliminary discussions had been conducted in
secrecy, so when the news broke, it took many executives by surprise.
McMahon recalls the announcement:

> There was no period of negotiation; the agreement in principle
> for merger was announced as a *fait accompli* in the public press
> by Mr. Ferguson and Mr. Sarnoff of RCA while Mr. Adams was
> on a tour of the Orient. Mr. Ferguson, who was kind of remote
> to many of us, was not available or prepared to talk about it in
> any depth, and Adams wasn't here for the next week.[51]

Some executives, however, had been involved in the merger discussion because of their proximity to Ferguson. Among these was Crawford, who recounted the details of an event that had the financial world
buzzing:

> General David Sarnoff wasn't there nor was Mr. Ferguson. . . .
> We talked generally about the company and about what kind of
> pension plans and contracts we had. All in the space of an hour
> and a half, we covered the whole company. Mr. Werner then set
> up a huge meeting in the RCA boardroom—where we had our
> bankers and their bankers, our counsel and their counsel; and our
> comptrollers and a lot of staff people, from A to Z. We went
> through a long program explaining how this matter was going

to be handled, who was going to have what responsibility, and how all the documents were going to get done. And, of course, this was going to be a statutory merger with the approval of each company's stockholders, and we were going to include it in our annual meeting proxy statement. Then we started work with Adrian Leiby, who was then the principal representative of Leboeuf and Lamb [St. Regis legal counsel], to work on this matter. We started the merger agreement.[52]

In addition to surprise, the general reaction was one of disappointment and apprehension. McMahon recalls:

It is difficult for me to say how people felt about it in its entirety; they were shocked and disappointed, as people always are in a situation like this. . . . I guess underneath it all, there was a unanimous feeling that when the final date at the end of February came, the merger wouldn't happen.[53]

Sloan speaks of the attitude of other company officers:

Yes, I would say that [negativism] was a very general feeling. Of course, this was very much a matter of thinking that they might lose their independence; because RCA was much bigger than St. Regis, chances were that they would have tried to flood our board. At that time they were probably four times our size.[54]

A sense of loss was felt by those whose long affiliation with St. Regis had developed loyalty and pride in the company. Storer recalls those emotions:

I think we all approached it with a certain amount of trepidation—and I'll say disappointment. We had lived through a period of seeing St. Regis grow and diversify very dramatically. I think you approach any acquisition in which you are the acquired company with a certain amount of fear as to what the future is, and a little loss of morale. Apparently this also began to take place at the board level.[55]

This complex of opinions, fears, and uncertainties was not without consequence. Some, such as Sloan, made their opinions known to Ferguson and to board members. The impact of negative reaction to the proposed merger apparently was strong enough to reverse the decision. Kneeland characterizes Ferguson at this time:

> Personally, I was never for the RCA merger and I had many long and bitter discussions with Roy on the subject; he was for it. You have to understand Roy; you might have known he was going to change his mind. I will never forget when it was just before the board meeting at which the RCA agreement would be voted on. And Roy just said to me, "You have always opposed this thing. I want you to come to lunch with the board and convince them that you are right and I am wrong." Obviously, at that point, he wanted the merger off.[56]

In February 1969 the St. Regis board of directors withdrew from the negotiations, to the relief and jubilation of company personnel.[57]

The conclusion of the 1960s marked the true watershed of Roy King Ferguson's long domination of the St. Regis Paper Company. Failure of the RCA merger and the split with Adams are believed by many observers to have resulted in Ferguson's eclipse. Accolades continued to be accorded him, and it was a rare day that he did not put in time at his Manhattan office. That he continued to carry weight in decision making is confirmed by his election as a full member of the board of directors, as chairman of its executive committee, and as a member of the new finance and audit committee set up in 1973.[58] Haselton confirms that Ferguson continued to be a factor:

> I believe until Roy left us permanently, he was extremely interested in the key elements of this company in almost the broadest practical way. . . . I've got to say, in a proportionately restrained fashion, that he had a very strong hand on things until he died.[59]

The company's future destiny now lay in the hands of new leadership. The newly structured top management continued to employ tools of intensive cost accounting, long-range planning, and other new methods with which they had become acquainted in the 1960s.

9
Capitalizing on Opportunity

The onset of the 1970s was a watershed for the nation, socially, politically, and economically. The social and economic decay of the decade produced a multiplicity of problems. The external problems strongly affecting American business enterprise were inflation, unemployment, shortages of resources, and costly pollution-abatement requirements. Further darkening this picture were increased worldwide instability and international fluctuations of purchasing power.

The strategies St. Regis employed during these years produced a corporate structure different from that of the past. The number of employees, facilities, and operations was reduced, but total production, earnings, and profits grew. The key to this apparent contradiction was skillful use of the human, material, and technological resources of the corporation.

After the best performance in its history in 1969, the company experienced a decline in earnings in 1970 and in 1971 suffered its worst year since 1954. St. Regis was not alone in its plight; other major producers were similarly affected. The profit-to-sales ratio of the paper industry dropped 0.6 percent below the level of all industry, and a 27 percent decline in net profits was registered in 1970. Net profits per share fell off sharply at International Paper, Kimberly-Clark, and Mead Corporation. St. Regis fared somewhat better, its earnings per share dropping only $.69 from the $2.98 level of 1969.

Paper industry wages, up to a record $6.4 billion in 1969, increased an additional $240 million in 1970, despite reduced demand and prices.

This was only the fifth time since 1946 that production figures declined; the addition of tonnage for the 1972-1974 period was set at 2.1 percent, the lowest rate in any three-year period since the war.[1]

History is a continuous process. Watersheds and turning points are, in actuality, artificial categories used by historians for purposes of analysis. The economic downturn that burdened the 1970s had been developing and was perceptible in earlier years. Its onset was predicted by many industrial leaders. At St. Regis this foresight was one cause of basic structural and functional reorganizations in the late 1960s. Refinement of the company's top management permitted the revision of the remaining administrative, financial, and operational functions.

The switch from expansive to intensive management policies in 1969 was only the beginning of a major transformation. After thirty-seven years of leadership, Roy Ferguson retired as chairman of the board in 1971, setting in motion a series of management changes that continued until 1973 when William Haselton became president. Ferguson's retirement symbolized one of the major changes in American business life in the second half of the twentieth century: the evolution of the decision-making process from individual to consensual action.

William Adams filled Ferguson's board position and William Caldwell attained the presidency. Adams retired in 1972 and was succeeded by George Kneeland as chairman of the board and chief executive officer. Further change occurred after the death of Caldwell in 1973. Caldwell's affiliation with the company had begun in 1939. Starting as an engineer, he had risen swiftly through positions in many divisions until he attained the presidency in 1971. He is remembered by Edward McMahon in this manner:

> Bill Caldwell was a good thinker and a deep thinker. He was always a very popular and well-respected fellow. He started out many years ago in the Panelyte Division in Trenton, and then went on to Kalamazoo; I knew him a little bit then. I got to know him well when he was manager of Pensacola—he was a very quiet guy with a lot of inner strength.[2]

Roy Ferguson died in December 1974. Recognition of his leadership during the Great Depression, World War II, and extended periods of company growth came from a wide range of associates. But his most important testimonial was the company he had guided over so many years. At the time of his death, St. Regis was one of the largest and most successful corporations in its industry and a major participant in the national and international economy.

Kneeland and Haselton offered the company tested ability when they assumed their respective responsibilities. Kneeland had started out as a mail boy in 1939 and was able to educate himself about the company even in this capacity:

> I came to New York in answer to an opening for a mail boy in St. Regis. So I got in line, and I got the job. . . . Being a mail boy was an advantage, for it opened my eyes as to what this company was all about at that point. All letters that came to the mail room were addressed to St. Regis Paper Company, and had to be opened and then delivered to individuals. I must admit I certainly got an education by reading all those letters. It taught me an awful lot about this company.[3]

Kneeland won the early attention of his superiors, including Ferguson, and moved steadily into positions of increasing responsibility. He advanced from order room production to assistant to the vice-president of the Kraft Division. In 1954 he became production coordinator for all divisions and later gained experience in marketing, finance, and administration.

William Haselton brought to St. Regis a background of diversity and achievement, including a doctorate from the Institute of Paper Chemistry and broad experience in the forest products industry. Haselton states his formula for successful development of a business leader:

> Surely, the knowledge and the insight derived from formal schooling . . . provides background, but only sustained experience "on the firing line" can instill the real know-how that a truly experienced manager has to have to excel at his profession. It is the day-to-day exposure on the job which serves to identify those individuals who will, through natural or acquired ability in the field of management, rise in their company to a position of increased responsibility.[4]

Selective growth, involving the dismantling of marginal facilities and cautious selection of new acquisitions, was the underlying premise in the early 1970s. St. Regis divested itself of operations that were unprofitable, too costly to operate, or that no longer fit into the basic line of business. This action was, in Haselton's words, "overdue when one considers the dates that the acquisitions of all the various companies took place—many, many years before." Haselton further explains the reduction:

> The thing that really catalyzed consolidation, however, was the somewhat dismal performance of the very early seventies. This made it mandatory, when we barely made our dividend one year, to go ahead and do what could and should have been done, perhaps, earlier. . . . So George Kneeland, to some extent Bill Caldwell, . . . and I cut down on the number of people—at the same time that sales and ultimately, of course, profits, were expanding. This was probably a unique opportunity that I only wish we could have again. . . . So that was the framework: it was an idea whose time had come, and it was accelerated by the need for improved earnings.[5]

The paring of outmoded or inefficient plants has continued, as St. Regis increasingly measures productive value by stringent criteria.

Equally vital to the belt tightening was the regrouping of production activities into more functionally profitable units. Insight into consolidation of the Gummed Products, American Sisalkraft, and Sherman Paper Products divisions, one of several significant reorganizations, is provided by McMahon:

> It did not make sense to keep the three divisions separate any longer. It got to the point where the three divisions were competing among themselves in many areas of the marketplace. . . . It has been very evident that the decision was the right one. Plus the fact that they have cut their overhead down and eliminated the number of executives they needed.[6]

McMahon also explains some of Robert Searle's actions in realignment of the Corrugated Container Division and the Flexible Packaging Division.

> When Bob Searle took over [as senior vice-president of Packag-

ing] . . . he used a zero-based budgeting concept. . . . It was a case of being overly fat, overly concentrated in the nonprofitable areas— all these outfits that really were not highly profit oriented.[7]

"This intermarriage and exchange of personnel and procedure, and this standardization," Searle states, "have tended towards making St. Regis a very strong packaging supplier."[8]

Recent acquisitions have been based upon the criteria applied to existing facilities: the degree to which a proposed purchase will strengthen or expand capacity or marketability. One example of such an acquisition was the merger of Southland Paper Mills, Incorporated, with St. Regis in 1977. A major manufacturer and marketer of newsprint, the east Texas firm's success had followed the widening prosperity of the South. Its subsequent growth reflects the philosophy underlying St. Regis acquisition policies.

In line with this conservative perspective, investment in new production facilities has been based upon projections of the national economy, industry patterns, and applicability of the additions to the overall operation. Thus St. Regis focused principally upon two large-scale additions to its primary capacity. Expansion of the Bucksport mill in 1977 has maintained St. Regis's supremacy in the lightweight coated publishing paper field. A joint venture with Svenska Cellulosa AB at Obbola, Sweden, involved an investment of $95 million in a linerboard machine. These major commitments of capital kept the company moving in a strong domestic market and gained a foothold in a potentially profitable foreign market. The domestic venture has proved by all odds the more successful, since demand for Bucksport's product has matched predictions of growth. The anticipated demand for linerboard in Europe, however, has fallen short of expectations.

In its 1977 annual report, St. Regis bemoaned the failure of its expectations of Swedish-made linerboard but also cheered the good results stemming from the improvements at Bucksport. These gave the company a total annual production capacity of 739,000 tons of lightweight coated paper and uncoated papers for magazines, directories, and catalogs. At the same time, these facilities produce 103,000 tons of specialty papers annually, chiefly for packaging. Any serious downturn in the economy, with attendant reductions in advertising, plus increased mailing costs, could transform this picture, however. So runs the hazardous course confronting the business leader.

More intensive use of natural resources was another strategy emphasized by Haselton and Kneeland. Revenues from oil, gas, and mineral
deposits first made an impact in 1972 and have continued to mount
steadily. St. Regis early realized that its timberland in southern Alabama and the Florida Panhandle might hold reserves of oil and gas. The
company owned three hundred thousand acres near a new well drilled
by the Humble Oil and Refining Company in Pollard, Alabama, in
January 1951. Company officials, with stockholder approval, amended
the articles of incorporation to allow development of mineral rights.
In 1953 the Stanlind Oil and Gas Company and the Sun Oil Company
began exploring for oil on St. Regis land, and a year later drilling
commenced.

The search for oil and natural gas was sustained at a moderate level
throughout the 1960s; the breakthrough occurred in 1970 when Humble Oil discovered oil on a St. Regis tract in northwest Florida. Andrew
Storer testified to the benefits provided the Pensacola mill by the Florida
natural gas operations:

> It had its major impact on the Pensacola mill, which we now
> [1975] fuel through a pipeline which we built across western
> Florida. . . . And the natural gas that is generated at wells on our
> land has made us self-sufficient at the Pensacola mill. So that's
> been the major impact on our own mills of that oil-gas situation.
> Over and above the earnings that have been, of course, substantial.[9]

In 1972 the first revenue from oil totaled slightly over $1 million.
The 1976 annual report claimed "significant contributions to earnings . . . from crude oil, condensate, pipeline gas, and sulphur, as well
as products from the gas processing plants such as ethane, propane,
butane, and natural gasoline." To maximize exploitation of these resources, the company has continued exploration in Alabama and western Florida.

The pressure to maintain a firm grip on growth and expansion was
not as strong in the international sector as it was domestically. The
momentum built up during the 1960s carried over St. Regis's foreign
activities successfully into the next period. Still, conditions abroad were
changing rapidly, as reflected by market demand.

The international demand for paper and paper products increased
at twice the domestic rate in the early 1970s. The company met this

demand by acquiring or building facilities in Britain, France, and Austria. Its domestic position in food equipment and consumer product lines was bolstered by purchase of operations in Canada, Great Britain, and Australia. Marketing distribution contracts were widened by the sale of St. Regis's food equipment and refrigeration business to A. P. V. Holdings, Limited, of England. In exchange, St. Regis received a 28 percent interest in the British company, which had a worldwide sales organization. By 1975 international operations had crested at 35 percent of St. Regis net profits.

Nevertheless St. Regis's international position was threatened by economic and political factors—recession, inflation, political instability, and the decline of the American dollar—in mid-decade. Most vulnerable to overseas conditions was the Obbola facility, a victim of the depressed linerboard market. Kraft activities were also weakened by poor demand and fluctuating prices. The worldwide uncertainties dictated cautious action by corporate leadership. But the company's successful international history allowed management to express an optimism for the future of its foreign enterprises.

One of the great issues of concern to the American public in the 1970s had been the state of the environment. The extent of the problem can be measured by the spate of legislation at both the federal and state level. As a major user of one basic resource, St. Regis's attention has moved to accommodate itself to legal mandates and also to acceptance of a responsible social role. In support of this attention, the company's expenditures during the decade have amounted to $200 million.

The paper industry had been concerned about the environment long before development of the pollution issue. In 1922 the industry had begun research on pollution abatement. It had established a research institution in 1943, the sole responsibility of which was the study of various means of reducing air and water pollution. Between 1943 and 1968, expenditures for improving environmental quality by the paper industry totaled $415 million. In the late 1960s St. Regis allocated $5 million for pollution reduction at Monticello and planned to spend more than $18 million for pollution control at other company plants.

But serious obstacles to complete elimination of pollution remained. Not the least of these was that at precisely the time when pervasive concern for the quality of life became most strongly expressed, St. Regis was scrambling hard to cut expenditures in the face of recession. It also became clear that no amount of expenditure could alter the fact that technology was still imperfect. Related to these difficulties was a more subtle problem. Paper mills, emitting highly visible air pollution and releasing enormous volumes of effluent, were easy targets for public criticism. Leaders of the paper industry like William Adams were candid about the need for progress in pollution control, but some critics were hesitant to recognize either past progress by the industry or its future plans for treatment facilities.

There were immediate and tangible benefits of pollution abatement. The high cost of installation of treatment facilities in older mills induced management to close these facilities. The industry closed about forty mills for this reason in 1971. Since older plants were often less profitable than newer ones, stringent pollution measures actually helped paper companies save money.[10]

Most of the St. Regis pollution-abatement projects were capital improvements that paid no dividends. Fortunately the government offered assistance in some areas. In 1970 St. Regis initiated a program jointly financed with the federal Environmental Protection Agency to develop means of improving water content. The pilot program was designed to demonstrate that water used in a kraft pulp and paper mill could be recycled by filtering effluent through activated carbon rather than treating and then discharging liquid waste. The second phase of the program, implemented in Pensacola in 1973, demonstrated that quality activated carbon could be economically produced from pulp mill residue by hydropyrolysis, a new chemical recovery process. This was the culmination of a system development of which every industry could be envious: a manufacturing process whose waste created its own purifying agent. The ultimate result was that kraft pulp and papermaking systems could reuse as much as 90 percent of their primary water.

Local communities assisted in rectifying pollution problems at Tacoma, Jacksonville, Pensacola, and Deferiet. The port of Tacoma issued $30 million in industrial bonds to finance pollution-control facilities at the Tacoma mill. The Jacksonville Port Authority sold $13 million in industrial development revenue bonds to underwrite construction of similar antipollution installations at the local mill. Escambia County of Florida issued $35 million in industrial revenue development bonds for air-emission control measures at Pensacola. The Jefferson County Industrial Development Agency sold $7 million worth of bonds to support the establishment of treatment systems at Deferiet.

Through the early 1970s, St. Regis sharply accelerated pollution-abatement expenditures. In the first six years of the decade, it spent over $114 million on treatment facilities. The magnitude of this program can be seen by comparing it to the approximate $100 million cost of the Ferguson mill in Monticello. The company received awards for pollution-control improvements from the American Paper Institute, the Environmental Protection Agency, and the Izaak Walton League.

Despite this response to environmental problems, the image of both the company and the industry remains poor. William Haselton states the problem: "The paper industry in total has done a tremendous job. As industries go, they are probably the best—without exception. Credit: very little."[11]

St. Regis's vast timberland holdings give it strength and potential in a world of finite resources. Its many years of operation and research have developed knowledge of several areas of business, but it is the human factor that has shaped and directed St. Regis. It has been the company's leadership—Sherman, Anderson, Gould, Carlisle, Ferguson, Adams, and now Kneeland and Haselton—that has formulated a remarkable record of success.

William Haselton, current president and chief executive officer, as of June 1980, provides a brief contemporary analysis of both the industry and the company that relates to these statements:

> The industry is viewed as being reasonably well-managed—not spectacular in its ingenuity and aggressiveness—but I think this is reflected in the fact that we are in a commodity business tied to natural resources. . . . I think that in the league we play in, we are viewed probably as above average as far as management is concerned. We are viewed as being in a potentially improving sector because land is limited, and natural resource-based companies are now looked upon as better risks for the next ten years than perhaps they were on average for the last ten.[12]

Senior executives have often comprehended the complex nature of their industry and the free-enterprise system in which it operates. This degree of perception is indicated by board Chairman George Kneeland. Responding to the statement that "St. Regis looked overseas to establish facilities on foreign soil," Kneeland said in 1975:

> People say that, but they really don't understand this business:

you have to examine the long-range picture. For example, our Obbola mill will certainly do better in the future than it is right now. . . . My point is that this is just a matter of the times: this is why you build a paper machine, not for one year, but for fifty. . . . Some people are very narrow in their perspective. One of Roy Ferguson's great philosophies was "awareness of opportunity." Something may not look like an opportunity at the moment, but don't worry about it: if it is sound, it will be good in the future.[13]

The assessment has been made both by those within and without the industry that St. Regis is basically conservative in its orientation. Haselton accepts the label but asserts the soundness of that philosophy for the future of the company:

It has currently been very difficult to cast off the old and embrace the new, because we are by nature a somewhat conservative company. . . . In any event, being conservative is probably the better of the two choices if you are in business for the long pull.[14]

APPENDIX I:
St. Regis Executives

GEORGE EGGLESTON DODGE	President	1899 - 1900
GEORGE W. KNOWLTON, JR.	President	1900 - 1908
GORDIAS H. P. GOULD	President	1908 - 1916
FLOYD LESLIE CARLISLE	President	1916 - 1934
	Chairman of the Board	1934 - 1943
ROY K. FERGUSON	President	1934 - 1957
	Chairman of the Board	1948 - 1971
	Chief Executive Officer	1957 - 1963
WILLIAM R. ADAMS	President	1957 - 1971
	Chief Executive Officer	1963 - 1972
	Chairman of the Board	1971 - 1972
WILLIAM R. CALDWELL	President	1971 - 1973
GEORGE J. KNEELAND	Chairman of the Board	1972 -Date
	Chief Executive Officer	1972 - 1979
WILLIAM R. HASELTON	President	1973 -Date
	Chief Executive Officer	1979 -Date

APPENDIX II:
St. Regis Officers as of July 1, 1980

WILLIAM R. HASELTON
President and Chief Executive Officer

GEORGE J. KNEELAND
Chairman of the Board

EDWIN H. JONES, JR.
Vice chairman of the Board, Chief Financial Officer and Director of International Operations

MALCOLM T. HOPKINS
Executive Vice President—Finance and Administration

EDWARD J. McMAHON
Executive Vice President—Operations

JOHN P. BERDOLT
Senior Vice President—Financial Systems and Controls

MICHAEL T. BIONDO
Senior Vice President—Consumer and Specialty Products

JAMES N. BOWERSOCK
Senior Vice President—Pulp and Paper Products

B. T. EDWARDS
Senior Vice President—Timberlands and Construction Products

L. DAVID MOORE
Senior Vice President—Packaging and Machinery Products Group

KENNETH D. BAILEY
Vice President and General Manager—So. Timberlands Division

ROBERT M. BYRNES
Vice President—Human Resources

HOMER CRAWFORD
Vice President and Corporate Secretary

KERMIT GREENE
Vice President and General Manager—Laminated & Coated Products Division

J. DUDLEY HAUPT
Vice President—Corporate Communications

C. BROOKS NEWSOME
Vice President—Purchasing

ROBERT R. KOLLMEYER
Vice President—Corporate Engineering

ELMER J. LOSO
Treasurer

RUSSELL R. MAJOR
Vice President and General Auditor

JOHN R. MEISTER
Vice President and General Manager—Container Division

ROBERT E. MILKEY
Vice President—Administration

ROBERT L. MYERS
Vice President—Technology

SANFORD G. SCHELLER
Vice President and Divisional General Manager—Consumer Products Division

ROY J. SIPPEL
Vice President and Divisional General Manager—Flex. Packaging Division

S. KEPPLE PRATT
Vice President and Divisional General Manager—Kraft Division

J. WILLIAM PRICE
Vice President and General Manager—Southland Paper Division

TED L. ROBINSON
Vice President and Divisional General Manager—Printing Paper Division

WILLIAM H. VERSFELT, JR.
Vice President and Divisional General Manager—Bag Packaging Division

MICHAEL J. WALSH
Vice President—Transportation and Distribution

Notes

INTRODUCTION

1. Thomas C. Cochran, *Business in American Life: A History* (New York: McGraw-Hill Book Company, 1972), p. 6.

CHAPTER ONE

1. Samuel W. Durant and Henry B. Pierce, *History of Jefferson County, 1797-1878: Some of Its Prominent Men and Pioneers* (Philadelphia: L. H. Everts and Co., 1878), p. 9.

2. Howard W. Palmer, "Sale of Remington Mills to International in 1889," *Watertown* (N.Y.) *Daily Times*, scrapbook 74, art. VII. One of a series of numbered articles written in 1920 on the paper industry of northern New York. (Future references to the *Watertown Daily Times* will be cited as *WDT*.)

3. Watertown Manufacturers Aid Association, *Watertown, N.Y., A History of Its Settlement and Progress, with a Description of Its Commercial Advantages, as a Manufacturing Point, Its Location, Its Unsurpassed Water Power, Its Industries and General Features of Attraction to Capitalists and Manufacturers* (1876), p. 3.

4. Central Trades and Labor Assembly, Watertown, New York, *Official Labor Day Program, 1899, "The Garland City," Watertown, New York: Exercises to be Held at Glen Park, September 4, 1899* (n.p.).

5. Harry F. Landon, *150 Years of Watertown* (Watertown: *WDT*, 1950), p. 18.

6. Watertown Manufacturers Aid Association, *Watertown*, p. 37; Landon, *150 Years*, p. 20.

7. George S. Knowlton, memo, 1944. This memo was inserted in *WDT*, scrapbook 74.

8. *Knowlton Brothers: 150 Years of Craftsmanship in Paper* (n.p., 1958). This booklet was produced by the Knowlton Company.

9. David C. Smith, *History of Papermaking in the United States (1691-1969)* (New York: Lockwood Publishing Co., 1970), pp. 29-30, 34. The authors of *Knowlton Brothers* and Taggart D. Adams, "The St. Regis Paper Company: 1899-1941" (Senior essay, Hamilton College, 1963), p. 9 concur that a reference to a "shelf machine" in the Knowlton Brothers papers alludes to a fourdrinier. See Smith for the logical reasoning of this contention. The Knowlton 1944 memo suggests that a cylinder machine was installed.

10. See Knowlton memo, 1944. This source is cited in *Knowlton Brothers*.

11. Thomas C. Cochran, *Business in American Life: A History* (New York: McGraw-Hill Book Company, 1972), p. 145; Dan Cahill memoirs, in possession of John Johnson, editor and publisher of *WDT*, p. 34. Joel H. Monroe, *Through Eleven Decades of History: Watertown, A History from 1800 to 1912, with Illustrations and Many Incidents* (Watertown: Hungerford-Holbrook Co., 1912), p. 135.

12. Monroe, *Through Eleven Decades of History*, p. 135; Landon, *150 Years*, pp. 25, 27.

13. *WDT*, scrapbook 74, art. III; *Knowlton Brothers*; Knowlton memo, 1944; 74; and Smith, *History of Papermaking*, p. 24, offer differing accounts and chronologies of the brief period between the retirement of Knowlton and the subsequent formation of Knowlton Brothers.

14. *WDT*, scrapbook 74, arts. V-VII.

15. Discussion of the Taggart bag operations is based on ibid., art. IX, and Durant and Pierce, *History of Jefferson County*, p. 149.

16. *WDT*, scrapbook 74, art. IV. See Smith, *History of Papermaking*, p. 123.

17. Adams, "St. Regis Paper Company," p. 11.

18. Smith, *History of Papermaking*, pp. 121, 130.

19. Ibid., pp. 63-64.

20. For more complete discussion of the reciprocal impacts of different industries, see Cochran, *Business in American Life*, and Smith, *History of Papermaking*.

21. Smith, *History of Papermaking*, pp. 132-33.

22. *WDT*, scrapbook 74, art. XXII.

23. Durant and Pierce, *History of Jefferson County*, p. 149; *WDT* scrapbook 74, art. V; and Smith, *History of Papermaking*, p. 134.

24. *WDT*, scrapbook 74, art. V.

25. Ibid., art. XIII. R.A. Oakes, comp., *Genealogical and Family History of the County of Jefferson, N.Y.*, 2 v. (New York, Chicago: Lewis Publishing, 1905).

26. *WDT*, scrapbook 74, arts. I, XIV.

27. Central Trades and Labor Assembly, *Official Labor Day Program, 1899.*

28. Ibid.

29. Ibid.

CHAPTER TWO

1. U.S. Congress, House, *Pulp and Paper Investigation Hearings*, 60th Cong., 2d sess., 4 vols., 1908-09. 1:967.

2. Ibid., 1:849.

3. Eunice Remington Wardwell, Louise E. Richter, and Harold S. Sutton, "Three Memoirs on St. Regis Paper Company History," oral history interviews conducted by Elwood R. Maunder and John R. Ross (Santa Cruz, Calif.: Forest History Society, 1976), pp. 5-8. Copies of interviews are on file at the St. Regis Records Retention Center in Watertown, New York. For another account of the construction of the Remington mill at Glen Park, see *WDT*, scrapbook 74, art. VII.

4. "The St. Regis Paper Company Incorporated," *Paper Trade Journal*, 11 February 1899. (Future references to the *Paper Trade Journal* will be cited as *PTJ*.)

5. Wardwell, Richter, and Sutton, "Three Memoirs," pp. 14-15 (Wardwell interview). Wardwell is the daughter of the late C. H. Remington, which explains her reference to the Andersons as "being on the other side of the camp as far as business is concerned." For another description of Anderson, see Homer A. Vilas and James E. Kussmann, "Evolution of a Paper Company: The Carlisle-Ferguson Years at St. Regis," oral history interviews conducted by Elwood R. Maunder and John R. Ross (Santa Cruz, Calif.: Forest History Society, 1977), p. 89.

6. Robert A. Rutland, *The Newsmongers: Journalism in the Life of the Nation, 1690-1972* (New York: Dial Press, 1973), pp. 253-55; Sidney Kobre, *Development of American Journalism* (Dubuque, Iowa: William C. Brown, 1969), pp. 349-55, 521-26; Allan Hutt, *The Changing Newspaper: Typographical Trends in Britain and America, 1622-1972* (London: Gordon Fraser, 1973), pp. 43-87; Edwin Emery, *The Press and America: An Interpretive History of the Mass Media* (Englewood Cliffs, N.J.: Prentice-Hall, 1972), pp. 333-34, 342-43.

7. Kobre, *Development*, pp. 493-507; Hutt, *Changing Newspaper*, pp. 78, 83; Emery, *Press and America*, pp. 333-34.

8. L. Ethan Ellis, "Print Paper Pendulum," appendix to Ellis, *Newsprint: Producers, Publishers, and Political Pressures* (New Brunswick, N.J.: Rutgers University Press, 1960), p. 10 and n. 1; "Watertown," *PTJ*, 16 April 1898. A general assessment of American business appears in the remarks of International Paper's Hugh J. Chisholm in *PTJ*, 4 June 1898.

9. *PTJ*, 28 May 1898, p. 452; Harold T. Pinkett, *Gifford Pinchot: Private and Public Forester* (Urbana, Ill.: University of Illinois Press, 1970), p. 32.

10. Gifford Pinchot, "The Sustained Yield of Spruce Lands," *PTJ*, 19 February 1898.

11. Andrew Denny Rodgers III, *Bernhard Eduard Fernow: A Story of North American Forestry* (Princeton, N. J.: Princeton University Press, 1951), pp. 260, 268.

12. House, *Pulp and Paper Investigation Hearings*, 1:881.

13. Ellis, "Print Paper Pendulum," p. 9.

14. Addresses by George C. Sherman, *PTJ* convention supplements, 19 February 1898, 18 February 1899.

15. "Paper Stock Soaring," *PTJ*, 27 August 1898; Ellis, "Print Paper Pendulum," pp. 24-25. In contrast to Ellis's estimate of IP's market percentage, George Sherman estimated IP's percentage of market in 1908 to be no more than one-third. See House, *Pulp and Paper Investigation Hearings*, pp. 961-62.

16. Address by George W. Knowlton, *PTJ* convention supplement, 15 February 1902.

17. *PTJ*, 16 April 1898, p. 317; Ellis, "Print Paper Pendulum," p. 25.

18. Address by George C. Sherman, *PTJ* convention supplement, 18 February 1899.

19. House, *Pulp and Paper Investigation Hearings*, 1:961-62.

20. *PTJ*, 13 September 1900, p. 323, 1 January 1898, p. 1, 7 May 1898, p. 396, 11 March 1899, p. 206.

21. Vilas and Kussmann, "Evolution of a Paper Company," p. 89. Other descriptions of the alleged contest for waterpower rights between St. Regis and IP appear in "The St. Regis Paper Company Incorporated," *PTJ*, 11 February 1899; "Sharp Contest for the Great Bend Water Power," ibid., 25 February 1899; *WDT*, scrapbook 74, art. XVII; and in a clipping from an unknown northern New York newspaper entitled, "Our Million Dollar Paper Plant to Rival the Paper Trust Which Tried to Kill It." The clipping was contributed to St. Regis by Jeannie Fox, an employee of the company, who believes that the article came from a Carthage, New York, newspaper.

22. Elisha P. Douglass, *The Coming of Age of American Business* (Chapel Hill: University of North Carolina Press, 1971), pp. 397-98. Phelps-Dodge developed from New England origins in about the 1830s and was involved in metal imports and exports until becoming involved

in the brass industry of the Naugatuck Valley of Connecticut. The company also speculated in metals and toward the end of the century developed one of the major copper mining enterprises in the West.

23. Data on the Dodge-Meigs interests are drawn from: "The St. Regis Paper Company Incorporated," *PTJ*, 11 February 1899; from *WDT*, 9 October 1941, 11 May 1943; and from law papers on file in the Jefferson County (N.Y.) Courthouse.

24. See *New Catholic Encyclopedia* (New York: McGraw-Hill, 1967), vol. 12; *Butler's Lives of the Saints* (1956), vol. 2.

25. Franklin B. Hough, *A History of St. Lawrence and Franklin Counties, New York, from the Earliest Period to the Present Time* (Albany, N.Y.: Little and Co., 1853) (facsimile edition; Baltimore: Regional Publishing Company, 1970), pp. 111-16, 176-77. See also T. Wood Clarke, *Emigres in the Wilderness* (Port Washington, N.Y.: Ira J. Friedman, 1967), pp. 182-94.

26. St. Regis Paper Company, Articles of Incorporation, 26 January 1899. See also *PTJ*, 11 February 1899.

27. St. Regis Paper Company, Minutes of Board Meetings, 28 February 1905, 9 April 1900, 11 February 1902. (St. Regis Paper Company, Minutes of Board Meeting, hereafter cited as Minutes.)

28. Ferris Meigs to George C. Sherman, 1 June 1899; Titus B. Meigs to Sherman, 2 June 1899; both in St. Regis Records Retention Center, Watertown, N.Y. (Future references will be WRC.)

29. Manufacturers Paper is described in the prospectus for St. Regis's first mortgage bond issue as follows:

> The Manufacturers Paper Company has been established for many years, and was the outgrowth of the sales department of the Hudson River Paper Co., the Montague Paper Co., and the Turners Falls Paper Co., all of which have been lately absorbed into the International Paper Company. The St. Regis Paper Company and the Taggarts Paper Co. have made substantially the same arrangements with the Manufacturers Paper Company as were formerly held by the Hudson River, the Montague, and the Turners Falls Paper Companies.

See also "To Sell St. Regis Paper," *PTJ*, 15 April 1899; Minutes, 22 March 1899.

30. Minutes, 11, 12 April, 12 July 1899.

31. It seems probable that Agricultural Insurance Company did consummate the informal agreement to purchase the bonds, although absolute proof of this has not been discovered. See Minutes, 19, 29, 31 May, 12 July 1899. Also see *WDT*, 1 November 1960, for a discussion of the Agricultural Insurance Company and Anderson's affiliation with it.

32. There is extensive coverage of work at the St. Regis millsite in *PTJ*,

under the following titles and dates: "The St. Regis Paper Company Incorporated," 11 February 1899, pp. 101-04; "Work on the Water Power," 15 April 1899, p. 309; "Correspondence: Northern New York," 6 May 1899, p. 378; "Correspondence: Northern New York," 13 May 1899, p. 399; "Correspondence: Northern New York," 20 May 1899, p. 434; "Work at St. Regis Mill Site," 3 June 1899, p. 7; "Carthage's New Industry," 10 June 1899, p. 44; "Estimates for St. Regis Mill," 13 July 1899, p. 201; "News from the Mills," 20 July 1899, p. 246; "Work at the St. Regis Plant," 27 July 1899, p. 265; "Northern New York Notes," 3 August 1899, p. 300; "Work at St. Regis," 24 August 1899, p. 408; "In Northern New York," 5 October 1899, p. 588. See also *WDT*, scrapbook 74, art. XVII; and Vilas and Kussmann, "Evolution of a Paper Company," p. 90.

33. "In Northern New York," *PTJ*, 5 October 1899, p. 588.

34. Original canal contract and amendments are in the F. A. Hinds Papers, Deferiet Mill. Copies of these are attached to *St. Regis Paper Company* v. *Metropolitan Paving and Construction Company et al.* Complaint, Deposition, and Exhibits (Sup. Ct. Jefferson County, 20 April 1899; Appellate Div. Sup. Ct. New York State, 27 April 1899; Sup. Ct. Onondaga County, 5 May 1900), on file at Jefferson County Courthouse, Watertown, N.Y.

35. Meigs to Sherman, 1 June 1899, WRC.

36. Ibid.; Minutes, 15 June 1899.

37. "Work at St. Regis," *PTJ*, 24 August 1899, p. 408; "Decision Reversed in Pulp Wood Case," *PTJ*, 22 November 1900, p. 654. See also House, *Pulp and Paper Investigation Hearings*, 1:851. This testimony contains a typographical error: "1200" should read "12,000."

38. Titus B. Meigs to Sherman, 2 June 1899, WRC.

39. Ibid.; George E. Dodge to John P. Badger, 22 November 1899.

40. Henry S. Graves to F. Meigs, 24 March 1897, Record Group 95, Records of the Forest Service, National Archives.

41. Pinchot to F. Meigs, 21 April 1899, 17 May 1899, Pinchot to Ferris J. Meigs, 9 May 1899, RG 95.

42. Pinchot to F. Meigs, 17 May 1899, Dodge to Badger, 22 November 1899, RG 95.

43. Dodge to Badger, 22 November 1899, WRC.

44. Dodge to Sherman, 25 April 1899, RG 95.

45. Minutes, 4 January, 15 May 1900.

46. Dodge to Badger, 22 November 1899, WRC.

47. Minutes, 3 January 1902.

48. Ibid., 4 April 1899, 21 November 1901, 25 September 1902.

49. House, *Pulp and Paper Investigation Hearings*, 1:943. For additional information regarding Alvah Miller's relationship to St. Regis, see Minutes, 9 April, 15 May 1900.

50. Rockefeller's program of land acquisition is chronicled in *PTJ:* 17 June, 20 July 1899, 9 January 1902; Minutes, 29 June, 10 July 1900.

51. Details of the case can be found in the complaint in *St. Regis Paper Company* v. *Metropolitan Paving and Construction Company et al.*, and in pertinent contracts and depositions in the F. A. Hinds Papers, Deferiet, New York, with copies at the Jefferson County Courthouse in Watertown, N.Y.

52. *PTJ*, 22 November 1900, p. 654; Minutes, 12 September 1900.

53. The St. Regis archives in New York City contain copies of some of the legal papers from *St. Regis Paper Company* v. *Santa Clara Lumber Company and Brooklyn Cooperage Company*.

54. *PTJ*, 15 January 1903, 18 May 1905, 11 October 1906, 18 July 1907.

55. Progress in St. Regis construction appears in *PTJ* under the following headings and dates: "Pushing Work on the St. Regis Mill," 21 June 1900; "News from the Mills," 12 July 1900; "Pushing Work on the St. Regis Mill," 23 August 1900; "Among the Mills," 4 October 1900; "News from the Mills," 1 November 1900; "Work at the St. Regis Mill," 13 December 1900; "Notes of the Trade," 3 January 1901; "Among the Mills," 28 February 1901; "News From the Mills," 7 March 1901.

56. Clarke, *Emigres in the Wilderness*, pp. 154-64; Minutes, 15 May 1901.

57. *WDT*, illustrated supplement, 30 October 1901.

CHAPTER THREE

1. Smith, *History of Papermaking*, p. 198.

2. *PTJ*, 5 December 1907.

3. *Paper Mill News*, 9 February 1907, p. 138.

4. Smith, *History of Papermaking*, p. 210.

5. *PTJ*, 29 May 1902.

6. Ibid., 19 December 1901.

7. *Encyclopedia of American History*, Bicentennial Ed., s.v. "Panic of 1907."

8. *PTJ*, 25 May 1911.

9. Ibid., 11 October 1906.

10. Ibid., 6 November 1907. George Knowlton stated in 1908: "While we claim to have won the suit . . . our loss by the abrogation of that contract is not less than $250,000, so we have to concede a loss, all told, of $300,000." Minutes, 10 June 1908.

11. *PTJ*, 10 October 1907.

12. Alfred L. Donaldson, *History of the Adirondacks* (1921; reprinted ed., New York: Century, 1977), 2:157.

13. *PTJ*, 22 August 1907.

14. Rodgers, *Fernow*, p. 277.

15. *PTJ*, 25 June 1903.

16. Rodgers, *Fernow*, p. 324.

17. New York State later enjoined the cutting on the contention that the forest was subject to cutting restrictions the state constitution and the courts found for the state. Ibid., p. 322.

18. Hearings before the New York State joint Senate and Assembly Forest Fish and Game Committees on Senate Bill No. 92, 20 February 1912. For a further discussion of Pinchot's role in this issue, see *PTJ*, 8 February 1906, 4 July 1907, 2 December 1911.

19. Wardwell, Richter, and Sutton, "Three Memoirs," pp. 1, 23.

20. *PTJ*, 6 February 1908.

21. House, *Pulp and Paper Investigation Hearings*, 1:852.

22. Thirty to fifty carloads were shipped daily from Brandreth Lake to Deferiet, *PTJ*, 13 February 1913. The Brandreth Lake purchase included all pulpwood on a tract of 30,000 acres, and J. N. MacDonald, a Carthage lumberman, was to operate the tract for St. Regis. Ibid., 29 February 1913. In 1909 St. Regis purchased about 7 million feet of timber from T. B. Basselin, whose sawmill had burned down that year. Ibid., 8 July 1909. In 1909 International Paper held 250,000 acres and Gould Paper Company, 118,000 acres. Ibid., 11 March 1909.

23. Ibid., 13 February 1908, 7 February 1907.

24. Ibid., 19 September 1901, 27 March 1902, 12 May 1904.

25. Ibid., 6 August 1903, 2 July 1908, 13 March 1902. In 1901 several eastern newsprint paper mills reduced hours from seventy-eight per week to sixty-five; this reduction of hours was accomplished without a reduction of wages and even some increases. Ibid., 4 June 1908.

26. Affidavit, Union Litigation, Supreme Court, Jefferson County, 19 March 1903, 11 April 1903; *PTJ*, 2 March, 2 April 1903.

27. *PTJ*, 2 April 1903, 9 June 1904.

28. Ibid., 7 November 1907; House, *Pulp and Paper Investigation Hearings*, 1:933.

29. *PTJ*, 22 October 1908.

30. Ibid., 29 October 1908.

31. Ellis, "Print Paper Pendulum," pp. 29, 34. See also Smith, *History of Papermaking*, pp. 206-07.

32. *PTJ*, 13 March 1902, 26 March 1903, 9 June 1904.

33. Ibid., 2 July 1908.

34. House, *Pulp and Paper Investigation Hearings*, 1:949.

35. *WDT*, 20 December 1915.

36. House, *Pulp and Paper Investigation Hearings*, 1:155; Ellis, "Paper Print Pendulum," p. 36.

37. Gardner later confessed that "the St. Regis people . . . lost money on our contract." House, *Pulp and Paper Investigation Hearings*, 1:572. Gardner showed an ambiguous compassion when he testified that although the papermakers might be "good fellows," they were "under orders to crucify us, and they do it, but they do it with as much consideration as possible, that is all." Ibid., 1:573.

38. See *PTJ*, 23 August 1906, 30 April 1908.

39. House, *Pulp and Paper Investigation Hearings*, 1:353-54.

40. Ibid., 1:933.

41. Ibid., 3:1978-79, 1987.

42. Ibid., 1:941.

43. The price of newsprint had actually been growing steadily for several years. In July 1902, it was $1.34 per hundred pounds, $1.39 in 1903, $1.41 in 1904, $1.54 in 1905, $1.52 in 1906, $1.59 in 1907, and $1.65 in 1908. Thus the price increases were certainly not unusual. See ibid., 1:944.

44. Ellis, "Print Paper Pendulum," p. 52.

45. Ibid., p. 50.

46. House, *Pulp and Paper Investigation Hearings*, 1:951-52.

47. Ellis, "Print Paper Pendulum," p. 21.

48. Ibid., pp. 78-80, 88, 84.

49. Knowlton's resignation statement is unsigned and undated, and is recorded in Minutes, 10 June 1908. See also Vilas and Kussmann, "Evolution of a Paper Company," appended interview with Carl B. Martin, p. 105.

50. Clarence L. Fisher, *History of Lyons Falls* (Boonville, N.Y.: Willard Press, 1918), pp. 24-25.

51. Ibid.

52. "Development of the Gould Paper Company," *WDT*, scrapbook 74, describes Gould as humble. Eunice Remington Wardwell remembers that Gould brooked no disobedience in Wardwell, Richter, and Sutton, "Three Memoirs," pp. 9, 13.

53. *PTJ*, 21 February 1909.

54. Ibid., 12, 19 August, 2 September 1909.

55. Minutes, 13 February 1912, 14 October 1913.

56. *WDT*, scrapbook 74, art. XVIII, 1920; Wardwell, Richter, and Sutton, "Three Memoirs," pp. 5, 9.

57. *WDT*, scrapbook 74; *PTJ*, 2 February 1912; Clarence A. Nugent, "First Operations at Herrings Mill Commenced in 1892," *St. Regis Northeasterner* (July-August 1964).

58. *WDT*, 1 November 1960; *PTJ*, 13 February 1908.

59. *PTJ*, 20 August 1914; Minutes, 15 September 1914. The company's officers at the time of Anderson's resignation were: Gould, president; Alvah Miller (representing H. G. Craig), vice-president; Sherman, secretary-treasurer; J. M. Sexsmith, assistant secretary-treasurer; Anderson, general

manager; and J. V. Baron, assistant general manager. See Minutes, 8 June 1914.

60. Minutes, 22 September 1914.

61. Ibid.

62. Ibid., 8 June 1915, notes his continued participation.

63. *PTJ*, 9 November 1916; *WDT*, 30 June 1920.

64. *WDT*, 3 May 1915; Smith, *History of Papermaking*, p. 232.

65. Letter of John H. Malin to D. J. O'Keefe, 24 June 1915; General Circular, 17 May 1915, IBPSPMW Executive Files.

66. Tylcoff to Malin, 26 April 1915, ibid. Tylcoff was loaned to Malin by the AFL to help organize the IBPSPMW.

67. *PTJ*, 13 May 1915.

68. Ibid., 12 April 1915; *WDT*, 12 April 1915; *New York Times*, 3 September 1915.

69. *PTJ*, 20 May, 13 June 1915. Many of the strikers were Polish, while the imported strikebreakers were mostly Italian. Ethnic conflicts between the two groups as well as competition for unskilled mill jobs were volatile factors in the conflict. IBPSPMW Labor General Circular, 21 March 1917. For list of strikebreakers, see *Paper Makers Journal* (October 1915): 45.

70. *PTJ*, 27 May 1915.

71. *WDT*, 29 May, 9 August 1915.

72. *PTJ*, 24 June, 19 August 1915; *WDT*, 11 August 1915.

73. *WDT*, 3 September, 20 December 1915.

74. Minutes, 13 October 1915; *PTJ*, 2, 23 September 1915; *WDT*, 6 September 1915.

75. IBPSPMW General Circular, 1 November 1915; *Paper Makers Journal* (August 1915): 10.

76. IBPSPMW, Circular Letters, 27 January, 11 April 1916; *PTJ*, 30 November 1916; Minutes, 1, 13 December 1916.

77. *PTJ*, 28 December 1916; Minutes, 14 March 1917. IBPSPMW, Circular Letters, 1, 20 March 1917.

78. Minutes, 1 December 1916.

79. Gould's share of the common and preferred stock in the company, together with proxies, and his son's interest, totaled 90 percent of the outstanding shares. Ibid., 17 May 1915; *WDT*, 10 October, 24 November 1916.

80. *PTJ*, 30 November 1916; *WDT*, 7 December 1916.

81. *PTJ*, 21 December 1916.

CHAPTER FOUR

1. *PTJ*, 6 May 1899, 29 January 1903, 31 January 1907, 6 January 1910; *WDT*, scrapbook 74, art. XIV, 1920; House, *Pulp and Paper Investigation Hearings*, 1:967.

2. *PTJ*, 28 January 1909, 1 October 1908.

3. Ibid., 13 January 1910. In 1907 Wisconsin became the first state to approve a water storage law. This act allowed power companies to use water dammed in reservoirs. Ibid., 27 June 1907.

4. See ibid., 6, 13 January 1910, 12 March, 17 October 1907.

5. Ibid., 6 January 1910, 14 March 1912. Smith's opinion was shared by Gifford Pinchot who stated that waterpower was "a natural monopoly" beneficial only as long as it remained supervised by government. Ibid., 30 November 1911.

6. *WDT*, scrapbook 74, art. XIV, 1920; *PTJ*, 15 November 1906; Smith, *History of Papermaking*, p. 161.

7. *WDT*, scrapbook 74, art. XXIX, 1920; Roy K. Ferguson, preliminary draft for Newcomen Address on St. Regis Paper Company and the Paper Industry; *WDT*, scrapbook 74, art. XXIX, 1920.

8. Testimony of Floyd L. Carlisle before the Commission on Revision of the Public Service Law of New York State, 19, 20 December 1929.

9. *PTJ*, 20 May 1909, 13 April 1916. Carlisle, who was one of the original members of the league, served as a director in 1912 and as third vice-president in 1916. Ibid., 24 June 1909, 28 March 1912, 16 March 1916. The passage of the 1915 Machold law, which gave power site owners the right to "form reservoir districts and regulate the flow of streams for the purpose of developing their water power," was attributed to the efforts of the league. Although later found unconstitutional, the law inspired Gould to formulate plans for a new local organization to implement its provisions. Because of the protracted labor strike of 1915-1917, he was unable to devote the necessary energy and time to that undertaking. Ibid., 25 November 1915.

10. Ferguson, Newcomen Address, p. 5.

11. *PTJ*, 12 November 1942.

12. St. Regis, Minutes of Stockholders Special Meeting, 11 June 1917.

13. Carlisle, testimony, 19, 20 December 1929.

14. *WDT*, 30 April 1921; Minutes, 17 October 1922; *WDT*, 6 June 1927; *PTJ*, 15 May 1913; *WDT*, scrapbook 74, 1920; *WDT*, 30 November 1920.

15. *WDT*, 1 December 1920.

16. *PTJ*, 18 May 1922.

17. See *WDT*, April-May 1921. On 30 April 1921, John N. Carlisle reported that the Northern New York Utilities Company was engaged in a reforestation project that had grown one-half million young trees that year and planned to plant an additional 100,000. *PTJ*, 5 February 1920. President F. L. Carlisle stated that combining the timberlands of the company and of its affiliates guaranteed future wood supply requirements for the next thirty years. St. Regis Paper Company, Annual Report, 1927; *PTJ*,

14 April 1927. (St. Regis Paper Company, Annual Report, hereafter cited as Annual Report.)

18. Oral history interview with H. V. "Pete" Hart conducted by Elwood R. Maunder at Fort Myers Beach, Florida, 10 April 1976, [10]. See also oral history interview with Paul M. Dunn conducted by Elwood R. Maunder at Corvallis, Oregon, 22 August 1977. The Carlisles' concern for reforestation is evidenced by their long-term membership in the New York Forestry Association and the Empire Forest Products Association; Floyd Carlisle was a sponsor of the Forestry School of St. Lawrence University. At the time of John Carlisle's death in 1931, the *PTJ* credited his influence for the initiation of industrial forestry by the Carlisle interests. *PTJ*, 12 November 1942, 30 July 1931.

19. Oral history interview with Andrew F. Storer, session I, conducted by John R. Ross, New York City, 17 September 1975, [3]; Minutes, 15 January, 30 September 1920.

20. Minutes, 4 November 1920; *WDT*, 6 November 1920; *PTJ*, 18 May 1922, 6 November 1924.

21. *PTJ*, 11 November 1920, 14 August, 11 September 1924, 25 November 1926, 23 June 1927; Hart interview, [8].

22. *PTJ*, 14 April 1921.

23. Ibid., 21 April 1921.

24. Ibid., 5 May 1921.

25. Ibid., 28 April 1921. Included in the list of paper companies holding such a position were St. Regis, Union Bag and Paper Company, International Paper Company, Sherman Paper Company, and nine others. See ibid., 2, 23 June 1921.

26. Ibid., 18 August, 6 October 1921.

27. Ibid., 4 May 1922. IP had been one of the original companies represented by Carlisle. Early in the dispute, IP broke away to initiate separate negotiations, and it established the open shop. Ibid., 18 August 1921, 20 April 1922.

28. Ibid., 27 April, 11 May 1922. Due to the abundance of unskilled laborers, strikebreaking became an additional method of undermining labor solidarity. The issue of standardized wage scales for unskilled labor was serious since approximately 50 percent of total union membership was drawn from this group. Ibid., 4 May 1922.

29. Ibid., 18 May 1922, 3 May 1923. The threatened radicalization of the unions did not materialize. Conservative labor leaders feared that the continuation of a hard line by management would push local leaders toward endorsement of Industrial Workers of the World policies, as had occurred in the case of woodsmen and lumbermen. Ibid., 11 May 1922.

30. Ibid., 25, 3 May, 3 August 1922.

31. Cochran, *Business in American Life*, pp. 161-62.

32. Roy K. Ferguson, "Remarks for the Orientation Meeting of April 4, 1955," p. 4, St. Regis Archives, New York City.

33. *WDT*, 25 November 1921.

34. Oral history interview with George J. Kneeland conducted by Elwood R. Maunder at New York City, 9 December 1975, session II, [5]. Wardwell, Richter, and Sutton, "Three Memoirs," p. 34.

35. Biography of H. Edmund Machold, *WDT*, February 1966 and 10 January 1916; Minutes, 14 January 1925.

36. IP and Great Northern are listed as numbers one and two. *PTJ*, 27 October, 3 November 1921, 19 January 1922; Minutes, 11 December 1922.

37. *PTJ*, 30 October 1924; *WDT*, 24 November, 5 December 1924.

38. See Carlisle, testimony, 19, 20 December 1929 (regarding Carlisle power network); Minutes, 17, 23 October 1922; *PTJ*, 2 November 1922.

39. *PTJ*, 17 January 1924; Minutes, 14 April 1926.

40. Minutes, 11 December 1925; Annual Reports, 1926, 1927.

41. Ferguson, Newcomen Address, p. 4; Ellis, "Print Paper Pendulum," pp. 117-23. From the first quarter of 1921 until the first quarter of 1922, the price of newsprint per ton fell from $130 to $70. The $70 rate remained fairly stable the following year, but by mid-1924 prices steadily dropped and continued to fall during the rest of the decade. This decrease in the price of newsprint precluded any further need for investigation by the government. Small manufacturers and small publishers had increasingly urged such investigations in the early 1920s after World War I government price controls had been lifted. Ellis, "Print Paper Pendulum," pp. 101, 111, 113, 114.

42. See Annual Reports, 1926, 1927, 1930; Ferguson, Newcomen Address, p. 5.

43. *WDT*, 4 December 1924; *Watertown Standard*, 19 February 1926; *PTJ*, 11 March 1926; Hart interview, [9].

44. Annual Report, 1926; St. Regis bought out IP's one-third share in the Vermont-New Hampshire tract in 1927; Annual Report, 1927. *PTJ*, 13 January 1927; Dunn interview, [69-70].

45. Annual Report, 1927; *WDT*, 27 January 1937.

46. Annual Report, 1928. This is the first listing of Panelyte Corporation. Annual Report, 1930; Ferguson, Newcomen Address, p. 9.

47. Testimonial Dinner, St. Regis Inn, 29 January 1942, Deferiet Files; *WDT*, 25 June 1928.

48. Wardwell, Richter, and Sutton, "Three Memoirs," p. 37; Ferguson, Newcomen Address, p. 8.

49. See T. H. Cosford, "A History of the Bates Valve Bag Company of West Virginia," unpublished manuscript (n.d.), and Edgar H. Hoppe,

"History of the Development of the Bates Valve Bag Packaging System," unpublished manuscript (1942), both in WRC.

50. Annual Report, 1930.

51. Ibid., 1930, 1931.

52. Ibid., 1927, 1930.

53. "Add to Tycoons," *Fortune* (August 1930): 51; *PTJ*, 9 January 1930; Annual Report, 1929.

54. Annual Reports, 1929, 1924, 1931; FTC Corporate Chart of the United Corporation as of December 1931, WRC.

55. Annual Reports, 1932, 1933, 1934, 1935, 1936.

56. Ibid., 1931, 1932, 1933.

57. Minutes, 13 June 1934; Annual Reports, 1925, 1927, 1928, 1930; Ferguson, "Remarks for the Orientation Meeting," p. 4.

CHAPTER FIVE

1. Roy K. Ferguson, "Address to the First Annual Meeting of the Multiwall Bag Division of the St. Regis Paper Company," WRC.

2. Oral history interview with Hugh W. Sloan conducted by James E. Kussmann, Elwood R. Maunder, and Mark H. Neuffer, New York City, 8 February 1977, [6]; oral history interview with William R. Adams conducted by Elwood R. Maunder at New York City, 9 December 1975, session II, [34].

3. Sloan interview, [22].

4. Oral history interview with Charles A. Woodcock conducted by John R. Ross at New York City, 27 October 1975, session II, [1]; Minutes, 2 February 1938.

5. Adams interview, session I; Woodcock interview, session II, [1-2]; Annual Report, 1921.

6. Minutes, 25 November 1936; Annual Report, 1936.

7. Ibid.

8. Annual Reports, 1938, 1940, 1941, 1942, 1943.

9. *PTJ*, 11 June 1931. The cultural grades of paper, however, did not fare as well as did board and wrapping grades. This poor performance was linked to the advertising industry, which recovered only after general business and sales had stabilized. During the early years of the depression, all advertising, except radio time, reflected the slump. The encroachment of radio upon newspaper advertising further reduced demand in this area. In 1930 major advertisers reduced their newspaper coverage by 12.5 percent but increased their radio advertising expenditures by 63 percent.

10. Ibid.

11. Ibid., 16 February, 19 January 1933.

12. Ibid., 20 February 1930.

13. Ibid., 18 February 1932, 19 February 1931.

14. Ibid., 2 February 1934. Not everyone sang the praises of the NRA, however. Royal S. Kellogg, forester and newsprint trade association executive, later recalled that the program was a mistake and that it did not benefit the paper industry at all: "All NRA ever did for the paper industry was to increase its manufacturing costs." Oral history interview with Royal S. Kellogg conducted by Elwood R. Maunder, Palmetto, Florida, 16 April 1955, [31-32].

15. Edward R. Gay, "The National Recovery Act and How It Affects Us," *Sixty East* (June 1933): 2.

16. *PTJ*, 22 February 1934.

17. "Codes and Cartels," *St. Regis-Bates Monthly News* (March 1935):1.

18. Annual Reports, 1936, 1937; "Notes on Paper Industry," 25 August 1937. This manuscript was found in company files in New York City and appears to be a report written by an outside management consultant.

19. Minutes, 22 May, 19 June 1935.

20. Annual Reports, 1939, 1937.

21. Ibid., 1936, 1937; Minutes, 22 July 1936; *PTJ*, 20 August 1936; "Notes on the Paper Industry," 25 August 1937.

22. Interview with Charles A. Woodcock conducted by John R. Ross, New York City, 24 September 1975, session I, [5-6].

23. Minutes, 19 November 1941; "Sixty East," *St. Regis-Bates Monthly News* (September 1941).

24. *PTJ*, 24 August 1933, 22 February 1934. Annual Report, 1940. *PTJ*, 22 July 1937. The Raymondville mill was sold in 1943.

25. Oral history interview with George J. Kneeland conducted by Elwood R. Maunder, New York City, 8 December 1975, session I, [6-7].

26. See Annual Reports 1937-1940. Kneeland interview, session I, [7]. Ted Gay, who served as director of the General Commodities Division of the War Production Board, reached a different conclusion about federal regulations. He believed they "were equitable because no one was satisfied" and that more stringent measures would be forthcoming "unless substantially greater conservation measures [in the uses of paper] are put into effect by business." *PTJ*, 17 February 1944.

27. Ferguson, Newcomen Address, p. 11.

28. Adams interview, session I, [28].

29. *PTJ*, 5 March 1942, 3 July 1941; See also ibid., 26 November 1942, 18 February, 23 March 1943, 18 May 1944; Annual Report, 1942; Ferguson, Newcomen Address, p. 11.

30. *PTJ*, 27 March 1941; Woodcock interview, session II, [8]; *PTJ*, 2 October 1941, 19 February 1942; Adams interview, session I, [30].

31. Annual Reports, 1942, 1943. See also Minutes, 20 May 1942.

32. Minutes, 17 July, 26 September, 25 October, 12 December 1944; Annual Report, 1944; *PTJ*, 4 October 1945.

33. Adams interview, session I, [6].

34. *PTJ*, 26 November 1942; oral history interview with Gardiner Lane conducted by Mark H. Neuffer, Bolton, Vermont, 8 June 1977, [6-9].

35. Woodcock interview, sessions I, II, provides information for this section.

36. Annual Report, 1944; oral history interview with Kenneth D. Lozier conducted by Elwood R. Maunder, Pompano Beach, Florida, 16 March 1977, [12-13].

37. Annual Reports, 1942, 1943.

38. See *PTJ*, 2 March, 14 December 1939, 26 September, 9 May, 2 February 1940; Annual Report, 1942.

39. Annual Reports, 1942, 1943, 1944.

40. Minutes, 15 December 1942, 8 December 1943; Annual Reports, 1942, 1943.

41. Minutes, 18 June 1941.

42. See Annual Reports, 1934-1944, for data relating to the following section.

43. Kellogg interview, [32]. *PTJ*, 4 June 1936. See also *PTJ*, 13 May 1937, 9 June, 19 May 1938, 28 May 1942 for coverage of St. Regis-Union negotiations.

44. *PTJ*, 20 June 1935.

45. Archibald Carswell, "Address to the First Annual Meeting of the Multiwall Bag Division of the St. Regis Paper Company," WRC.

CHAPTER SIX

1. St. Regis Paper Company, *International Division Monthly Bulletin* (January 1947): 1.

2. William R. Adams, "Remarks at a Meeting of the New York Society of Security Analysts, Incorporated, on August 2, 1962."

3. Marshall McLuhan, *Understanding Media: The Extensions of Man* (New York: McGraw-Hill, 1964), pp. 7-21, 45.

4. *PTJ*, 5 July 1945, 27 February 1947, 26 August 1948.

5. Oral history interview with J. McHenry Jones conducted by Elwood R. Maunder, Pensacola, Florida, 21 March 1977, [22-24, 42-50].

6. *PTJ*, 25 August 1949, 3 March, 3 November 1958.

7. Annual Reports, 1939, 1947. St. Regis's position as a major force in

the paper industry was indicated by its statistical comparison with the other two ranking leaders, International Paper and Crown Zellerbach. See "Relative Sales Position of North American Companies Which Reported Sales of Paper and Paper Products above $100,000,000 in Their Fiscal Years Covered by This Statistical Comparison," *PTJ*, 15 July 1957.

8. For detailed account of St. Regis's move into the South, see Jones interview. See also oral history interview with Marcus Rawls conducted by Elwood R. Maunder, Jacksonville, Florida, 16 April 1976; Hart interview, [16-18].

9. Information and figures for discussion of St. Regis's rise in the postwar period are drawn from Annual Reports, 1945-1960.

10. Documentation in the Time Inc. Archives, New York City, covers a wide range of relations with St. Regis. See also Storer interview, session I, [5]. Annual Reports, 1945, 1946; oral history interview with Jack W. Hartung conducted by John R. Ross, New York City, 8 October 1975, [1]. For additional comments on the Time operations, see oral history interview with Jack E. Wilber conducted by Mark H. Neuffer, New York City, 18 July 1977.

11. Minutes, 20 June 1951, 13 April, 20 June 1956; Annual Report, 1956.

12. Hartung interview, [1, 5].

13. Minutes, 20 March 1946, 21 June 1950. See also Adams interview, session II, [24]; *PTJ*, 7 February 1946.

14. For fuller detail and excellent pictures of working conditions in the cement industry, see *Packaging Magic: The Story of Packaging in the Cement Industry* (New York: St. Regis Paper Company, 1958). The history of the Bates Valve Bag Company has received the most thorough study of any part of St. Regis history. Cosford, "History of the Bates Valve Bag Company," traces the origins of the first prominent St. Regis subsidiary. Two other histories written by former St. Regis employees are also valuable sources: O. R. Johnson, "St. Regis Overseas Operations: 1923-1964" and Hoppe, "History of the Development."

15. Minutes, 13 December 1950, 10 December 1952. See also Kussmann interview II, session I, 17 October 1975, pp. 43-44; Sloan interview, [4-10]; Kneeland interview, session II, 9 December 1975, [22].

16. Inman F. Eldredge, *The Four Forests and the Future of the South* (Washington, D.C.: Charles Lathrop Pack Foundation, 1947), provides a rich insight into the development of southern forest resources. See also Inman F. Eldredge, et al, *Voices from the South: Recollections of Four Foresters* (Santa Cruz, Calif.: Forest History Society, 1977), pp. v-ix, 1-62, 222-28.

17. *PTJ*, 26 August 1937. See also ibid., 15 March 1934; Lozier interview, [14]; Rawls interview; Storer interview, session I, [3].

18. The personal files of J. McHenry Jones provide rich documentation

on the origins of the Florida Pulp and Paper Company, and the Alabama Pulp and Paper Company and their relationship to St. Regis Paper. These records are available to scholars at his law offices in Pensacola, Florida. See also Jones interview; Annual Report, 1946; Rawls interview, [6-7, 9-10]; oral history interview with A. B. Recknagel conducted by Elwood R. Maunder, Tucson, Arizona, 28 October 1958, [37]; *PTJ*, 23 February 1950. Hugh W. Sloan contends that the initial kraft pulp produced at Pensacola by Florida Pulp and Paper Company compared unfavorably with West Coast kraft pulp. See Sloan interview, [6-7].

19. Jones interview, [13-16]. See also corporate records and correspondence files of Florida Pulp and Paper Company and Alabama Pulp and Paper Company in Jones collection, Pensacola, Florida.

20. Allen to Ferguson, 30 December 1948. Attachments to this letter include final annual reports of both the Florida Pulp and Paper Company and the Alabama Pulp and Paper Company and cite Ferguson as chairman of the board and Allen as president and general manager of each. A. D. Pace is listed as a member of the executive committee of each company. Copies of documents were made available by Jones.

21. Jones interview, [19-21a]. See also Annual Reports, 1946-1950; Rawls interview, [17]; *PTJ*, 28 December 1950.

22. *PTJ*, 20 June 1946. See also Jones interview, [31-36].

23. *PTJ*, 11 September 1947; Annual Report, 1947; Kneeland interview, session II, 9 December 1975, [27]; see also Rawls and Jones interviews for discussion of timberland acquisitions and the role of Albert Ernest.

24. Jones interview, [42]; Rawls interview, [4, 9]; *PTJ*, 11 September 1947, 1 August 1952. See also Eldredge, *Voices from the South*, pp. 72-88, 225, 228.

25. George Kneeland discusses the negative aspects of the kraft plant expansion in the South: "We had in mind building the biggest bag plant in the world when we built at Pensacola. But we got involved in many, many problems in its operations and in service to customers, and today it's not the biggest bag plant. It still is in physical size, but it isn't run that way. It was a mistake in judgment. Fortunately . . . we rectified without any big material damage to either venture [speaking also of Pollock]." Kneeland interview, session I, [20]. See also Annual Report, 1949; oral history interview with Reginald L. Vayo conducted by Mark H. Neuffer, New York City, 17 May 1977, [4-6, 20-21].

26. For information and data concerning the Hinton Mill project, see Annual Reports, 1954, 1963; and Storer interview, session I, [9, 10]; Dunn interview, [81, 82]; Hart interview, [23-25].

27. Discussion of Multiwall Division during this period drawn from Annual Reports, 1948-1959; Woodcock interview, sessions I, II; Storer interview, session II.

28. Woodcock interview, session I, [11, 12]; oral history interview with Bernard W. Recknagel conducted by Mark H. Neuffer, New York City, 6 April 1977, [12].

29. Recknagel interview, [7].

30. Storer interview, session II, [5-6]; Woodcock interview, session I, [6-13].

31. Storer interview, session II, [6].

32. Annual Report, 1949; Storer interview, session II, [9].

33. Annual Report, 1949; Woodcock interview, session I, [13]. See Wilber interview, [27], Vayo interview, [16], for a more thorough discussion of Hoppe's importance to both the stepped-end pasted bag and to the international licensee program. Both Wilber and Vayo credit Hoppe with maintaining the foreign licensee program during World War II.

34. Annual Reports, 1947-1949, 1952.

35. Ibid., 1956, 1957. Arthur Chandler, *Strategy and Structure* (Cambridge, Mass.: MIT Press, 1962), confirms this analysis. See his introductory chapter for the significance of long-range planning in the effective operation of business enterprise.

36. Vayo interview, [4-5]. The significance of the Kress purchase is articulated by Vayo: "It was decided that the Container Division would become a unit of St. Regis and that Mr. Philip B. Duffy, who had been executive vice-president of F. J. Kress Box Company, would become vice-president of the new St. Regis Container Division. One of Kress's big customers was H. J. Heinz, and Duffy was the man who originally converted Heinz from wooden boxes to fiber containers. From that point on, the Container Division was built up to what it is today." Ibid., [4].

37. Annual Reports, 1954-1958.

38. Recknagel interview, [10].

39. Annual Reports, 1955, 1956. Kneeland interview, session II, [38, 40]; Storer interview, session II, [1].

40. Annual Report, 1956.

41. Oral history interview with Joseph Rosenstein conducted by Mark H. Neuffer, Dallas, Texas, 6 June 1977, [18-23]. Rosenstein, connected with Pollock since the late 1940s, discusses the development of polyethylene in detail.

42. Annual Report, 1956.

43. Vayo interview, [4].

44. Minutes, 17 December 1958.

45. Annual Report, 1961; Minutes, 23 October 1963.

46. Annual Reports, 1947, 1953, 1955; Minutes, 16 June 1953, 26 January 1955. See Vilas and Kussmann, "Evolution of a Paper Company," pp. 45-46, 53-54, for the following: "When I came to Panelyte, for two years— probably through 1947 and into 1948—we made nothing but reinforced lami-

nated plastics. . . . At that time the injected-molded thermal plastic materials were taking a place in the refrigeration field in which Panelyte was very strong. We were the principal supplier of inner door liners for refrigerators right after the war. . . . We began to see that the compounded curves that were being engineered into refrigerator doors would not allow us to mold them with the sheets of kraft paper and phenol formaldehyde. So around that time in Trenton, New Jersey, we started putting in a thermal plastic operation in which we had some of the largest injection-molded presses built and installed at that point." Kussmann further explains in this interview St. Regis's decision to withdraw from the injection-molded plastics field. Just as independent converters in the paper industry were vulnerable to the competition of totally integrated paper companies, paper companies such as St. Regis were not in a good position to supply themselves with the raw materials for making plastic. This was evidently a much-discussed issue among top and middle management, and the subject is dealt with in detail in the Recknagel interview, [17-18].

47. Annual Reports, 1957, 1960; *PTJ*, 7 January 1957. See also Paul Neils, *Julius Neils and the J. Neils Lumber Company* (Seattle: Frank McCaffrey Publishers, 1971), pp. 86-87.

48. Annual Reports, 1957, 1958; *PTJ*, 25 February 1957.

49. Adams interview, [13].

50. Annual Reports, 1940-1959. The 1946 transaction with Time Inc. included 70,553 acres from the Dead River Company in Maine. Acquisition of 82,000 acres from the Ellsworth Forest Products Corporation of Ellsworth Falls, Maine, further augmented St. Regis's holdings.

51. Annual Report, 1948; *PTJ*, 22 January 1948; Storer interview, session II, [3, 4]; A. B. Recknagel interview conducted by Elwood R. Maunder, 28 October 1958, [45].

52. St. Regis Woodlands Manager and Forester Paul M. Dunn and his predecessor H. V. Hart both suggest that during these years of accelerated acquisition, the company's professional foresters devoted as much of their time to land purchase as they did to developing and maintaining management programs. Dunn interview, [25-27]; Hart interview, [19-24].

53. Dunn interview, [32-33, 75, 76, 80, 81]; *PTJ*, 12 November 1954; Rawls interview, [14]. Rawls believes that it was this method of raw material acquisition that enabled St. Regis to expand as it did in the South because "they didn't have to utilize all their capital to buy land."

54. *PTJ*, 2 May 1952.

55. Ted Gay was highly regarded by those who knew and worked with him. His influence was frequently noted in history interviews conducted by the authors. See B. W. Recknagel interview, [16]; Lozier interview, [3, 16]; Woodcock interview, session II, [3]. Andrew Storer identified Gay

as one of the three architects who determined St. Regis's course in the 1950s. Storer interview, session I, [6].

56. Annual Reports, 1945-1953.

57. B. W. Recknagel interview, [16]; Kneeland interview, session I, [13-17]; Hartung interview, [13]; Lane interview, [16-17]; *PTJ*, 8 August 1955.

58. Roy K. Ferguson, "Remarks at the St. Regis Paper Company Orientation Meeting of April 4, 1955." Kneeland interview, session I, [13-18].

59. Kneeland interview, session I, [17].

CHAPTER SEVEN

1. U.S. Bureau of the Census, *Statistical Abstracts of the United States* (Washington, D.C.: Government Printing Office, 1963), pp. 219, 317-22; ibid. (1971), pp. 209-11, 305-09; *PTJ*, 18, 3 January 1965.

2. *PTJ*, 28 November 1960, 29 May, 23 October 1961, 25 January 1962. *PTJ*'s issue of 21 May 1961 noted that in 1961 it took $17 to produce a dollar of profit, while in 1945 only $8.10 was needed for the same earning.

3. *PTJ*, 21 May 1961, 28 January 1963.

4. Annual Report, 1963.

5. Vilas and Kussmann, "Evolution of a Paper Company," pp. 71-72.

6. Storer interview, session III, [9, 15-17]; oral history interview with Edward J. McMahon conducted by Mark H. Neuffer, New York City, 15 April 1977, session II, [9-11]; Annual Report, 1965, p. 10.

7. See Thomas C. Cochran, "The Sloan Report: American Culture and Business Management," *American Quarterly* 24 (Winter 1977): 476-86.

8. Oral history interview with William R. Haselton conducted by Maunder and Neuffer, New York City, 21 January 1977, session I, [27]. The acquisition policies of the 1950s and early 1960s are also discussed in the Kneeland interview, session I, [6]; Vilas and Kussmann, "Evolution of a Paper Company," p. 54; oral history interview with Robert F. Searle conducted by Neuffer, New York City, 10 May 1977, [9]; Storer interview, session I, [8, 9].

9. Kneeland interview, session I, [6].

10. Vilas and Kussmann, "Evolution of a Paper Company," p. 54. A stronger criticism of Ferguson's acquisition policies is registered by Joseph Rosenstein: "I think it is safe to say—maybe this characteristic of some of Roy Ferguson's other acquisitions—that this was not a very thoroughly researched acquisition. [Pollock]. To the best of my knowledge, no one from St. Regis ever set foot in the Pollock operation before the decision was made to acquire it." Rosenstein interview, [13].

11. Searle interview, [9].

12. This summary of the positive and negative conditions of managerial integration is drawn from two major sources: factual data and subjective commentary. The former are derived from the company's annual reports and the latter from oral history interviews with William R. Haselton, George J. Kneeland, James E. Kussmann, Robert F. Searle, and Andrew F. Storer.

13. See Kneeland interview, session I, [6]; Vilas and Kussmann, "Evolution of a Paper Company," p. 5; Searle interview, [9]; Storer interview, session I, [8, 9]. Major discussion of this subject is also given in Haselton interview, sessions I, II.

14. Information for the discussion of St. Regis's program of growth, diversification and integration was drawn from Annual Reports, 1947-1962.

15. Annual Report, 1952; Wilber interview, [66-67]. William R. Adams states that after World War II, research was done outside the company: "Through the Institute of Paper Chemistry and at the Forest Products Laboratory . . . and a few places like that. I think I speak for the industry, although my experience only relates to St. Regis, in saying that we had no research." Adams interview, session I, [16].

16. Lane interview, [19].

17. Annual Reports, 1962, 1963, 1964.

18. Storer interview, session III, [6].

19. B. W. Recknagel interview, [10]; Storer interview, session III, [6]; Wilber interview, [43-45].

20. Searle interview, [5].

21. Haselton interview, session I, [20]. The organizational change was announced in Annual Report, 1963. See also Kneeland interview, session II, [28, 42].

22. Discussed in Searle interview, [3-5].

23. Ibid., [4-5].

24. Sloan interview, [17-18]; Haselton interview, session I, [19].

25. Haselton interview, session I, [19-20].

26. Federal Trade Commission Decisions, 1966, p. 66, Federal Trade Commission Library, Public Reference Branch (SIR), Washington, D.C.

27. Oral history interview with Homer Crawford conducted by Elwood R. Maunder, Mark H. Neuffer, and James E. Kussmann, New York City, 9 February 1977, [18a].

28. Ibid., pp. 17, 18a; Federal Trade Commission Decisions, 1966, p. 66. Philip B. Duffy is first noted as a vice-president of St. Regis in the 1960 Annual Report.

29. Haselton interview, session I, [8].

30. Ibid., [18-20].

31. See Annual Reports, 1955-1960; Rawls interview, [4-13].

32. See Dunn interview, [90-93].

33. Rawls interview, [4-5].

34. Ibid., [16].

35. Ibid., [1-2].

36. Annual Reports, 1945, 1950.

37. Ibid., 1957.

38. Jones interview, [44-52]; Kneeland interview, session II, [25-26].

39. Jones interview, [49-51]; Kneeland interview, session II, [25].

40. Annual Reports, 1959-1962, 1964.

41. Kneeland interview, session III, [40].

42. Annual Reports, 1959, 1960, 1964.

43. Minutes, 22 July 1964. Storer interview, session III, [22-23]; Rosenstein interview, [25].

44. Annual Report, 1960. The Rosenstein interview, [19-20], discusses Central Waxed Paper and its relationship to the Pollock operations.

45. Annual Report, 1960; Storer interview, session III, [5].

46. Minutes, 10 November 1960; Annual Report, 1960; Storer interview, session III, [5].

47. Annual Report, 1965; Vayo interview, [4, 13]. Vayo credits his success to others, and to a decision made by the company in 1952:

> A key decision on the company's policy for the sale of kraft paper that was made April 11, 1952. Prior to that time, if the Bag Division needed more paper, the Kraft Division would give it to them. They just went in and were able to requisition it and take it. But at this meeting in 1952 with Messrs. Gay, Carswell, Hahn, Versfelt, Dixon, and Adams in Mr. Ferguson's office, I was instructed to carry out a policy of maintaining, to the best of my ability, full production on all kraft paper machines of the company. In order to implement this policy, it was decided that the outside customers of the Kraft Paper Division should receive equal treatment with our various converting divisions, such as the Bag Division. Treating inside and outside on an equal basis is what permitted us to be so successful in the Kraft Division.

48. Annual Reports, 1954-1955, 1958.

49. Minutes, 13 July 1960. Reginald Vayo explains the formation of St. Regis International: "The International Corporation was a Panamanian company located in the West Indies, in Nassau. The Kraft Division used Nassau as an export office; we invoiced our linerboard there. The key exports handled in Nassau were of linerboard to England and the Continent. The U.S. Government offered a special tax incentive for building up overseas, and the profits were not taxable until they were brought back to the States." Vayo interview, [12].

50. Annual Reports, 1964, 1965.

51. Ibid., 1959; Sloan interview, [14].

52. Woodcock interview, session I, [19].

53. Annual Reports, 1961, 1963, 1964. Storer interview, session III, [10]. The status of Panelyte is also discussed in Adams interview, session I, [29-30]; Hartung interview, pp. 10-11. Sloan recounts his version of the sale following his appointment to the Panelyte Division: "Look, Roy, if I can get our book value plus the losses we've sustained over the years, will you let me sell it? [Ferguson responded in the affirmative.] On the sale of the Panelyte operations, we got our depreciated investments, plus the losses, back." Sloan interview, 8 February 1977, [23].

54. Vilas and Kussmann, "Evolution of a Paper Company," pp. 45-57.

55. Ibid., pp. 70-71.

56. Ibid., p. 72.

57. "Adams's Remarks at the Annual Meeting of Stockholders," 23 April 1964.

CHAPTER EIGHT

1. Annual Report, 1967; *PTJ*, 24 February 1969, 22 July 1968, 16 March 1970.

2. William R. Adams, "Remarks to a Group of Boston Security Analysts on October 23, 1969."

3. William R. Adams, 12 July 1965.

4. Ibid., 27 September, 30 August, 27 September 1965. However, by September 1965, Kimberly-Clark, IP, and Mead had increased prices because of unprecedented demand for paper products. Weyerhaeuser increased packaging prices 3 percent and St. Regis announced spot price increases of ten dollars per ton for coated publication papers.

5. Annual Reports, 1965-1970.

6. Ibid., 1965, 1970.

7. Adams interview, session I, [17-18]. See also Adams's Remarks at the Annual Meeting of Stockholders, 23 April 1970, pp. 3-7.

8. *PTJ*, 20 June 1966. For a discussion of the role of public relations in the business organization, see Vilas and Kussmann, "Evolution of a Paper Company."

9. Vayo interview; Storer interview, session III; Annual Report, 1965; *PTJ*, 7 June 1965.

10. Annual Report, 1965. For a discussion of formation of the International Division, see Vayo interview.

11. *PTJ*, 1 March 1965, reports 360,000 acres, while Annual Report, 1965, claims 350,000.

12. Annual Reports, 1965, 1966.

13. Vayo interview, [9].

14. Kneeland interview, session I, [8].

15. Annual Report, 1965.

16. Ibid., 1966.

17. Ibid.; Vayo interview, [6-8].

18. Annual Report, 1967.

19. Ibid., 1968.

20. Ibid., 1970.

21. Ibid., 1965.

22. Ibid., 1966. The 1977 Annual Report celebrates the merger and notes the company's reentry into the newsprint business.

23. See Woodcock interview, sessions I and II, [19-22], [40-41].

24. Annual Reports, 1967, 1969; *PTJ*, 11 September 1967.

25. *PTJ*, 20 November 1967.

26. Annual Report, 1966; Minutes, 25 April 1968.

27. Annual Report, 1965.

28. Ibid.

29. Minutes, 27 March 1968; Haselton interview, session I, [24].

30. The same practice of eliminating wholesalers where possible, plus the connections gained with Wheeler, led to St. Regis's later acquisition of Iowa Prestressed Concrete, a licensee of Span-Deck. Span-Deck, a prestressed concrete producer, had made inroads into a market previously dominated by wood: construction of high-rise buildings of all kinds. Headquartered in Nashville, Span-Deck itself was ultimately purchased in 1971. *PTJ*, 5 May 1968, p. 53. See also Haselton interview, session I, [20-24], and Storer interview, session III, [13-15], for a discussion of this area.

31. Annual Report, 1969.

32. Storer interview, session III, [14]; *PTJ*, 13 May 1968.

33. Annual Report, 1967.

34. Statistics of timberland acquisition patterns were taken from ibid., 1965-1968.

35. Ibid., 1965.

36. Ibid., 1969.

37. Haselton interview, session II, [20-21]. Haselton further details the land-development fiascos of other forest products firms: "Consider some of the greatest blunders our industry has made. IP, Boise, and Fibreboard were overly eager to get into land development, went overboard into an area where they personally had no direct experience in management, and found to their horror that they were burned beyond belief as far as dollars are concerned." See also Crawford interview, session II, [58-59], for additional coverage of St. Regis land development.

38. Annual Reports, 1960-1969. See figures for the entire decade in ibid., 1969, [6-12, 38-40].

39. Haselton interview, session II, [3].

40. Ibid. Haselton continues his comments on the reorganization and its status in the early 1970s: "The only change since then was when Alex Smalley retired [1973]. His group, which was about $50 million in sales, had been flying in the same league with a group of $700 million in sales and $500 million in sales. It seemed ridiculous to continue the three group concept domestically; and in the interest of efficiency and economy I merged the groups... with the one that Bob Searle headed."

41. Annual Report, 1969.

42. Russell R. Major, personal communication, 20 July 1979.

43. Minutes of Special Meeting of the Board, 8 January 1969; Crawford interview, session II, [36-37].

44. McMahon interview, session I, [22, 24].

45. Kneeland interview, session III, [43].

46. Vilas and Kussmann, "Evolution of a Paper Company," p. 59.

47. Storer interview, session III, [18].

48. Sloan interview, [20].

49. Vilas and Kussmann, "Evolution of a Paper Company," p. 59.

50. Minutes of Special Meeting of the Board, 8 January 1969.

51. McMahon interview, session II, [1].

52. Crawford interview, session II, [38].

53. McMahon interview, session II, [1].

54. Sloan interview, [21].

55. Storer interview, session III, [18-19].

56. Kneeland interview, session III, [43].

57. Minutes, 26 February 1969; Crawford interview, session II, [39-40]; Kneeland interview, session III, [43]; Storer interview, session III, [19].

58. Annual Reports, 1969-1973.

59. Haselton interview, session I, [31].

CHAPTER NINE

Unless listed as a formal note, all statements of fact are from annual reports.

1. Discussion of the industry's status has relied heavily upon three sources: 1970, A Test of Stamina (New York: American Paper Institute, 1971); Richard A. Donnelly, "Less Excess Capacity Sooner or Later Will Give Them a Lift," Barrons, 14 June 1971; and a special issue of Magazine of Wall Street, 22 November 1971, devoted exclusively to the paper industry.

2. McMahon interview, session II, [2].

3. Kneeland interview, session I, [2].

4. William R. Haselton, "Remarks at the Eighteenth Industry Seminar at the Institute of Paper Chemistry on June 14, 1973."

5. Haselton interview, session II, [4-5].

6. McMahon interview, session II, [8].

7. Ibid., [8-9].

8. Searle interview, [10-16].

9. Storer interview, session III, [4].

10. The foregoing discussion used *Magazine of Wall Street*, 22 November 1971, as a source.

11. Haselton interview, session II, [16]. Pollution-abatement practices are also discussed in Crawford interview, session II, [27-36].

12. Haselton interview, session II, [14].

13. Kneeland interview, session III, [46].

14. Haselton interview, session II, [20-21].

Notes on Sources

Heavy reliance was placed on records held by the St. Regis Paper Company at its New York City offices and in its Watertown, New York, records retention center. Eventually all historical materials will be transferred to Watertown. Central to the study, as well, were numerous interviews with company officials who had firsthand knowledge of management, marketing, manufacturing, product research, and land management. Elwood R. Maunder and Mark H. Neuffer conducted most of the interviews, with John R. Ross and James E. Kussmann conducting the remainder. Interviews with the following people added immeasurably to this study: William R. Adams, Kenneth A. Arnold, Archibald Carswell, Lauge Christensen, John D. Clifford, John E. Cowles, Homer Crawford, Paul M. Dunn, Harold V. Hart, Jack W. Hartung, William R. Haselton, Edwin H. Jones, Jr., J. McHenry Jones, George J. Kneeland, James E. Kussmann, Gardiner Lane, Kenneth D. Lozier, Carl Martin, Edward J. McMahon, Marcus Rawls, A. B. Recknagel, B. W. Recknagel, Louise E. Richter, Joseph Rosenstein, Robert F. Searle, Hugh W. Sloan, Andrew F. Storer, Harold S. Sutton, Reginald L. Vayo, Homer A. Vilas, Eunice R. Wardwell, Jack E. Wilber, and Charles A. Woodcock. These interviews are on file at the Watertown records center.

Also of value were collections of historical materials held by individuals and related firms. *North American Forest History: A Guide to Archives and Manuscripts in the United States and Canada*, compiled by Richard C. Davis (ABC-Clio Books for the Forest History Society, 1977), offers entree to pertinent unpublished sources.

Historians have not studied the paper industry as extensively as they have other elements of the forest products community. Nonetheless historical and contemporary technical literature is voluminous. For a historical context, see Ronald J. Fahl, *North American Forest and Conservation History: A Bibliography* (ABC-Clio Books for the Forest History Society, 1977). The early years of paper history in context with other aspects of forestry and forest industries is included in E. N. Munns, *A Selected Bibliography of North American Forestry*, 2 vols., USDA Misc. Pub. No. 364 (1940). *The Bibliography of Pulp and Paper Making*, compiled by the TAPPI Committee on Abstracts and Bibliography, is a detailed listing of technical literature from 1900 to 1971.

Certain works and collections were especially influential throughout this study. David C. Smith, *A History of Papermaking in the United States (1691-1969)* (New York: Lockwood Publishing Co., 1971) and U.S. Congress, House, *Pulp and Paper Investigation Hearings*, 60th Cong., 2d sess., 1908, provided much factual information and useful interpretations. The *Paper Trade Journal* and *Paper Makers Journal* were only two of the valuable trade journals used. Published annual reports of the St. Regis Paper Company and the unpublished minutes of its board of directors' meetings were also sources of essential data and insights. Labor's view is amply contained in the records of the International Brotherhood of Pulp, Sulphite, and Paper Mill Workers, which are held in New York City at the headquarters of its successor, the United Paperworkers International Union.

Index

Acquisition policy of management, 66, 99, 107, 112–113, 123–125, 151, 165

Adams, William R., 80, 87, 88, 93, 117, 119, 127, 132, 140, 142, 144, 145, 155, 157, 162, 168, 169

Adirondack forests, overcutting of, 17

Adirondack League Club, 91

Administration, vice-president for, 154

Advance Planning Executive Committee, 106

Advertising, 16, 117; forest-oriented campaign, 123; for rags, 7; wartime, 89

Africa: Capetown, 110, 139; Durban, 139, 148; Johannesburg, 139, 148; Port Elizabeth, 139; Salisbury, 139; Zambia, 148

Agricultural Insurance Company of Watertown, 24, 26

Air pollution. *See* Pollution

Ajax Box Company, 108

Alabama: industry in, 99, 100, 135; land-holdings in, 100, 166

Alabama Pulp and Paper Company, 100, 101

Alberta, Canada, 102, 152. *See also* Hinton, Alberta

Alberta Hi-Brite pulp, 152

Allen, James H., 99–101, 133

Allentown, Pennsylvania, 85

Aluminum Company of America, 75

Amalgamated Packaging Industries, 139, 148

American Can Company, 110

American Federation of Labor, 43

American Forest Products Industries, Incorporated, 113

American Forestry Association, 41

American Newspaper Publishers Association, 39

American Paper and Pulp Association (APPA), 17, 37–38, 47, 48, 50, 82, 83–84; labor policy, 67; News Division, 15, 18, 31

American Paper Institute, 169

American Protective Tariff League, 38

American Publishers Association, 48

American Pulp and Paper Mill Superintendants Association, 68

American Sisalkraft Corporation, 127, 138, 164

American Superpower Corporation, 75

Anderson, David M., 7, 10, 13–15, 51, 59, 61, 62, 169; financial holdings of, 54–55; as founder of St. Regis, 21–34; labor negotiations, 44; land deals, 20, 53

Andersson barker, 135

Anti-pollution legislation, 122

Anti-trust rulings, 111

APPA. *See* American Paper and Pulp Association

Appliances, household, 107, 111
A.P.V. Holdings, Limited, 167
Argentina, subsidiaries in, 147
Arkell and Smiths, 124
Armour, Philip D., 53
Arnold, Kenneth, 105, 126
Asphalt-laminated bag paper, 105, 138
Association of Newsprint Manufacturers, 84
Atlanta Film Converting Company, 138
Atlas Box Company, Limited, 110
Atlas Plywood Corporation, 98–99
Attleboro, Massachusetts, 127, 138
Australia, operations in, 138, 147, 167
Australian Consolidated, 147
Austria, facilities in, 167

Badger, John P., 30
Bag Division, 92, 103–105, 130, 140, 149–150
Bag-filling machines, 98, 104, 117
Bagley and Sewall Company, 26
Bag patents, expiration of, 103
Bags, 70, 84–85, 117; multiwall, 73, 77, 85–86, 95, 98, 139, 150; sales of, 103–105; special use, 89
Baking industry, bags for, 104
Banana boxes, 110, 139
Bank of Nova Scotia, 102
Barcelona, Spain, plant in, 147
Basselin, T. B., 66
Bass Rock, Louisiana, 100
Bates, Adelmer, 74, 98
Bates, Limited, 138
Bates, R. M., 98
Bates International Bag Company, 74, 81
Bates Valve Bag Company, 73–74, 81, 86
Bearce, George, 98
Beaunit Mills, Incorporated, 88
Beaver River, St. Regis water rights on, 65
Becker, Folke, 131, 132
Beebee, Levi, 4
Belden and Seely, 24
Belgium, bag plant in, 147
Benefits, employee, 92
Benson, George J., 25
Biondo, Michael T., 128

Birmingham, Alabama, 74, 109, 130
Birmingham Paper Company, 130, 137
Black River, 3–4, 12, 13, 35, 40, 61–62; canal construction, 23, 24–25, 32, 33–34. power plant, 63; St. Regis mill, 24–26, 32–34, 59; St. Regis water rights, 65
Black River Canal, 62
Black River Power Association, 62
Black River Valley, 9; International Paper in, 20; labor issues in, 56
Bleaching process for groundwood pulp, 90
Boer War, 16, 18
Bogalusa, Louisiana, 99
Bomb-bay doors, 111
Book paper, groundwood, 90
Booneville, New York, 62
Boxboard, folding, 96
Boxboard Division, 137
Boxes, 107–108; South African production of, 110; wooden, 112
Brazil, subsidiaries in, 147
Bread wrappers, 96, 108, 109
Brewton, Alabama, 100
Bridge construction materials, 131, 151
Britain, facilities in, 138, 167
British Sisalkraft, Limited, 138
Brooklyn Cooperage Company, 33, 41–42
Brooklyn Standard Bag Company, 85
Bryant Paper Company, 96
Bucksport, Maine, 96–97, 137, 150, 153, 165
Buffalo, Niagra and Eastern Power Company, 75
Building materials, 131, 138, 151
Bunn, William, 123
Burke, John, 68
Burns, Celestine C., 58, 59, 71
Burns, Matthew, 91–92
Bush, Clayton, 89
Bushman, Robert P., 117
Butler, J. W., 46

Caldwell, William E., 118, 148, 154, 155, 162, 164
Cambridge, Ohio, 108, 111
Cambridge Corrugated Box Company, 108
Cambridge Molded Plastics Company, 111

Camden, Arkansas, 99
Camp Tylcoff, 57
Canada: Alberta, 102, 152; Cap Rouge, Quebec, 67; Dryden, Ontario, 74, 103; Hinton, Alberta, 102–103, 126, 152–153; logs from, 17–18; newsprint from, 51, 72; pulp supplies from, 43, 51, 102, 115; Three Rivers, Quebec, 74, 103; Vancouver, B.C., 103
Canadian paper and pulpwood, tariffs on, 19, 47, 49–50, 71–72
Canadian Securities Corporation, 66–67
Canadian timberlands, 66–67, 102, 152
Canal, construction of, 23, 24–25, 32, 33–34
Cancell, Benton, 119, 130, 131, 132, 133
Cantonment, Florida, 101
Capetown, South Africa, 110, 139
Cap Rouge, Quebec, 67
Carey, J.T., 45, 56, 68
Carlisle, Floyd Leslie, 11, 53–54, 58–59, 61, 64–65, 69, 73, 76, 77, 79, 116, 169; electric power investments, 75–76; labor relations, 58, 67–68, 92; reforestation program, 65–66; waterpower interest, 63–64
Carlisle, John N., 11, 64, 65, 71
Carlisle, William S., 11
Carnegie Steel Company, 25
Carswell, Archibald, 92, 104, 117, 119, 128, 130
Carthage, New York, 32, 70, 72, 97, 115
Carthage Lumber Company, 40
Carthage Power Corporation, 73
Cartons, folding, 96, 107, 108, 137, 150
Caswell, Gurdon, 4–5
Catalog paper, 71, 72, 75, 82, 90, 96, 165
Caughnawaga Indians, 22
Cellophane, 109
Cement bags, 82, 98; paper for, 70
Central America: Costa Rica, container plants in, 110; Guatemala, container plants in, 110; Panama, 110, 139, 148; Puerto Rico, 103
Central Waxed Paper Company, 138
Champion, New York, 35
Champion Paper Company, 65, 70, 73, 80

Chemical industry, move into, 112
Chemical Packaging Corporation, 103
Chemical Warfare Service, 89
Chemi-pulp process, 86
Chesapeake-Camp Corporation, 86
Chester Packaging Products Company, 109–110
Chicago, 74, 108, 137, 138
Chile, school of forestry in, 133
Chipping equipment, 135
Civil Rights Act of 1964, 122
Civil War, paper needs of, 6, 7
Civil Works Administration, 82
Clearcutting, 136
Closed shop, 57, 59, 68; opposed by Gould, 55
Clow, Peter, 55
Coated papers, 150, 165
Cochran, Thomas C., x, 5, 68
Coin wrap, 97
Colonial Trust Company, 24
Color supplements to newspapers, 16
Columbia, subsidiaries in, 147
Conical containers, 139
Conservation concerns, 17, 40, 122–123
Conservation nature of St. Regis, 170
Consolidated Edison, 76
Consolidated Paper Corporation of Montreal, 140
Construction materials, 131, 138, 150–151
Consumer products lines, 137
Container Division, 130, 131, 150
Containers, marketing of, 106–107
Continental Can Company, 110
Continental Paper Company, 56
Contractors, for St. Regis construction, 24–25, 32
Cook Not Mad, The, 5
Cooper, Abe, 115
Cornell, John E., 74
Cornell Bag Corporation, 81
Cornell Multiwall Valve Bag Company, 74
Cornell Paperboard Products Company, 137
Cornell University: experimental forest, 17, 41; State College of Forestry at, 17, 41–42

Corrugated boxes, 95, 107, 108, 110, 139, 148
Corrugated Container Division, 164
Cost-accounting procedures, 155
Costa Rica, container plants in, 110
Cotton goods, manufactured in Watertown, 4
Covington, Kentucky, 74
Cowles, David S., 48, 50
Cowles, John, 147, 154, 155
Craig, H. G., and Company, 32, 46, 47, 49
Crawford, Homer, 130–131, 155, 157–158
Creamery Package Manufacturing Company, 127, 137–138
Crepe paper, 97, 115
Crosby Lumber and Manufacturing Company, 152
Crown Zellerback Corporation, 84–85, 109
Cullen, R. J., 99
Cupples-Hesse Company, 137
Cutting practices, 17, 41, 136
Cutting rights, ix, 43, 101, 114, 134, 145, 152

Dallas, Texas, 108, 109, 127
Dana, Samuel T., 133
Davis Sewing Machine Company, 11
Dayton, Ohio, 137
Debarking equipment, 135
deCamp, Julia L., 52
Decker (mill superintendant), 44
De Feriet, Jenika, 34
Deferiet, New York, 20, 34; labor problems at, 44, 56–58; mill at, 39, 59, 86, 90, 96–97, 137, 172; pollution control measures at, 168; research and development at, 106
Denmark, box factory in, 148
Depression, economic, 39, 75–79, 81; recovery from, 82–87
Dexter, Michigan, 112
Diana Paper Company, 73
Directory paper, 70, 71, 72, 75, 90, 96, 165
Distribution system, 151, 167
Divestiture of operations, 130–131, 141, 164
Divisional vice-presidents, 155

Dixon, Willard J., 80
Dodge, George E., 21, 34; as founder of St. Regis, 21–32
Dodge, Meigs and Company, 21; deceptive representation of forest land, 22–23, 28–30
Dodge, William E., 21
Domtar Packaging Company, 150
Doors, manufacture of, 112
Drexel and Company, 75
Dryden, Ontario, 74, 103
Dry land log-handling facility, 151
Duffy, Philip B., 130–131, 154, 155
Dunn, Paul M., xi, 114, 123, 133
Du Pont scientists, collaboration with, 90, 105
Durban, South Africa, 139, 148

Eagle Lodge, 43
Earnings, 121, 144–145, 154, 161, 166
East Norfolk, New York, 70
East Pepperell, Massachusetts, 74, 97
Economic cycles in paper industry, 18–19
Economy, national, 121–122, 139, 142, 143–144, 161–162; depressed, 39, 75–76, 79–82; growth of, 93, 95, 112; postwar, 93–95; prosperous, 38–39; recovery from depression, 84–86; Trade Expansion Act, 139
Ecuador, container plants in, 110, 139
Eggleston, New York, 34
Eight-hour day, 38, 44–45, 49, 56, 58
Electrification of paper industry, 62–63, 76; advantages to papermakers, 65, 72
Emeryville, California, 130
Empire Wood Pulp Company, 53
Employment figures, 95
Employment policies, 122
Empsall, Frank A., 59, 71
Engineering Contract Company, 32
Engineering Division, 126
Engineering and Machine Division, 104
England, operations in, 138, 167
Envelopes, 137
Environmental concerns, 17, 122–123, 141, 143, 167–169

Environmental Protection Agency
    Program, 168, 169
Equal opportunity employment, 122
Ernest, Albert, 101, 113, 117, 133–134
Escambia County, Florida, 168
Essay on Man (Pope), 5
Everett, Washington, 151
Executive development policies, 117–119
Executive vice-presidents, 154
Expansion, excessive, 121–122
Experimental forests, 17, 41–42, 114,
    136–137
Export volume, 148

Fairbanks, Jason, 4
Family holdings, in South, 135
Farming, company land used for, 153
Federal Trade Commission (FTC) investi-
    gation, 110–111; decision, 130–131
Felts Mills, New York, 10, 13
Ferguson, Hardy S., 101
Ferguson, Roy King, 64, 69, 73, 74, 76,
    77, 79–81, 96, 100, 108, 113, 117, 140,
    141, 170; labor relations, 92; management
    techniques, 98–99, 118, 124; merger
    with RCA, 155–159; retirement of, 162
Ferguson Mill, 145, 146–147; cost of, 169
Ferguson Technical Center, 127–128
Fernow, Bernhard Eduard, 17, 41–42
Fiberboard, 107, 108
Fiber containers, 147
Finance, vice-president for, 154
Financing, original, of St. Regis, 23–24
First National City Bank, 79
Fisher, Mary L., 40, 52
F. J. Kress Box Company, 107, 131
F. L. Carlisle and Company, Incorporated,
    69, 70, 75, 76
Flexible Packaging Division, 108, 109–110,
    130, 138, 150, 164
Florida: industry in, 99–100; landholdings
    in, 99–100, 152, 166
Florida Pulp and Paper Company, 99–100
Flower, George W., 11
Flower, Roswell P., 11, 20
Folding boxboard, 96
Folding boxes, 108, 110, 139

Folding cartons, 96, 107, 108, 137
Fon-du-lac Paper Company, 52
Food Equipment and Consumer Products
    Division, 154, 155, 167
Food packaging, 108, 109, 138, 150
Food Processing Equipment Division, 130
Fordney-McCumber tariff, 71
Foreign investment, 103, 107, 110,
    138–140, 145, 146–147, 165, 166–167
Forest, Land and Mill Company, 23
Forest Products Division, 131, 132,
    150–152
Forestry, 99, 101, 113–115, 133; experi-
    mental, 17, 41–42, 114, 136–137;
    industrial, 113–114; land use, 153–154;
    New York State College of, 17, 41–42
Formica, 111
Fourdrinier, Henry, 5
Fourdrinier, Sealey, 5
Fourdrinier paper machines, 5, 7, 16;
    rebuilt, 86
France, facilities in, 167
Franklin, Virginia, 86, 103
Franklin County, New York: forestry
    experiment in, 17; lumber mills in, 21;
    sale of land in, 23
Freeman family, 20
Frozen food wrappers, 108, 109
Fruman, Oscar, 110
Fruman's Properties, Limited, 110, 148
FTC. *See* Federal Trade Commission
Fullerton, Kenneth B., 23, 32, 46
Fullerton, California, 130
"Full wagon" sales strategy, 108
Furman, H. F., 71
F. W. Williams, Limited, 138, 147

Galena, Ohio, 112
Gardner, W. E., 47–48
Gas reserves, ix, 166
Gay, Edward R., 80, 83, 116, 118, 119, 127
General Container Corporation, 107, 137
General Paper Company, 45
Georgia-Pacific Corporation, 110
G. H. Mead Company, 82
Gibson, J. W., Company, 101
Glass containers, 107, 147

Glassine paper, 95, 109
Glass-packaging companies, in paper
    business, 110
Glenfield and Western Railroad Company,
    52
Glen Park, New York, 6, 10, 14
Godbout timber tract, 66–67, 72
Goodwill, value of, 73, 81
Gould, Gordias Henry P., 46, 51–53, 54,
    61, 62, 63, 169; labor relations, 55–59;
    resignation of, 58–59
Gould Paper Company, 20, 52, 56
Government regulation, 83–84, 143–144
Grading of paper, 86
Grain bags, 98
Graves, Henry Solon, 28, 29
Gray's Harbor County, Washington, 152
Grazing, company land used for, 153
Greaseproof paper, 109
Great Bend, New York, 10–11, 13, 35
Great Bend Paper Company, 10
Great Southern Lumber Company, 99
Great Western Bag Corporation, 149–150
Greeley, William, 113
Grinding of wood for pulp, 8
Grocery bags, 139, 149
Groundwood paper, grades of, 86
Groundwood pulp: bleaching of, 97; devel-
    opment of, 8–9; wartime use of, 90
Grower's Container Corporation, 107, 108,
    109, 130
Guatemala, container plants in, 110
Gummed products, 96, 97, 108
Gummed Products Company, 108, 127, 164

Hahn, Willard E., 104, 117
Hall, A. H., 6
Hamilton County, New York, cutting of
    timber in, 91
Hanna Paper Corporation, 70–71, 76, 80
Hardwood, use of, 41
Harmon Paper Company, 65
Harnit, Joseph, 80
Harrisville, New York, 73, 115
Harrisville Paper Corporation, 72–73, 81,
    115
Hart, Pete, 113, 133

Hartung, Jack W., 97
Haselton, William R., 123–124, 129, 130,
    131–132, 151, 153–155, 162, 163, 164,
    166, 169, 170
Hemlock Experimental Forest, 136
Hennepin Paper Company, 96
Herkimer County, New York: cutting of
    timer, 91; timberland purchased in, 66
Hermitage, 34
Herring, William P. "Buffalo Bill," 53, 116
Herrings mill, 53, 59, 70, 73, 97
Herty, Charles H., 99, 150
Herzberg Mullone Automatic Products,
    Limited, 110
Hewson, Thomas A., 126
H. G. Craig and Company, 32, 46, 47, 49
Highway construction products, 131, 152
Hinds, Frank A., 24
Hinton, Alberta, 102–103, 152–153;
    expansion of mill, 126
Hoe, R., & Company, rotary presses, 16
Holding companies: St. Regis, 64–65, 71,
    116; Taggart Corporation, 73
Holyoke, Massachusetts, 43
Hoppe, Edgar, 105
Housing products, manufacture of, 131,
    150–151
Houston, Texas, 149
Howard Paper Mills, Incorporated, 127,
    137
Howland, Maine, 98–99
Humble Oil and Refining Company, 166
Hydroelectricity, 62–63, 64, 76. See also
    Waterpower
Hydropyrolysis, 168

IBPM. See International Brotherhood of
    Paper Makers
IBPSPMW. See International Brotherhood
    of Pulp, Sulphite and Paper Mill Workers
Indian River, 61
Inheritance taxes, 135
Institute of Paper Chemistry, 131
International Brotherhood of Paper Makers
    (IBPM), 43–45, 56, 58, 68, 91–92; praise
    of Sherman, 55
International Brotherhood of Pulp, Sulphite

and Paper Mill Workers (IBPSPMW),
  56–58, 67–68
International Brotherhood of Stationary
  Firemen, 58
International Division, 145, 146–149, 155,
  166–167
International Division Monthly Bulletin, 93
International operations of St. Regis, ix,
  103, 107, 110, 138–140, 145, 146–149,
  165, 166–167
International Paper Company (IP), 18–20,
  52, 72, 95, 100, 161; labor relations, 45;
  price-fixing charges, 47; waterpower of,
  62
Iowa Prestressed Concrete Company, 151
IP. *See* International Paper Company
Izaak Walton League, 169

Jacksonville, Florida, 101, 126, 130, 168;
  port of, 147; shipping from, 148, 168
Jacksonville Port Authority, 168
Jefferson Board Mills, 53
Jefferson County, New York, 3
Jefferson Paper Company, 53
Jefferson Power Company, 53
Jersey City, New Jersey, 130
J. H. Sankey and Sons, Limited, 138
J. Neils Lumber Company, 112, 132
Johannesburg, South Africa, 139, 148
Johns-Manville, 73
Jones, J. McHenry, xi, 117, 135
J. P. Lewis Company, 91
J. P. Morgan and Company, 75
J. W. Gibson Company, 101

Kalamazoo, Michigan, 96–97, 141, 162
Kamyr process of pulping, 102
Kapowsin region, Washington, 152
Kavanaugh, John A. C., 82
Kellogg, Royal, 91
Kimberly-Clark, profits of, 161
Klickitat, Washington, 112
Kline Manufacturing Company, 112
Kneeland, George J., 86, 98–99, 101, 117,
  118, 124, 135, 147, 154, 162, 163, 164,
  166, 169–170; views of RCA merger,
  156, 159

Knickerbocker Trust Company, 39
Knowlton, George W., Jr., 6, 10, 19, 31,
  51, 62
Knowlton, George W., Sr., 5
Knowlton, John C., 6
Knowlton Brothers, 6, 7, 31
Kosterville, New York, 52
Kraft Division, 97–102, 110, 130, 139, 146,
  149
Kraft paper, 73, 74, 75, 76–77, 84, 85,
  97–102, 117; market, 95, 97, 101–102,
  167; output, 102, 115; polyethylene-
  coated, 105, 109; raw materials for,
  84–85, 102; reinforced, 138
Kress, F. J., Box Company, 107, 131
Kuka-Shark, 149
Kussmann, James E., xi, 123, 124, 141–142,
  145–146; views of RCA merger, 156, 157

Labor costs, 38, 48–49
Labor-management relations, 43–45, 55–59,
  67–69, 91–92
Lake Logging Company, 90
Laminated products, 96, 108, 111
Land Development Division, 153–154
Land purchase policy, 113, 114, 145
Land use theories, 40–42, 113, 114–115,
  153–154
Lane, Gardiner, 89, 117, 118, 127
Lath, 112
Latin America, subsidiaries in, 110,
  147–148
Leboeuf and Lamb, 158
Leiby, Adrian, 158
Lewis, Harry S., 65
Lewis, J. P., Company, 91
Lewis County, New York, 3; timberland
  purchase in, 66
Libby, Montana, 112
Linerboard, 107, 110, 165, 167
Little Falls, Minnesota, 96
Loblolly pine (Virginia and North
  Carolina), kraft paper from, 86
Lone Star Bag and Bagging Company, 103
Long-range Planning and Policy Com-
  mittee, 123
Longview, Washington, 109

Los Angeles, California, 74, 137, 149
Louis Calder Foundation, 149
Louisiana: industry in, 99, 100; land-holdings in, 146, 152
Louisiana Pulp and Paper Company, 100
Louisville, Kentucky, 150
Lozier, Kenneth D., 89–90, 104, 117
Lubbock, Texas, 103
Lufkin, Texas, 137, 149, 150
Lumber, production of, 96, 150–151
Lumber and Plywood Division, 130
Lumber companies in paper business, 110
Lumber industry, 9, 112, 132, 150–151; Southern, 135
Lyon, Lyman R., 52
Lyon & Gould, 52
Lyon's Falls, New York, 52

McArdle, Richard E., 133
McGowin family, 135
Machold, H. Edmund, 70, 71
McIntyre, W. E., 44
Mackey, James, 44
McLuhan, Marshall, 94
McMahon, Edward J., 154, 162, 164–165; views of RCA merger, 155–156, 157, 158
MacMillan family, 100
McMillen, Charles, 86
Magazine paper, 71, 165
Mahaney, C. Russell, 111, 117
Maine, landholdings in, 152, 153
Maine Seaboard Paper Company, 96
Malin, John H., 56, 58
Maltby, Ralph, 80
Management policies, 123–125, 161; switch in, 162; vertical organization, 129–130
Manila paper, 7, 53
Manufacturers Paper Company, 23, 46, 51
Manufacturing Development Department, 106
Marathon Corporation, 115
Marketing, 103–105, 106–107, 116, 128–129; international, 167
Marketing Analysis Department, 128–129
Marketing and Communications, vice-president for, 154
Marsh, George Perkins, 122

Martin, Carl B., 80
Mason, David, 113
Mayer, Oscar, Company, 105
Mead, G. H., Company, 82
Mead Corporation, profits, 161
Meigs, Ferris J.: as founder of St. Regis, 21–32; misrepresentation of forest land, 22–23, 28–30; pulpwood supply contract, 32–33
Meigs, Titus B., 21, 22, 27
Menominee, Michigan, 74
Merchandising tags, 137
Mergenthaler, Ottmar, 16
Mergers, 18, 82, 110, 135, 151, 155–159, 165
Merrian, Florence L., 52
Metal containers, 107
Metal-packaging companies, in paper business, 110
Metropolitan Paving, 32
Michigan Molded Plastics Company, 112
Middle management committee, 117–119, 125, 127
Middleton, DeWitt C., 59
Milk cartons, paper, 139
Miller, Alvah, 32, 46, 54, 71
Miller, Warner "Wood Pulp," 9
Millers, multiwall bags used by, 104
Millfields Cardboard Box Manufacturers, 110
Milwaukee, Wisconsin, 137
Mineral region, Washington, 152
Mississippi, landholdings in, 146, 152
Mix, James T., 46
Mobile, Alabama, 100
Modern Valve Bag Company, 85–86
Mohawk-Hudson Power Corporation, 75
Molded plastics, 111–112
Monopoly, charges of, 46–47
Montana, timberland in, 112
Montgomery Ward, catalog paper for, 72
Monticello, Mississippi, 142, 145, 146, 169; pollution control in, 167
Moose River Lumber Company, 91
Morgan, J. P., and Company, 75
Morristown, New Jersey, 150
Mt. Wolf, Pennsylvania, 107

Muir, John, 122
Multiple product recovery, 114
Multiwall Bag Division, 92, 103–104, 130, 149–150
Multiwall bags, 73, 77, 84–86, 95, 98, 103–105, 139, 150
Murray, Edward G., 117
Murray Bag and Paper Corporation, 149–150

Nashua River Paper Company, 97–98
National Bank and Loan Company, 53
National Containers, Limited, 110
National Kraft Container Corporation, 130
National Packaging Company, Limited, of Johannesburg, 148
National Paper Corporation, 115
National Paper Products Company, 84–85
National Paper Trade Association, 84
National Recovery Administration (NRA), 82–84, 86
National Union Bank, 53
Natural gas, 166
Natural resources: depletion of, 143; private control of, 64; use of, 167
Nazareth, Pennsylvania, 74
Neils, J., Lumber Company, 112, 132
Neopac, 148
Neoprene-impregnated paper, 115
New Deal, 81; and paper industry, 82–84
New England Power Association, 72
New Hampshire-Vermont Lumber Company, 72
New Pacific Coal and Oils, Limited, 102
Newspaper circulation, increase in, 15–16, 52
Newspaper publishers, and paper industry, 19, 46–50
Newsprint: manufacture of, 7, 9–10, 16–17, 18, 150; pricing problems, 18–19, 45, 48–49; production of, 75; rag content of, 9; sales of, 45–49
Newton, Massachusetts, 137
New York, forests in, 9, 17, 114
New York State Board of Mediation and Arbitration, 57

New York State College of Forestry at Cornell, 17, 41–42
New York State Conservation Commission, 62
New York State Flood Commission, 61
New York State Forest Service, 136
New York State Public Service Law, Revision, 63
New York Telephone Company, 72
New York World, 16, 19, 59
New Zealand, 138
Niagra Hudson Power Corporation, 75
Nicaragua, plants in, 139
Nifty brand school supplies, 137
Norfolk, New York, 70, 76, 115
Norris, Charles, 70
Norris, John, 19, 46–47, 48
North Canadian Oils, Limited, 102, 153
Northeastern Power Corporation, 71, 72, 75
Northeastern wood resources, wartime demand on, 91
Northeast Forest Research Council, 133
Northern New York Development League, 62, 64
Northern New York Paper Manufacturers Association, labor relations, 56
Northern New York Trust Company, 53, 59, 64, 69
Northern New York Utilities Company, 65
North Kansas City, Missouri, 89, 103
Northwest Door Company, 112
North Western Pulp and Power Company, 102, 153
Norway spruce, planting program, 42
Norwood, New York, 70
Norwood & St. Lawrence Railroad Company, 71
NRA. See National Recovery Administration

Oakland, California, 74
Oakmont, Pennsylvania, 74
Obbola, Sweden, 165, 167, 170
Oil reserves, ix, 166
Ontario Paper Company, 10, 20
Operating divisions, 155
Operations, vice-president for, 154, 155

Oriental Bag Company, Limited, 103
Orientation program, for young executives, 118–119
Oscar Mayer Company, 105
Oswego, New York, 73, 74, 97, 115
Oswego Board Corporation, 73, 81
Oswego Machine Division, 90, 104
Other Paper Products Division, 137
Ottmeier, William M., 101
Owens Illinois Glass Company, 110

Pace family, 99–100
Pacific Northwest, wartime restrictions, 90
Pacific Pulp Mill Company, 74
Pacific Waxed Paper Company, 109
Packaging, 88–89; revolution in, 93–94, 106
Packaging Division, 108, 138; vice-president of, 155
Pagenstecher, Albrecht, 32
Panama: container plants in, 110, 139; paper mill in, 148
Panama City, Florida, 100
Pancake mix, bags for, 150
Panelyte Corporation, 73, 76, 81
Panelyte Division, 88, 111, 117, 139, 141, 162
Paper, x; consumption figures, 121, 144; production figures, 93, 94–95; uses of, 72, 88–89, 93–94, 95, 99
Paper industry, 94; diversification of products, 72, 93–94; early, 5–10; economics of, 38–39; environmental concerns, 167–168; growth of, 9, 10, 121–122, 139–140, 144; labor relations, 43–45, 55–59, 67–69, 91–92; packaging revolution, 93–94; production costs, 38, 44, 48–50, 121; production figures, 94–95, 162; relocation of, 114–116; restraint of trade, 39; socioeconomic pressures, 161–162; technological advances, 5, 8–9, 16–17; wartime, 87, 89
Paper Trade Journal, 45, 48, 82, 83
Paraffin cartons, 108
Payne-Aldrich Tariff, 50
Pensacola, Florida, 99–100, 101, 102, 103,

105, 115, 162; natural gas fuel, 166; pollution control program, 168; sale of plywood plant, 151; seed orchard, 136
Personnel and New Developments, vice-president for, 154
Personnel policies, 118–119
Piercefield Paper Company, 20
Pinchot, Gifford, 17, 23, 28–29, 42–43, 122
Pine, Southern: forestry practices, 101; loblolly, 86; newsprint from, 150; uses of pulp, 99
Pinkett, Harold T., xi, 17
Pioneer Mill, 4–5
Piping, polyethylene, 110
Pittsburgh, 107
Plasticized paper, 97
Plastic products, 140, 141, 147, 150; diversification into, 73, 95; molded, 111–112; wartime production, 88
Plywood business, 96, 112; decline in Northwest, 151
Pollard, Alabama, 166
Pollock, Laurence S., 108, 130
Pollock Division, 127
Pollock Paper Company, 107, 108–109
Pollution, 85, 122–123, 143; control of, 167–169
Polyethylene products, 105, 109–110, 150
Ponce Cement Corporation, 103
Poplar, pulp from, 41
Port Elizabeth, South Africa, 139
Portland, Oregon, 112
Power Corporation of New York, 70–71
Power grid, establishment of, 70, 75
Price, Overton, 29
Price-fixing, in paper industry, 46–49
Price of paper, 46–47; and production capacity, 82; and production costs, 121; and wood pulp revolution, 18–19
Printing industry, technological advances, 16
Printing paper, 95, 96–97, 117, 137
Printing Publication and Converting Paper Division, 96–97
Printing Paper Division, 96–97, 127, 130, 137, 150

Product development, 89, 95, 149
Product Development Department, 106, 126
Production: capacity, 94–95, 96, 97, 115, 165; costs of, 38, 44, 48–50, 95, 121; excessive, 81, 95, 110, 144; increases in, 86, 93
Productivity, increase in, 38–39
Product line, ix–x; diversification of, 71–75, 95–96
Public Affairs Department, 145–146
Public relations, 123, 141–142, 145–146
Public utilities, St. Regis ventures, 63, 65, 75
Public Works Administration (PWA), 82
Publishers: and paper industry, 19; and price of paper, 45–48; prosperity of, 38
Puerto Rico, operations in, 103
Puget Sound area, 90, 132; aerial survey, 134
Pulitzer interests, 59
Pulp: Alberta Hi-Brite, 152; sources of, 8
Pulp and Paper Investigation Hearings, 37
Pulpboard, 96
Pulp mills, bleached sulfite: Deferiet, New York, 86; Hinton, Alberta, 102
Pulpwood, 146; supply problems, 32–33, 38, 65, 114; tariff issue, 50. *See also* Timberlands
Pulpwood waste, building materials from, 73
Puyallup River Valley, Washington, 152
PWA. *See* Public Works Administration

Quinlan, Joseph A., 116–117
Quality control, 126

R. W. Paper Company, 109
Radio Corporation of America (RCA) merger, 155–159
Rags: paper made from, 5, 9; sources of, 7–8
Rail transportation, 40, 41
Randers, Denmark, box factory in, 148
Raquette River, St. Regis water rights on, 65

Raquette River Power Company, 71
Rawls, Marcus, 133, 134
Raw materials, 40, 96, 112–113, 114, 132–137; for plastic products, 141; rags, 7–8; sources, 99–101, 146, 152–153; wartime, 90–91
Raymondville, New York, 70, 76, 86
Rayon, 88
RCA. *See* Radio Corporation of America
Real estate business, 154
Reciprocity Act, 50
Recknagel, A. B., 113–114, 115, 133
Recknagel, Bernard W., 104, 108, 117–118, 128, 129, 130, 154
Reconstruction Finance Corporation, 100
Reed, Robert W., 126
Reforestation, 42–43, 65–66, 134, 136–137; attempts, 41–42; in Northeast, 114
Refrigerator parts, 111
Regis (Saint), Jean François, 21–22
Reinforced papers, 138
Remington, Alfred D., 6, 9–10
Remington, Charles H., 14, 42, 70
Remington, Illustrious, 6
Remington Paper and Power Company, 59, 65
Remington paper mills, 20
Research, 123; center for, 127–128
Research and Development Department, 105–106, 126
Resources, natural: depletion of, 143; private control of, 64; use of, 167
Restraint of trade by papermakers, 39
Reuben, Frank, 102
Reynolds, Frank, 20
Rhinelander Division, 149; reforestation by, 137
Rhinelander Paper Company, 108–109, 127, 131–132
Rhodesia, interests in, 139
R. Hoe & Company, rotary presses, 16
Rice, Clarke, 5
Richmond, Indiana, 111
Richmond Molded Plastics Company, 111, 112
Riparian rights, 64. *See also* Waterpower

Robert, Nicholas-Louis, 5
Rockefeller, William, 32
Rogers, F. L., 66
Roosevelt, Theodore, 37, 39
Rosenstein, Joseph, 109
Royal Bank of Canada, 102
R. W. Paper Company, 109

St. Paul & Tacoma Lumber Company, 112;
  reforestation, 134
St. Regis-Bates Monthly News, 84
St. Regis Company of Canada, Limited,
  66–67, 81, 103; sale of, 140
St. Regis Consumer Packaging Center, 50
St. Regis Container Corporation, 108
St. Regis Development Committee, 106
St. Regis Falls, New York, 21
St. Regis International, 139, 145
St. Regis Kraft Company, 74, 81
St. Regis Paper and Bag Corporation of
  Puerto Rico, 103
St. Regis Paper Company, ix–x, 13, 21, 75;
  acquisitions, 66, 70–71, 72–75, 90,
  96–115, 137–138, 151, 152; acquisitions
  policies, 66, 99, 107, 112–113, 123–125,
  151, 165; capital investments, 145;
  capitalization, 22, 40, 75, 81, 91, 95,
  145; conservative nature of, 170; consolidation, 126–140, 142, 145, 164; cutting
  rights, ix, 43, 101, 114, 134, 145, 152;
  diversification, 71–75, 115, 125; divestiture, 130–131, 141, 164; earnings, 121,
  144–145, 154, 161, 166; electrification
  of plants, 61, 72, 76; employment, 95,
  122; expansion, postwar, 95–115, 126,
  142, 146–149; financing, original,
  23–24; founding of, 22–34; as holding
  company, 64–65, 71, 116; income, 95,
  149; incorporation of, 13–14, 21, 22;
  international expansion, ix, 103, 107,
  110, 138–140, 145, 146–149, 165,
  166–167; labor relations, 44, 56–59,
  67–68, 91–92; landholdings, 23, 40, 43,
  66–67, 72, 90, 96, 112–113, 114,
  133–134, 137, 145, 146, 152, 157, 166;
  land purchase policy, 113, 114, 145;
  leadership, quality of, 169; mergers, 18,
  82, 110, 135, 151, 155–159, 165; name,
  origin of, 21–22; natural resources, 166;
  organizational changes, 96, 106, 112,
  117–119, 123, 126, 129–132, 154–155,
  162; output, 53, 100, 103, 165; profits,
  121, 154, 161, 167; records, early,
  13–14; recovery from depression, 84–86;
  reforestation, 42–43, 65–66, 134,
  136–137; research and development,
  105–106, 127–128; sales figures, 84, 91,
  95, 108, 125, 139, 148, 149, 152; sales
  practices, 46, 103–105; southward expansion, 86, 95, 99–101, 114, 117; supply
  policy, 65, 96, 114, 145, 152; utility
  holdings, 63, 64, 75–76; waterpower
  interests, 61–62; westward expansion,
  74, 95. *See also* Knowlton Brothers;
  Pioneer Mill; Taggarts Paper Company
St. Regis Sales Corporation, 81, 117
St. Regis Securities Corporation, 81
Sales figures, 84, 91, 95, 108, 125, 139,
  148, 149, 152
Sales meeting, first annual, 104
Sales practices, 89, 103–105; of newsprint
  industry, 45–48
Sales strategy, "full wagon," 108
Salinas, California, 108, 130
Salisbury, Rhodesia, 139
Salt Lake City, Utah, 103, 150
San Leandro, California, 150
Santa Clara Lumber Company, 17, 21, 41;
  land sale, 23; misrepresentation of
  timber yield, 28–30; ownership, 27–28;
  pulpwood contract, 26, 27–28, 32–33;
  resolution of suit, 39, 40, 51
Sankey, J. H., and Sons, Limited, 138
Sarnoff, David, 157
Sartell, Minnesota, 96–97
Savannah, Georgia, 100, 103
Sawmills, acquisition of, 112
Scandinavia, pulp from, 90, 97, 98, 102,
  115, 139
Schmidt and Ault Paper Company, 137
Schoellkopf family interests, 75
Scholarship program, 136
School supplies, 96
Scrimgeour, A. C., 46

S. D. Warren Company, 63
Searle, Robert F., 124, 128–129, 164–165
Seattle, Washington, 74
Seed orchard, 136
Seip, Russell G., 101
Self-opening sacks (SOS bags), 149
Selling all the way through, 89, 104–105
Seminole Chief machine, 126
Senior vice-presidents, 154–155
Set-up boxes, 110
Shane, Samuel, 141, 145–146
Shelter, Timber, and Land Management Division, 153, 155
Sherman, Charles Augustus, 10
Sherman, George C., 10, 13–15, 18, 19, 20, 40, 46, 50, 51, 53, 114, 116, 169; as founder of St. Regis, 21–34; labor negotiations, 44, 56; ouster of, 54–55; on price-fixing, 48–49; on reforestation, 42–43, 50; and waterpower, 13, 61–62
Sherman, Wooster, 6
Sherman Anti-Trust law, 38
Sherman family, 116
Sherman Paper Products, 137, 164
Sisalkraft Holdings, Limited, 138
Skenandoa Rayon Corporation, 88
Sloan, Hugh W. "Pete," 80, 128, 130, 140; views on RCA merger, 156–157, 158, 159
Smalley, Alex, 130, 154, 155
Smith, David C., xi, 7
Smith, Herbert Knox, 62
Smith, W. T., Lumber Company, 135
Sociological factors: in growth of paper industry, 15–16, 94, 122, 143, 161; in lumber industry, 135; in product development, 71–72
Soda process of wood pulping, 8
Soderhamn chipper, 135
Sodium peroxide bleaching process, 90, 97
Solid Cardboard Box Manufacturing, Limited, 110
Soper, Frederick J., 22
SOS bags. See Self-opening sacks
South Africa, expansion in, 110, 139, 148
South America: Argentina, subsidiaries in, 147; Brazil, subsidiaries in, 147; Chile, school of forestry in, 133; Columbia, subsidiaries in, 147; Ecuador, container plants in, 110, 139; Nicaragua, plants in, 139; Surinam, 110; Venezuela, box factory in, 148
Southern Kraft Corporation, 99, 100
Southern paper industry, 99–102, 135
Southland Paper Mills, Incorporated, 137, 149, 150, 165
Southward expansion, 86, 95, 99–101, 114, 117
Spain, Barcelona, plant in, 147
Span-Deck, 151
Spanish-American war, 16, 18
Specialty bags, 110
Specialty papers, 72–73, 97, 115, 165
Spruce, Adirondack, overcutting of, 17
Stanlind Oil and Gas Company, 166
Stepped-end bags, 150
Storage systems, needed for water control, 61
Storer, Andrew, 102–103, 105, 128, 138, 151, 156, 158, 166
Strikebreakers, 56–57
Strikes, 44, 56–57, 67–68
Strymen, 119
Sugar industry, multiwall bag use, 85
Sulfate process, 102, 115
Sulfite process of wood pulping, 8; first use of, 9–10
Sulfite Pulp Manufacturers Research League, 131
Sulfite waste liquor, 109, 131–132
Sulfurous acid, 8
Sun Oil Company, 166
Superior Paper Products, 107, 108
Superior Pine Products Company, 101
Supply problem, long-term solution to, 40–41. See also Raw materials
Surinam, container plants in, 110
Sutton, Harold S., 69
Suwanee Forest: harvesting rights, 101; reforestation, 134
Svenska Cellulosa AB, 165
Sweden, operations in, 165, 167
Systems selling, 128

Tacoma, Washington, 74, 112; housing
  boom, 150–151
Tacoma Kraft Mill, 85, 90–91, 97, 103,
  112, 115, 130, 148, 152; expansion
  of, 95, 150–151; modernization program,
  126; plywood plant closed, 151; pollution
  control, 168
Taggart, Byron Benjamin, 6–7, 10, 11, 61,
  62
Taggart, William W., 7, 10, 11, 22
Taggart Brothers Company, 7, 9, 53, 70, 73
Taggart Corporation, 73, 80, 86
Taggart family, 13
Taggart Oswego Paper and Bag Company,
  73
Taggarts Paper Company, 10–11, 13, 14,
  23, 32, 44, 54–55, 56
Tanning industry, in Watertown, 4
Tapes, sealing, 108
Tariff: on Canadian paper and pulpwood,
  19, 47, 49; Fordney-McCumber, 71;
  Payne-Aldrich, 50; Underwood Tariff
  Act, 50
Taylor, John B., 65
Team concept of management, 129–130
Technical Development Department, 89
Technical Planning Department, 126–127
Technical Services and Quality Control
  Department, 126
Technological advances, 16–17, 105–106,
  135; fourdrinier machines, 5; pulping
  processes, 8–9
Technological operations, reorganization
  of, 126–128
Textile bags, 85, 103
Thiokol Corporation, 141
Thor Corporation, Allied Paper Division,
  97
Thorne Loomis and Company, 75
Three Rivers, Quebec, 74, 103
Three-tour day, 38, 44–45, 48, 49, 56, 58
Tilden, John M., 7, 10, 14
Tilden Paper Company, 10
Timberlands, 17, 23, 40, 43, 66–67, 72,
  90, 96, 102, 112–113, 114, 133–134,
  137, 145, 146, 152, 157, 166
Time Inc., paper mills of, 96

Toledo, Ohio, 74
Torula yeast, 109, 131–132
Toweling, 115
Trade Expansion Act of 1962, 139
Transvaal Box Manufacturing, Limited,
  110
Tree farm movement, 113, 134, 136
Tree nurseries, 101
Trenton, New Jersey, 73, 111, 141, 162
Troy, Montana, 112
Troy, Ohio, 108
Truman, Harry, 89–90
Tylcoff, Joseph, 56

UBPM. See United Brotherhood of Paper
  Makers
Underwood Tariff Act, 50
Union Bag and Paper Company, 100, 133
Union Camp, 133
Union City, California, 150
United Brotherhood of Paper Makers
  (UBPM), 43
United Corporation, 75–76
U.S. House Select Committee to Investigate
  the Pulp and Paper Industry, 45–49

Vancouver, B.C., 103
Vayo, Reginald, 107, 110, 117, 130,
  138–139, 146, 155
Veneer plant, 151
Venezuela, box factory in, 148
Versfelt, William H., Sr., 80, 116
Vice-presidents: for administration, 154;
  divisional, 155; executive, 154; for
  marketing and communications, 154; for
  operations, 154, 155; of Packaging
  Division, 155; for Personnel and New
  Developments, 154; senior, 154–155
Voelter, Heinrich, 8
Voelter grinders, 8, 9, 16

Wages: increase in, 38–39, 44, 161; re-
  duction in, 67–68
Wagner Bag Company, 103
Wallpaper, all wood, 10–11
Wall Street Journal, 141

War: Boer War, 16, 18; Chemical Warfare
  Service, 89; Civil War, paper needs of,
  6, 7; Northeastern wood resources, war-
  time demands on, 91; Pacific Northwest,
  wartime restrictions on, 90; raw materials,
  in wartime, 90–91; Spanish-American
  War, 16, 18; World War II, 86–89,
  91, 114
War Production Board, 87, 90
Warren, S. D., Company, 63
Warren Parchment Company, 65
Washington, landholdings in, 112, 152
Wasps, papermaking by, 8
Waste materials, use of, 135
Watab Paper Company, 96
Water control, 153
Water pollution. *See* Pollution
Waterpower, 23, 61–63, 64, 76; of Black
  River, 3–4; and industrial growth, 13;
  rights to, 20
Water recycling, 168
Water storage system, 61, 62
Watertown, New York, 3–12, 115–116;
  bag manufacturing plant, 73, 97;
  drought, 52–53; fires, 4, 6; industriali-
  zation of, 4–6; leadership of, 11; paper-
  making developments in, 9–10
Watertown Daily Times, 34–35
Watertown Steam Engine Company, 10
Water transportation of logs, 40–41
Water use, 62
Waxed paper, 75, 108, 109
Webster's Spelling Book, 5

Weidmann Stave and Heading Mills, 32
Western Star, 126
Western Valve Bag Company, 74
West Fork Timber Company, 91
West Indies, office in, 139
Westinghouse, 111
West Nyack, New York, 127–128
Weyerhaeuser Timber Company, 109, 110
Wheeler Lumber Bridge and Supply
  Company, 151–152
Wilber, Jack, 127
Wildlife development, 153
Willapa County, Washington, 152
William R. Adams, 148
Williams, F. W., Limited, 138, 147
Willson, S. L., 83–84
Wilson, James, 41
Wisconsin: plants in, 150; reforestation in,
  137
Woodcock, Charles, 89, 104, 140
Wooden boxes, 112
Wood pulp technology, 8–9, 18
World War II, 91; depletion of forests,
  114; paper industry in, 86–89
Wrapping materials, 75, 108
W. T. Smith Lumber Company, 135

Yonkers, New York, 109–110
York, Pennsylvania, 137

Zambia, investments in, 148
Zellerbach, 84–85, 109

DATE DUE

GAYLORD			PRINTED IN U.S.A.